BOXING FOR CUBA

An Immigrant's Story Of Despair,
Endurance & Redemption

BOXING FOR CUBA

An Immigrant's Story Of Despair,
Endurance & Redemption

GUILLERMO VINCENTE VIDAL

GHOST ROAD PRESS

Boxing for Cuba.
Library of Congress Cataloging-in-Publication Data.

The material in this book is written to the best of the author's
recollection.

Photos by Guillermo Vincente Vidal.

Ghost Road Press
ISBN (Trade pbk.)
13 Digit 978-0-9789456-0-2
10 Digit 0-9789456-0-3
Library of Congress Control Number: 2007921501

Ghost Road Press
Denver, Colorado
ghostroadpress.com

A mis padres,
Roberto y Marta Vidal,
que sacrificaron todo;

A mis hermanos,
Roberto y Juan Vidal,
que me ayudaron a sobrevivir

To my parents,
Roberto and Marta Vidal,
who sacrificed everything;

To my brothers,
Roberto and Juan Vidal,
who helped me survive

"If I had known what life in exile was going to be like," my father said often over the years, "I would not have chosen it."

The rest of us knew precisely what he meant: if any of us could have foreseen the physical and mental suffering, the rupture exile would bring to our family, the madness it would engender in my parents, the myriad daily challenges posed by a new culture that seemed strange in every way, perhaps not one of us would have opted for the path we chose.

Yet, in the end, I know I believe in the truth of an old Cuban saying more than I believe in anything else: "No hay mal que por bien no venga."

Even out of the worst of it all, good things come.

Contents

Uno

The Center of the Universe

Our house in Camagüey was named for a bar of soap. "La Villita Candado," it was called, and Candado was a popular bath soap in the years before Fidel and his fierce *compañeros* swept down out of the Sierra Maestra and wholly changed our lives. The house had been a wedding gift to my parents from my paternal grandfather, who purchased it sometime in the 1940s from the family who had won it in a contest of sorts. As an advertising scheme, the soap company had built several modest *villitas* in cities across Cuba, announcing that a corresponding number of tokens—allowing the bearer to claim one of the houses—had been buried in bars of Candado. Sales of Candado soared; the tokens ultimately emerged from a few precious bars, and each of the houses retained minor renown for many years afterward in a nation where, for many people, owning a home was only a dream.

In my family's case, it wasn't our luck but our larger family's prosperity that had allowed us to make La Villita Candado our home. Good fortune, in fact, seemed to abandon us entirely beginning at a time when I was eight years old. And our prosperity—such as it was—was the thing that ultimately labeled us enemies of the people, set our small world on its end, and profoundly altered the life I otherwise might have lived.

§ —— ᵺ

In my earliest years in Cuba, however, I was buoyed by the absolute certainty that the city of Camagüey—the third largest in my country—lay at the lush center of the universe. Our home was situated on Carretera Central, the busiest street in town, and the house and its ample garden were surrounded by a stucco and wrought-iron fence that made our home feel like a grand fortress to my two brothers and me. Despite our seasoned tree-climbing skills, we couldn't scale the high fence, yet we didn't mind. The fence simply seemed to define the boundaries of an amusement park that was exclusively ours, the twins—Roberto and Juan, whom we called Kiko and Toto—and I enchanted each day by the rainbow-striped lizards that raced to escape our grasps and the slippery tadpoles that swam in the huge earthenware pot called a *tinajon*, which captured rainwater from the roof. We built exotic cities for ourselves among the jungle of fruit trees and shrubs and vines, played cowboys and Indians, embarked on daring safaris, and fought great battles against injustice of every kind. We endlessly climbed the great mango tree—its highest branches, even back then, visible throughout the neighborhood—knocking its wonderful fruit to the ground with our fists, rocks, and sticks.

We marveled at our friend Marcelo, the gardener, a young *campesino* in his twenties already missing his front teeth. Like so many people from the country, Marcelo seemed to find a way add the word *chico*, kid, to almost every sentence he spoke, and his accent was thick enough that sometimes we simply guessed at what he was saying, yet he was lithe and strong and adept—the kind of young man boys like us couldn't help but be fascinated by—and the fact that he used his machete to cut the lawn rather than the mower my father provided was proof to the three of us that he was man of exceptional skills.

It may have been true throughout Cuba in those pre-revolution years, but in our case at least, Marcelo and the others who worked for Mami and Papi were woven tightly into the broad fabric of our family. We all were related somehow, if only by our daily proximity to each other and the fact that all of us—boys and servants alike—

depended for our survival on my father's business acumen and my mother's complex kinds of acceptance. Our nannies Romelia and her daughter-in-law Emilita; Gladis the cook; Ismaela, Felix, and El Negrito Juan—the three of them having worked for my grandparents since Mami herself was a child—were people with whom I shared both love and relation, despite the fact that, in the case of Gladis and El Negrito Juan, it was a kinship plainly complicated by color.

Like the United States, Cuba had been stricken by the blight of racism since the earliest days of the slave trade, and because Gladis was black, none of us considered it unacceptable that she was confined to the kitchen and virtually never ventured into other parts of the house. Her coal-skinned boyfriend wasn't allowed to enter the house at all, and I remember him often waiting patiently for her to come out the back-door and join him for a bit, the two of them stealing kisses until the teasing my brothers and I made them suffer—as well perhaps as the demands of our dinner—would send him off to another Cuba, one the three of us knew nothing about. El Negrito Juan, who lived in tiny room at the back of my grandfather's medical clinic, would seldom venture farther than our front porch. He was a kind and gentle man who had been devoted to my mother since she was a small child, and the two of them shared an important bond, one that somehow cut through the prejudices and terrible affronts of that era.

My mother was still a small girl when people began to comment about her extraordinary beauty. Marta Teresa Ramos Almendros, they would insist, surely would grow up to be the most beautiful woman in Camagüey, and their predictions proved correct. But Mami's charm, her social graces, her family's wealth and position, and her beauty—the attributes that had drawn my father to her—masked a deep insecurity and a strangely incurable loneliness, the products of wounds she had begun to suffer early in life.

She was born in 1924 to Juan Ramos Garcia, a well respected Camagüey physician, and Rufina Almendros Boza, herself a storied beauty from one of the city's wealthiest families. My grandfather owned a large home near the city center, one that housed his medical clinic as well, and my grandmother decorated the house with furniture, paintings, and statues she imported from Europe. Dr. Ramos and his young wife wanted for nothing; they led a charmed life, and they lavished attention on their two children, no doubt in part because my grandfather had lost his own mother when he was just five, was raised by an aunt when his father no longer would do so once his wife was dead, and struggled to achieve success, working his way through medical school, then serving as an army doctor for many years before he married Rufina and opened his private practice.

I often suspect that great equalizing forces exist that do not allow even the most fortunate people to live their lives free of suffering, and no doubt that lesson first came to me in the stories I heard from my mother about how her family's world shattered when she was five—at the time when her younger brother, Juan Benito, contracted a disease Dr. Ramos diagnosed as polio.

Juan Benito, called Nene, or Baby, was only three when his father—a man quite confident in the belief that his intelligence and the sheer force of his will were enough to allow him to accomplish virtually anything—first began to restrain the whole of his son's small and twisted body in steel and plaster casts for months at a time in hopes that the confinement would prevent his bones from growing crooked in ways they dramatically had begun to do. My grandfather studied his son's condition exhaustively, tried every treatment about which he read, and experimented with some of his own design, yet always without success. Each time he cut the casts away, Nene's body had grown more twisted, and with the failure of each successive treatment, my grandparents began to more sadly confront a heartrending truth: Nene could not be cured.

To help compensate for their son's suffering, his parents increasingly focused their lives on him, virtually never letting him out of their sight, both of them sinking into terrible depression and despair as their son grew ever more disabled. And in much the same way that my grandfather had been orphaned by his mother's death and his father's subsequent abandonment of him, Mami, in turn, was forsaken by her parents' desperation over their son's awful fate. The two children adored each other, and both had brought their family great joy, but increasingly my grandparents made Nene and his suffering the totality of their world, one that contained very little room for my mother. Of course, she too was traumatized by what Nene was forced to endure, yet she was still a young girl, and she found it almost impossible to understand why her brother's disease also seemed to push her parents ever farther away from her.

Ismaela, her nanny, Felix, a lab technician in Dr. Ramos's clinic, and Juan, a custodial jack-of-all-trades, did their collective best to offer Mami the love and attention she longed for—tender, parental kinds of care that extended well into the 1950s, by which time she had become a mother herself—yet despite their best efforts, they could not fully replace the love my grandparents now seemed strangely incapable of offering her.

As she grew older and the measure of her beauty became apparent to everyone who met her, the blessing of her good looks was also transformed into something of a curse, not only for Marta, but for her parents as well. People cruelly—and all-too openly—referred to the two Ramos children as "the beauty and the beast;" the recognition of their daughter's loveliness only added to her parents' anguish over the continuing physical deterioration of their son, and it grew increasingly difficult for Marta herself to accept her beauty without feeling deeply guilty as well. Why should good fortune have come to her and not to her beloved brother? How could her future burn bright at the same time his was growing dimmer, his body becoming ever more twisted, misshapen, and repellent to others?

To Marta, there simply seemed to be no meaningful explanation. Her parents did not notice her distress, let alone attempt to console her; friends and extended family members invariably would express delight in her beauty and sympathy for her brother in the same breath, and inevitably in my mother's mind, the two circumstances became maliciously linked. Still a young girl, the only thing she believed she could do in response was to dedicate herself to filling with joy those aspects of Nene's life that had been left empty by his disability. Instinctively, she was sure she never could be a good enough sister, but her attempt to succeed nonetheless became her consuming passion. She focused all her energies and activities on her brother, trying her best to make each day as entertaining and as fun for him as possible. She pointedly declined invitations from friends that weren't extended to her brother as well, and she silently acquiesced when her parents announced one day that she could no longer bring girlfriends to their home: Nene might develop a crush on one of them, they whispered to her, then suffer the added humiliation of a broken heart. It was that kind of obsessive protectiveness that came to consume their home. The family's pleasures most often were forced, even counterfeit; the daily tensions grew huge, and although Nene's worsening condition was impossible to ignore, everyone nonetheless rigidly refused to admit that anything other than polio might be the cause of their collective pain.

My grandfather was a dedicated and by-all-accounts capable physician; he worked tirelessly, if in vain, to help his son, and I'm sure he must have been at least privately aware that Nene suffered a more rare and insidious disease than polio, in fact. Although he would never have a definitive diagnosis, by the time he was a teenager he was terribly disabled and disfigured, and surely calling the disease polio—one common in that era, and which was acquired rather than congenital—was an attempt both to make Nene himself feel less like a freak and to lessen the family's sense of shame.

It may have been because of that same kind of shame—or the cumulative effects of his stress or simply his ongoing grief—but whatever the cause, eventually my grandfather began to seek comfort in the arms of women other than his wife. His absences from home grew lengthy and impossible to ignore; rumors of his liaisons began to circulate openly, and they eventually reached my grandmother's ears, of course. Rufina became obsessed with finding proof of her husband's indiscretions; she threatened divorce—something quite scandalous in the Cuba of the 1940s—and she and her husband began to fight violently, Rufina screaming at her husband at the top of her lungs, breaking objects the two of them treasured, and terrifying her teenage children. On the day my mother came home and shared the news with Nene that, while out in the streets of Camagüey, she had inadvertently spotted their father arm-in-arm with a woman much younger than him, the two children were terrified that it would be only a matter of time before their parents divorced and they were abandoned by their philandering father.

Despite those tensions and the challenges she faced, there also were many pleasures in my mother's life, and among the most important were the weeks she and Nene spent each summer at the family's sugar plantation near the city of Cienfuegos on the southern coast. Away from their parents, the two lived free from the myriad rules, regulations, and slow-burning anger that filled their days in Camagüey; no one who looked after them on the plantation worried unnecessarily about Nene's fragility, and the children were free to play with whomever they chose. And as Marta grew older, on languorous summer evenings she would go to dance-halls in Cienfuegos with fellow teenagers from the plantation, where boys would line up to take turns dancing with the *patron's* beautiful daughter.

In time, young men began to pay similar kinds of attention to her back home in Camagüey. Although never a spectacular student, she loved to paint and sculpt, and she adopted an unmistakably artistic flare in her dress as well. The beautiful Marta was gregarious and charismatic, and by the time of her *quinceañera*, the celebration of her formal coming-out on her fifteenth birthday, she had emerged as a belle of Camagüey's social scene. At each elaborate *fiesta* and at social events of every kind, she was the center of attention, something she had longed to be in the years since her parents had stopped seeing her when her brother's needs began to grow great.

Mami was intoxicated by people's fascination with her, and their enthrallment seemed to make her feel whole. Buoyed by the press of attention people paid her in the ensuing years, she went to college, earned a degree in education, then worked as an assistant in my grandfather's clinic, and began to imagine finding the perfect husband—a stable, ambitious, and good man who would shower her with the kind of love her parents never had. But deep inside, the injuries her parents' abandonment caused didn't heal. She now incessantly sought out acceptance from others, and no amount of attention ever seemed enough for her. Like her mother, she could quickly become enraged; she regularly suffered severe bouts of depression, and something else troubled her profoundly as well: although she very much wanted children of her own one day, children whom she knew she could love and nurture in every important way, she was secretly afraid that Nene's disease was hereditary, and that one of her children—or all of them perhaps—would be born a beast as well.

My mother was twenty-five when the twins arrived. Kiko—Roberto—was born first by fifteen minutes. Being nominally the elder would always allow him to claim a bit of seniority—and it meant that he was the one who received my father's name, of course—but the price he immediately paid was the bumps and bruises he suffered in passing first through the birth canal. In addition to being traumatized by that passage, he was skinny and small and certainly not a pretty baby. His incrementally younger brother Juan, in contrast, slid out easily and without a scratch. Named Juan Antonio after his two grandfathers, Toto was big and strong and healthy in every way, and it seemed obvious that he had been stealing more than his share of the sustenance in his mother's womb.

News about the twins' appearance on the scene spread rapidly throughout Camagüey, and everywhere my parents went people were eager to have a look at Roberto and Marta's fine new *chicos gemelos*. Invariably, they were impressed by what a beautiful baby Toto was; it was Toto to whom people made eyes and who they wanted to hold—and their fascinations with only one of his sons annoyed the hell out of my father. He responded by lavishing *his* attentions solely on his namesake son, doing his best to ensure that Kiko received as much care and affection as Toto did, doing so often enough that soon my mother was certain that Kiko was my father's favorite.

A year and half later, I slithered kicking and screaming from my mother's womb. I was fat as a Buddha and a mama's boy right off the bat, crying whenever I lost sight of her, demanding her constant attention, and predictably, I suppose, my father grew convinced that my mother cared more for me than her two older sons. The truth was that although both denied having a favorite child, each of my parents did, and for Kiko and me, being allied with a particular parent—whether we had chosen to be or not—would prove to be a painful curse.

Unlike my brothers, whose names were family names, I was named after our neighbor, an auto mechanic. Mami and Papi's sedan seemed to need constant tinkering at the time, and Memo—a nickname for Guillermo—was a mechanic they trusted and liked. He was at work on the car's transmission, in fact, on the morning I was born, and so I became his curious namesake, though instead of being called Memo, I became "Guille," a name that somehow stuck.

Soon after I arrived, my mother became seriously depressed, lacking the energy to get out of bed, able to do nothing more than lie with me and feed me—a postpartum reaction that few people understood in those days, least of all my father. As far as Papi was concerned, the attentions she paid me were simply proof of her tendency to make poor choices, and her lengthy depression was only one more manifestation of her erratic behavior. Unlike the birth of the twins, which had brought them some months of respite from their combat, my appearance unfortunately had the opposite effect, initiating a model of conflict that continued throughout my parents' lives together, one in which Kiko, Toto, and I became their battleground, their prisoners of war, and their uncomprehending victims.

By the time I was old enough to remember, Mami and Papi could muster a reason to fight almost any time or anywhere. Whatever its catalyst, the normal pattern was one in which Papi would emerge the victor of sorts in a shouted war of words, then Mami, in turn, would fly into hysterics—hurling dishes, vases, and anything else within reach into the walls or onto the tiled floors. I can't be sure why her sons also began to seem fair game, but while I was still a toddler, she began to turn her anger on us as well, sometimes striking one of us with her open hand or her fist, sometimes becoming so enraged that Romelia or Emilita, our nannies and de facto bodyguards, would have to tackle her and hold her down to keep us from suffering serious injuries at her hands. It was my brother Kiko who was always my mother's first choice as a target, certainly because he was my father's openly acknowledged favorite—Mami imagining that hurting Kiko was the only way in which she could injure her husband, on whom she otherwise couldn't land meaningful blows.

Papi, in turn, would attempt to provoke her further by becoming oblivious to my very existence. He would look right through me, as if I'd simply vanished into the thick tropical air, offering the rewards of his fatherly attention to my twin brothers but not to me, even though I sat on the floor between them. Papi hit me only a handful of times over the years, but the way in which he could utterly vanquish me from his life wounded me every bit as much as fists ever did.

Toto wasn't immune to their wounds, of course, and like Kiko and me, he was terrified on those occasions when Mami's furies literally would last for days, her tantrums continuing without release until Papi would summon wonderful, patient Ismaela, still Mami's great consoler, to come to La Villita Candado to hold her, to talk quietly with her, and somehow to settle her at last. And like Kiko and me, on many nights Toto would lie awake for hours listening to our parents raging in the dark of the night.

As children, we wondered, of course, how an argument could flare when the lights were out and everyone presumably had gone to sleep. It wasn't until many years later—when Mami explained that my father had completely lost his sexual interest in her after I was born—that the reasons for their late-night screaming began to make some sense. She often would awaken, she said, from a dream in which my father announced he was leaving her for another woman. She then would waken him and beg him to ease her fears; he would tell her she was insane, and the pyrotechnics would erupt. At the time, the only thing the three of us could be sure of was that our three beds were not safe havens from the storms in our home; that at any time of the day or night peace was very precarious, and our lullabies, such as they were, likely would be screeching, swearing, crying, and the crash of shattering objects.

The fact that people throughout the neighborhood often would speak in hushed tones—conversations my brothers and I nonetheless readily overheard—about the battle that had been fought at La Villita Candado the night before helps explain how serious and how common the combat was between my parents. Yet, in time, at least they learned to flee from their suffering. Papi threw himself into his work and business investments and stayed away from home as much as he could. Mami's refuges were Camagüey's tennis club and country club, where she spent innumerable hours with friends. She loved to shop, and neither she nor my father nor the three of us children ever lacked for money. Our family led an idyllic life—or so it appeared to those who lived far enough away from the sounds that bespoke the truth.

It's one of the miracles of childhood, I suppose, that kids can so constantly find happiness amidst their sorrows and fears. My brothers and I certainly possessed that remarkable resiliency, and because of it, I'm sure I remember those early years in Cuba with much more fond nostalgia than tangled regret.

If we had to watch and listen to our parents brutalize each other, we also were regularly assured by them that we were safe and deeply loved; my father even communicated his care for *me* in ways that subtly worked their way inside and offered me a budding sense of my place in the world. Mami was beautiful and vivacious when her mood arced upward rather than down. She would spend hours preparing herself to go out—her dark hair and make-up perfect, her nails painted bright red, her tight-waisted dresses accentuating her fine figure, one that would engender whistles from men on the street, I remember, when she occasionally wore peg-legged pants—and like the legions of Mami's friends in Camagüey, we loved to be with her.

Every bit as important as our mother, the people who worked for us offered us the most staunch and critical kinds of support. It was Romelia who really had charge of the house. Without bearing a title, she commanded the other servants, and she possessed the ability to be relaxed and alert to dangers at the same time. She was stocky and short and would take each of us into her cuddling embrace several times each day. She loved us, we knew, and it was Romelia who constantly soothed our wounds—our scrapes and contusions as well as the serious injuries that were less easy to see.

When one of us was ill with mumps, measles, or a high fever, Romelia readily presumed it was because we were possessed by spirits and that it was time to *cortar las ojas*, or cut the leaves, as she would say. She was a devoted practitioner of Santería—the blend of Catholicism and African Yorùbá beliefs widely practiced in a number of Caribbean countries—and would bring avocado leaves stripped from a tree in the garden to my bedside, place them on the floor, then have me stand on the leaves in my bare feet. As she mumbled words I couldn't understand, she would cut to pieces the parts of the leaves still exposed with a kitchen knife while Mami watched in silence, obviously hopeful herself that the ritual would be efficacious. And it was: invariably I was much better the following day, whether from the simple power of suggestion, or because of Romelia's spectral skills with knives and leaves.

Romelia's daughter-in-law Emilita, a plain young woman in her early twenties, was as beautiful as Mami in our eyes. She had no children of her own, so we were the beneficiaries of her bountiful maternal instincts; she was playful and full of fun and could be counted on to join in our games and garden adventures. Emilita and Romelia took turns spending the night at our house, and my memories are bright with waking up each day to one of their smiling faces.

Although we virtually never entered the house's white-tiled kitch-en, the glorious food Gladis created there kept my baby fat from fall-ing away and ensured that my brothers and I seldom dawdled when we were called to the table. She served steaming white rice with vir-tually everything—most often chicken, pork, and the ubiquitous ground-beef dish called *picadillo*, and I loved the name we gave to simple black beans and rice—*moros y cristianos*, Moors and Chris-tians—almost as much as I craved the staple itself. We ate wonder-ful fruits like guava and mamey year-round, and my brothers and I relished *tostones*, fried plantains, and *plátanos dulces*, sweet bananas, as if they were boyhood's best prizes.

Papi's treasured fifty-gallon aquarium, filled with strange and fasci-nating fresh-water tropical fish, occupied a place of honor in the dining room. His glass *pescera* brought him as close in Camagüey as he could get to the undersea wonders that always had lured him, and, like Papi, I remember staring at it for hours with almost as much rapt attention as I also regularly paid to the large, oval-tubed television that com-manded notice in a corner of the white-tiled living room. My broth-ers and I loved watching American westerns and *Flash Gordon*, and I was personally such a fan of Broderick Crawford's *Highway Patrol* that I could proudly growl out the words in English, "Set up a roadblock!" Televisions, of course, were far from commonplace in Cuba in those days, and surely the opportunity to watch it was partly the lure when friends and family members occasionally came to visit.

Among those infrequent guests, perhaps my favorite was Ismae-la, who for my mother had been the blessed combination of Rome-lia and Emilita rolled into one, and who was elderly now, or so it seemed to Kiko, Toto, and me. She had silver hair and a heavy fig-ure, and I remember relishing my too-infrequent opportunities to sit in her broad and welcoming lap, listening to her stories about Mami's adventures and many misdeeds back when she was our age. Felix had never been married, and so my mother was his closest claim to a daughter, and we were like his grandchildren. He always had hard, bright-colored sugar candies for us when he came to vis-it; he taught us cubilete, a classic Cuban betting game employing poker dice, which we would play with him for hours. I still cherish a photograph I have of me standing beside him, my fat little arm on his shoulder, Felix looking at me with a kind of tenderness I never received from my father. Felix worked as a lab technician for my grandfather, Dr. Ramos, and was a colleague and close friend of El Negrito Juan, the two men living in small rooms at the back of the clinic. Juan's skin, I remember, was as dark as a moonless night; he often wore a broad-brimmed felt fedora, even in the most sultry weather, and as we sat on the porch with him on his visits, it was obvious that, like Felix, our mother—the very Mami whose moods somehow could transform her into a different person—mattered enormously to him as well.

The two boys who lived next door—one of them was also named Kiko and his brother was Oriol—were our fast friends and our regular nemeses, and hardly a day passed when we did not spend time with them, our respective parents aware that we belonged to different social strata, if we as yet were not. Unlike the three of us, sheltered and undeniably pampered behind the wall of La Villita Candado, Kiko and Oriol Marín were free to roam the streets of Camagüey; they were bold, foul-mouthed, and obnoxious. Kiko and Oriol fascinated us, and simply being with them made us braver in misbehaving than we ever were on our own.

One time, when Kiko and Oriol were with us in our garden, we heard loud and unusual moans and groans coming from the open window of a house that backed up immediately against our back fence. The four of us snuck a peek into the window and observed a young couple energetically making love. The two were *singando*, Kiko Marín explained—doing the horizontal mambo, something adults seemed to think was important to do—and we watched and listened and giggled at what a ridiculous thing it was. The commotion continued for some time and when at last it was finished and we could see that the bed was now empty and carefully made, neighbor Kiko's roguish mind was seized with a great thought. Why didn't we accessorize the love-bed with some shit conveniently supplied by our dog Lucky? It sounded like winning plan to the four of us, and we searched the grass and found four fresh helpings, then used a shovel to lift them across the fence, through the open window and place them on the smooth bedspread. Oriol, my brothers, and I rolled laughing on the lawn and delighting in our cleverness while Kiko ran home to fetch shit supplied by his own dog, and by the time our work was done, the whole of the bed was adorned. It was a brilliantly funny thing to do, we all agreed, before we moved on with the pressing pursuits of the day.

After dinner that evening, we were watching our favorite television comedy, *Casos y Cosas de Casa*—about, as it happened, a young bachelor and his sidekick who constantly created mischief—when the doorbell rang and I suddenly froze, remembering rather vividly now the love making and the array of turds from earlier in the day. Emilita went to the door, and quickly returned, urging my mother to go speak with an angry gentleman, and, quite predictably, I suppose, within seconds she was answering his fury with loud shouts of her own. Their argument grew animated, even by Mami's standards, and it was interrupted only by her repeated trips into the living room to ask us if, in fact, we were responsible for defiling the neighbors' bedroom. We denied that we were, of course, and added tears to our denials, and finally, in an act of betrayal that Judas himself would have admired, we blamed the incident on our neighbors Kiko and Oriol. They must have snuck into our garden and done it when we weren't watching, we insisted in the midst of our sobs, and although Mami surely knew how unlikely that was, she went out once more and furiously told the neighbor to take his complaint to the Marín's house, then came inside and we all returned our attention to the television, never speaking about the matter again.

We discovered the next day that Kiko and Oriol, in turn, had blamed the dog-shit deed on us. But they were punished, while we were not, and neighbor Kiko was angry with us for some time afterward for ratting him and his brother out. Like he did on that occasion, we could count on Kiko to invent the cleverest kinds of capers, but he was hot-tempered and always quick to throw punches, and it was specifically for that reason that Papi once suggested we invite him and Oriol to join us at our favorite place in all the world.

Papi christened the little beach cottage at Playa Santa Lucia he built especially for us *Casa Rojugui*—the latter a word of his own making that combined the names Roberto, Juan, and Guillermo. A twelve-mile long, white-sand beach on a peninsula separated from the Cuban mainland by salt-flats and mosquito-ridden marshland, Playa Santa Lucia lay beside a reach of the Caribbean where the water was clear and calm and astonishingly shallow, and where the world's second-largest coral reef lay only a mile off-shore, a magical, other-worldly place where Papi had snorkeled and scuba-dived since he was a boy himself.

At Santa Lucia, our lives had no boundaries. Our parents' obsessive worries about us vanished there, and we were free to roam the long shoreline—fishing from the *muellecito* that reached out into the bay like a narrow finger, swimming, snorkeling, splashing in the warm sea that always greeted us with open arms. Santa Lucia was the place where once we pulled a three-foot octopus from the shallow, aquiline water, where we would marvel at sand-crab invasions of the beach when the moon was full—so many of them crawling onto the sand that it was almost impossible to walk without crushing one or getting pinched by an angry claw—where following the heavy rains of spring, *millions* of mosquitoes would seek us out as prey. We would race toward the cottage as a black cloud of the beasts blew toward us, and even inside the house, we had little choice but to dive into bed under the mosquito nets that offered us only meager protection.

For boys like us, the beach at Santa Lucia and little Casa Rojugui were the heaven we would have made if God had given us tools. Yet it wasn't a place that was entirely free from the world's complications. Papi had built the two-bedroom, cinderblock cottage early in the 1950s fully a mile away from his brother's and sister's vacation homes—*their* houses built side-by-side so everyone in the extended family could be together on holidays. Tio Antoñico and Tia Elda had been hurt by his decision to build at a distance; they couldn't understand why Papi hadn't similarly wanted us to be near all the fun, and it wasn't until years later that he confessed that he simply wanted to ensure that Antoñico, Elda, and their families wouldn't be frightened by the terrible fighting on nights that were otherwise hushed except for the gentle break of the waves.

Papi himself was always relaxed and at ease at Santa Lucia. He told us repeatedly that he had built the cottage for us, and I loved the fact that in naming it Rojugui, Papi had seemed to define the three of us as equals and had, with a single word, transformed the three of us into one. Rojugui was a name that in the coming years would symbolize for me the bond between my brothers and me that unquestionably helped us survive the blows that were aimed at us, and it was at Casa Rojugui where Papi first taught us to defend ourselves.

My father had been a talented boxer in his younger days—it was the one sport he truly excelled in and loved—and, in retrospect, I realize that because of this, it was a certainty that we would be boxers as well. He purchased two good pairs of gloves for us to share, transformed the cottage's carport into an open-air ring, and for many hours a day on those beach excursions he would instruct us in the techniques that the boxers of his era liked to call "the sweet science." We would take turns sparring with Papi so we could learn basic footwork, balance, punches, and strategy, and before long, of course, it was time to fight each other, then to lure our neighbors Kiko and Oriol to the beach so we could pummel the hell out of them.

As usual, Toto picked up the sport immediately. He was quick and well balanced; he had a great jab and a stinging right hook that he could land at will, and it wasn't long after we began to box that both Toto and Papi were relishing the fact that he could so deftly beat his brothers. Our neighbors were next in line, and at first they were utterly unsuspecting of the trap that was being laid for them when we invited them to join us at the beach. Quite predictably, Toto beat both boys to a pulp—as he did every friend or cousin who entered the makeshift ring with him. Papi would beam with pride— convinced that it was entirely clear to all that Toto had received his skills from him—and it wasn't long before Kiko and Oriol began to decline invitations to join us at the beach.

My brother Kiko and I were enormously proud of Toto, and not solely because of his boxing talents. Among the three of us, Toto was always the best swimmer; he invariably caught more and bigger fish than we did, and it was Toto on whom girls at our school could always be counted on to develop a swooning crush. He was our hero—his strength, athletic abilities, and handsome good looks seemed as reliable to me as the sun coming up in the morning—but my brother could also be quite stubborn and rebellious.

When Toto was in the third grade, he already was powerful and self-possessed enough that by force of will he was able to beat back my mother's strange insistence that he memorize his textbooks. Toto believed her demands were plainly unfair, and in response he vowed to *appear* to be studying—studiously turning pages and mumbling as if he were diligently memorizing—yet when she quizzed him, invariably he could recite next to nothing. This frustrated Mami enormously, and Toto continued the studying ruse over a long enough stretch of time that eventually she came to believe that Toto simply wasn't very bright. She stopped punishing Toto for what she previously had believed was his laziness; she stopped quizzing him entirely, and in the eyes of Kiko and me, Toto emerged as an even greater hero than before, having defeated Mami at her own game without suffering further consequences.

Kiko remained shorter and skinnier than his twin. Although he was not uncoordinated, he appeared awkward and ungainly in comparison with his brother, and somehow accidents always sought him out. It seemed as though if anyone threw a stone into the air in any direction, you could be sure it would find a way to land on poor Kiko's head. He wasn't a bad boxer so much as an *unusual* boxer; he had a strange and complex defensive style that emerged from his deep desire to take as few punches as possible. He seldom threw a punch and focused instead on blocking everything that came his way, and when his opponent did manage to land a blow, Kiko had the curious ability to be able to fold the whole of his body around the offending fist. Papi called him "Merengue"—he could collapse like a hill of whipped egg whites, my father would tell him—and you can be sure it was a name Kiko deeply disliked.

Kiko's bad luck could readily get him into trouble, and if he was planning any mischief, I tried to stay clear of it because I knew instinctively that the outcome had little likelihood of being good—the full force of Mami's wrath coming down on my father's namesake son time after time after time. I worried a lot about Kiko in those days because my mother so often aimed her anger at him. He was the first to be spanked or hit when Mami would lose her temper, and if Mami was mad at Papi, it went without saying that she was angry with Kiko as well. Mami would fly full force at Roberto when he was just seven and eight and nine, and her wrath would be such that Romelia and Emilita would have to hold her until she was calm. I believed Kiko was in real danger, and I admired enormously his ability to take Mami's punishment just as he so deftly took the blows in the ring.

Because my baby fat had stuck with me, I had to endure plenty of teasing. I also seemed certain to catch every childhood disease making the rounds in Camagüey, and the asthma I suffered regularly kept me home from school. I did my best to be the equal of my older brothers, and to prove that status I would fly like Superman from Toto's high bunk-bed onto my single bed below, dive into the bathtub from the sink in our house's small bathroom, and perform sloppy summersaults from the high-dive at the country club. I'd willingly agree to be my brothers' front-man in mischief—all of us aware that whatever punishment from Mami came my way for a given misdeed would be less than what she would otherwise dish out to them. I was a better student than either of my older brothers, but that was a meager triumph, of course, and Papi said plainly that I was a worthless boxer often enough that I really hated the sport. If Toto was the Muhammad Ali of our house and Kiko the Ken Norton, I was nothing more than the bum of the month, and Papi made sure I understood that.

There had been a time in Papi's life when he believed he was a contender. But although he once might have had a shot at real success in the ring—even being tabbed in his early twenties to spar with Cuba's renowned lightweight champion Kid Gavilan—his own boxing days ultimately came to a close well before he became a father.

He was born Roberto Emiliano Vidal Pares in September 1920, the youngest child of Antonio Vidal Bautista and Caridad Pares Nuñes, each of whose parents had immigrated to Cuba from Spain late in the nineteenth century. "Don Antonio," as he was widely known in Camagüey, was a successful businessman and, by every account, an ogre of a father. Each afternoon, Don Antonio's two sons and two daughters were bathed and dressed by servants in preparation for his arrival home, then were required to be waiting for their father at the front door, where he would greet the girls with a perfunctory hug, the boys with a handshake. At the formal dinner that followed, the children were not allowed to speak unless they were spoken to, and, if called upon by their father or mother, their answers were expected to be brief. Because Papi always had suffered a deeply embarrassing "machine-gun" stutter, he prayed as he silently ate each night that he wouldn't be called on—afraid that the way in which he spoke would disgust his father, even as he knew he could count on his mother Caridad's constant encouragement and concern.

Roberto's stutter seemed to worsen when he was around other children, no doubt because he was ridiculed by them so often—in class at school, reciting poetry or speaking his lines in plays, and, particularly painfully for him, at those times when he mustered the courage to talk to a girl. When one of his peers would mimic him, his quick temper would flash white-hot. He regularly tore into brawls with the boys who taunted him and quietly fumed at the girls. He spent his childhood in alternating states of humiliation and anger. Papi loved and admired his older brother Antonio, whom everyone called Antoñico. It didn't help, however, that Antoñico was nothing short of perfection—tall and handsome, athletic and strong, enormously popular among the boys and capable of making the girls of Camagüey swoon.

Papi spent as much time as he could in Antoñico's company, in hopes in part that his brother's debonair ways would rub off on him, and also because he knew he could count on his brother to protect him. I could always see Papi's pride in Antoñico rise in his chest—even decades later—each time he told us about how much the two boys hated the piano lessons their parents required them to take. The piano instructor's home was a string of blocks from their own, and young toughs in the neighborhood ridiculed the Vidal brothers en route. It was clear they were *maricones*, faggots, the kids would taunt, because they played the piano, and throughout each lesson Papi and Antoñico could concentrate on little else except the gauntlet they would have to run when the hour was up. Virtually every piano lesson was capped by a fistfight, and Papi insisted to us that he literally wouldn't have survived those return trips from the piano teacher's if it hadn't been for his big brother's courage and physical prowess.

Because he longed to be strong and fearless like his brother, Papi began to box. He developed a disciplined training regimen, honed his skills, brought real passion to his new sport, and in time he became known as one of Camagüey's most promising young boxers, patterning his fighting technique after Billy Conn, the American light-heavyweight who on a night in New York in June 1941 very nearly defeated the colossal Joe Louis. Papi repeatedly watched newsreels of the famous fight, noting how Conn's flurry of quick jabs had softened Lewis up for the challenger's heavy blows. Papi lent Conn's style a Cuban-accent, developed it to perfection, and it was soon there-after that he caught the eye of Kid Gavilan's manager. But accord-ing to my father, because Papi moved too constantly and wouldn't let Gavilan tag him with his big punches—least of all his trademark "bolo punch," with which Gavilan swung his whole arm like wind-mill before finally landing what was often a knockout blow—he was only invited to spar with the champion a single time. Papi's oppo-nents seldom, if ever, hurt him, he liked to proclaim, yet the truth is that his nose had been broken a dozen times, something that was obvious to my brothers and me and everyone else. What once had been a fine, strong Roman nose now lay utterly flattened on his face, a condition of which I suspect Papi was secretly proud.

Although my father never overcame his stutter and the shame it caused him, he did begin to gain confidence in himself and willed for himself a bright and successful future. He became a fine student, worked tirelessly at Casa Vidal, his father's appliance store, and my grandfather Don Antonio began to believe that it was his younger son, rather than the elder, who would be best to command the family businesses one day. While in college, both boys spent a year abroad at Bridgewater College in Virginia, learning English, delighting in the comparatively permissive American culture, and falling in love with Ella Fitzgerald and Big Band jazz.

Once he had completed his bachelor's degree, Papi debated wheth-er to become a doctor or a pharmacist, ultimately deciding on the later, he told us, because, "All the men went into medicine and all the women went into pharmacy. I wanted to be with the women." In time, he left the prestigious University of Havana with a long-ing to become someone special, a three-pack-a-day smoking habit that helped him demonstrate his sophistication, and a doctorate in pharmacology, a degree that quickly helped him land a job as a sales representative for a pharmaceutical company, traveling throughout Cuba's eastern provinces.

Papi was in Santiago de Cuba in early in 1942 when he received an urgent message that Don Antonio had been severely injured in a car accident. He rushed home to Camagüey to find his father on his death-bed, or so it appeared. During the visit, his father begged Roberto in whispers to quit his job, move home, and take up the family business-es. The appliance and furniture store, operated at the time by Antoñico and his brother-in-law Aquiles, was veering toward bankruptcy; a number of rental properties were faring better, and Don Antonio himself still oversaw the operation of the profitable Hotel Residencial. It's a simple twist of fate, of course, that often points you toward your destiny, and after acquiescing to what he believed was his dying father's final request, Papi soon discovered work at which he truly excelled, work that allowed him to exhibit the tenacity he first learned as a boxer.

Every decision he made and each action he took seemed to bring the store ever more solidly out of its financial hole; his analytical mind, perseverance, and willingness to work hard lead to the store's recovery; Don Antonio almost miraculously recovered as well and began once more to oversee his hotel; and by the time late in the 1950s when dictator Fulgencio Batista's regime was about to collapse—his brutal rule hated by the privileged and poor alike, Cuba's stark economic inequities heating like a pot about to boil over—Papi had secured for his family Camagüey's sole franchises for Philco and Amana appliances, a Fiat automobile dealership, and a mattress factory as prized additions to Don Antonio's prior holdings. In a nation in which entrepreneurial success came only to a relative few, my father seemed born to make money; he loved his accumulation of wealth and the status it brought, and he devoted huge energy to being viewed by others as a proud member of the city's business and social elite. He still stuttered—terribly sometimes—still was tremendously insecure in ways that haunted him, but unlike boxing, in the world of business, it seemed, Roberto Vidal would succeed.

It is amazing to me to remember how very insulated our lives were at La Villita Candado. At the beach at Santa Lucia and in Casa Rojuqui, we were free as the gulls and pipers that plied the shores. But in Camagüey—perhaps because Papi recalled all-too clearly the beatings he had taken on the city's streets as a boy—we lived in a kind of protective isolation from the poverty, hardships, and cold complexities of contemporary Cuban life, and the Camagüey I knew was an exotic realm into which Kiko, Toto, and I virtually never ventured on our own.

The city—first called Santa Maria del Puerto Principe—was founded on Cuba's northern coast in 1514, but its early residents suffered such repeated pillaging from Caribbean pirates that they moved the entire settlement inland in hopes of escaping the banditry. Yet when the infamous British privateer Henry Morgan and five-hundred men sacked dozens of Cuban settlements and fortifications in 1668, they virtually destroyed the new Puerto Prinicipe, and in response, this time the city's residents vowed to rebuild what would henceforth be called Camagüey as a kind of illogical labyrinth, its new streets twisting, turning, and dead-ending unexpectedly, the maze an attempt to dissuade invaders of every sort from entering and risking being trapped and ambushed before they could attack or flee.

On its flat inland plain, the city lay in the rain-shadow of Cuba's high Sierra Maestra and rainfall was scant enough that the enterprising Camagüeyanos also fashioned huge earthen jars—like the one we employed at La Villita Candado—to capture run-off from roofs during the rainy season. These *tinajones* were everywhere, and, together with the warren of narrow and interwoven streets, for centuries they remained the foremost symbols of the city, and they are what I remember most particularly of the town of a hundred thousand people in which I spent those early and abruptly ended years.

Although I couldn't know it at the time, the first glimpse of the city my brothers and I saw from behind the wall of our home pointed eerily toward our future. Immediately across the Carretera Central from our house was El Asilo Padre Valencia, an asylum named after the priest who had founded it many years before, an austere and forbidding place that housed the very poor and the utterly hopeless—shoeless, sometimes toothless people in ragged clothes who included both the elderly and children who had been orphaned or abandoned—and it was the asylum that my brothers and I first would think of when, in Colorado in the autumn of 1961, we discovered that we had been sent to an orphanage, the asylum a place whose image would utterly torment my parents when they learned in letters where their young sons now lived.

Because Papi insisted on spending as much time at Casa Vidal as he could, it was Mami who was our chauffer on most of our excursions out into Camagüey. A notoriously bad driver, she could make the shortest of journeys an adventure—the combination of her frightful driving and the city's twisting cobblestone streets ensuring that our outings were every bit as harrowing as they were fun. Five days

a week we donned the short pants and blue shirts we were required
to wear and traveled to El Colegio Champagna, a parochial school
run by the Marist Brothers, and on occasional Sundays we drove to
mass at La Iglesia de Las Mercedes, the church where my parents had
been married. A visit to my grandfather's medical clinic—even when
we were sick—meant we would see our great friends and mentors
Felix and Juan, and, of course, our grandparents and Tio Nene. We
loved having the run of Don Antonio's five-story Hotel Residencial,
where we would join our cousins in mischief of every sort, including
the time we enraged our grandfather by spitting from a hotel balcony onto pedestrians on the sidewalk below. And there was always
something special about our trips to Casa Vidal, which proudly occupied a corner of the Plaza de las Mercedes. I loved to walk the aisles
among the many white-enameled and round-shouldered refrigerators and ranges, the marvelous portable dishwashers you could con-
nect with hoses to a kitchen sink, the big-eyed television sets in their
boxy wooden cabinets; and the patio furniture in rainbow colors
that seemed to offer everyone a life of pleasure and ease. There was
something pleasingly contemporary, progressive, and abundant in
the dazzling array of wares, and I was quietly proud that Papi was
the greatly respected *dueño* in charge of it all.

The modern world was a wonderful place, Casa Vidal seemed to
affirm in 1956, and my father and mother and Kiko and Toto and I
couldn't imagine looking toward the future with anything other than
anticipation and swelling confidence. Good fortune had visited us in
so many forms, we knew. We were as lucky as the handful of Cubans
who once had won houses in bars of soap, and our corner of Cuba,
Papi and Mami assured us, was the center of the universe.

El Negrito Juan, Tío Nene, and Feliz outside my grandfather Dr. Ramos' clinic in the late 1950s

Dos

A Wonderful Time to be Alive

D uring the half-century since Fidel Castro returned home to
Cuba and turned our world upside down, it has been impossible for me not to note the many things the magnetic leader
of the Cuban revolution and my father shared in common. In January
1959, Papi first responded to the nearly impossible news that Fidel and
his rag-tag army had seized power from Batista's forces with something
akin to giddy delight. He came, in time, to despise Castro with every
emotion inside him, believing Fidel had destroyed Cuba, *knowing* he
had shattered everything Papi had achieved. Despite that hatred, my
father continued throughout his life to express great admiration for
Castro's boldness and his brilliance—qualities I know Papi wanted to
believe he shared with the man who so profoundly changed his life.
He remained keenly and painfully aware, I know, that—unlike Fidel,
who had actualized his dreams—my father, for his part, had not.

Although Papi was older than Fidel by six years, the particulars of
their early lives were strikingly similar. Both were born far to the east
of the seat of Cuba's political and financial power in Havana. Both were
the sons of authoritarian, well-to-do men who pushed their sons to
accomplish great things; both earned graduate degrees from the University of Havana, the nation's most prestigious school; both lived for
a time in the United States before returning home—each man fascinated by the culture and history of the huge country to the north, each

choosing to take his bride to the U.S. on his honeymoon. And they were alike in more subtle ways as well: Papi had grown up shamed by his stuttering while Fidel was humiliated by the fact that his mother was his father's cook rather than his wife and that therefore he was illegitimate in many eyes. Both worked ceaselessly to earn their fathers' respect; both brought fiery intensity to the goals they set for themselves; both crafted complex, pain-riddled relationships with their children, and it's intriguing to me as well that although both men were deeply romantic, both suffered—and were largely responsible for—embittered relationships with the women they loved.

What Papi set out to do soon after he began to prove himself as a businessman was, plainly and simply, to marry above his class. Although he was confident that his burgeoning wealth one day would allow him to reach the level of Camagüey's social elite, my father was well-aware that *that* status was something he still only aspired to, and he also understood that in order to achieve his goal, his stuttering, introversion, and insecurity had to be modulated by a mate who was everything he wasn't in that regard—by a woman who was gregarious, always at ease, charming, and beautiful.

Marta Teresa Ramos Almendros seemed stunningly qualified in every way to become his wife when Papi met her, and he immediately set out to win the glittering socialite and prove something important about himself in the conquest: although Antoñico was the heart-throb of all the eligible young women in Camagüey, *he* would be the one who would woo, then wed, the most desirable of them all.

For her part, Mami was looking for a way out of her parents' home. Life there, with its constant focus on misshapen Nene and his chronic suffering, had been brutally hard in many respects, and she had an unwavering sense that she deserved better. She was nineteen years old—it was certainly time she found her husband—and Roberto Vidal seemed a perfect catch. He was well-educated; his success rebuilding one of his father's businesses recently had made him the talk of Camagüey's financial community, and as my grandfather, Dr. Ramos, reminded his daughter, her prospective father-in-law could provide an essential safety net, should Roberto's successes ever turn sour.

Their courtship was short and predictably tumultuous, given their oil-and-water natures. Papi was logical and unemotional; Mami was unpredictable and hot-tempered. Each was aware of those stark dissimilarities, but they were differences the two determinedly chose to deny. Because their dates were almost always chaperoned by their parents, it was all-too-easy to delude themselves into believing that they would be blissful, in fact, once they finally could be alone. Their wedding on a brilliant Saturday in June 1947 at the Iglesia de las Mercedes—in the same plaza where Casa Vidal proudly stood—was the social event of the season, and the next day the at-least-outwardly perfect couple was off on a month-long honeymoon in Miami.

Their first home in Camagüey was at the Hotel Residencial—a circumstance neither of them wanted to endure for long. Mami complained ceaselessly about Papi's meddling family, and he was deeply embarrassed—right from the beginning—by their loud and frequent arguments, which he was certain everyone in his larger family could hear. Within a few months, they moved to La Villita Candado—a belated wedding gift from Papi's parents—but the change of address didn't offer them better days. Roberto was utterly unprepared to deal with Marta's wild emotional swings and her constant need to be pampered, and she, in turn, was baffled and bitterly hurt by his sarcasm, stubbornness, and cruelly demeaning behavior. Almost daily, the most minor disagreement would trigger a battle that would burn hot for hours, and by the end of their first year together, they were miserable and Papi—he liked to insist in retrospect—was ready to call it quits.

As my father repeatedly would tell the story years later, one day he insisted that Mami pack all her belongings because their marriage was over. He was "returning" her to her parents, he told her, yet once they entered her parents' home and he was reminded of the unhappy life she would have to lead once more, he took pity on her and decided to "keep her" instead. Papi would tell us this story only when Mami was within earshot, of course—only to inflict a bit more of the kind of pain that was so characteristic of their interactions—and it was a story I never believed. If my father ever had made such an absurd announcement, in fact, I know my mother would have exploded immediately, and probably violently, and certainly wouldn't have obediently packed her bags. And I'm equally sure that my proud and commanding grandfather would have throttled my father—accomplished boxer or not—had Papi announced his inconceivable plan to hand his daughter back. Yet my father's fictitious tale does reveal something of the dynamic that defined their marriage throughout its course—Papi forever presenting himself as a person of superior character who had more important things to do than deal with a wife who bordered on insanity, that proclamation triggering in Mami the wild-eyed wrath that succeeded only in further reinforcing the image he crafted of her.

Were they ever in love? I hope so, but I doubt it, and it saddens me to think that perhaps they experienced nothing at all of the delight most couples share, at least in their earliest days. What happiness they hoped to create together evaporated immediately into the often-stifling tropical air, and, from the beginning, theirs was a wild and chaotic conjugal bond, one that was strangely symbolic of the way in which the whole of the Cuban culture soon would turn on itself with rage.

Like a slow-moving tropical storm that is inexorably on its way, deep societal unrest had begun to build in Cuba in 1952 when Fulgencio Batista, who had been democratically elected to a four-year term as president in 1940, returned to Cuba from exile in Florida and seized power by coup d'etat. The United States quickly recognized the new government; U.S. corporations established themselves on the island in unprecedented numbers, and a flood of American tourists soon joined them, lured particularly by legally sanctioned casino gambling—controlled by the Italian mafia, to whom Batista had open and obvious ties.

Throughout the twentieth century, the gap between Cuba's wealthy and its desperately poor had widened enormously, and it appeared to most that Batista now was intent on widening that chasm further. His military commanders kept the peace only with the most heavy-booted kinds of brutality, and his regime was corrupt from bottom to top, thousands of professionals and business people like my father necessarily acquiescing to a system of widely legitimized bribes and kickbacks in order to thrive.

Fidel Castro was a twenty-six year old graduate in law from the University of Havana in 1952, an idealistic and fiercely patriotic young man who was planning to run for parliament at the moment that Batista seized power. Castro led a court challenge against Batista, accusing him of violating the Cuban constitution, but his petition was refused. In angry response, he organized an armed attack against army barracks in the cities of Santiago de Cuba and Bayamo on the early morning of July 26, 1953—quixotic assaults that almost certainly were doomed to fail against Batista's well-trained and heavily-armed forces. Over eighty attackers were killed in the chaotic melees; Castro was taken prisoner, tried, and sentenced to fifteen years in jail.

In hopes of preventing the popular Fidel from becoming widely seen as a martyr to his reformist cause, Batista chose to release him from prison in May 1955; Castro fled into exile, first to the United States and then to Mexico, and although he would not be heard from again for more than a year, his obsession with defeating Batista now was total. He vowed never to rest until the dictator was forced from the island, convinced that in response to his skilled leadership of a small revolutionary force, hundreds of thousands of Cubans would join in a popular insurrection.

On December 2, 1956, eighty-two insurgent exiles—who had dangerously overcrowded a sixty-foot pleasure yacht on its voyage across the Gulf of Mexico from the Mexican city of Tuxpan—disembarked on the southern coast of Cuba's Oriente province. Lying in wait for them was a battalion of Batista's army. Only twelve of the invaders survived the bloody assault, among them Fidel, his brother Raul, and an Argentinean physician-turned-revolutionary named Ernesto "Che" Guevara, the guerillas escaping into the Sierra Maestra to regroup and, then quite incredibly, to claim victory. "We have already won," Castro declared from his remote mountain hideout. He and merely a dozen *compañeros* were pitted against a force of fifty-thousand regular soldiers equipped with state-of-the-art weaponry supplied to Batista by the United States, yet only twenty-five months later, Fidel's audacious claim would prove brilliantly prescient.

In spite of his two disastrous military failures, Fidel's tiny militia soon began to grow in great numbers, hundreds of poor *campesinos* and disaffected and otherwise hopeless young men from the cities joining him with a proud sense of their collective purpose, buoyed by Castro's bold rhetoric and his belief in the inevitability of their cause. I remember seeing graffiti everywhere in those days that read "Viva Fidel" and "Fidel Si, Batista No," the scrawled slogans the work of wonderfully fearless people, I imagined. Although hundreds of thousands of Cubans saw Batista as a ruthless and brutal pimp exploiting his citizens for his own gain, most were afraid to express their beliefs publicly for fear they or their families would be punished or killed. Privately, however, people cheered the revolutionary army on. Fidel's progress was the constant topic of discussion whenever we gathered with my father's family—Tio Antoñico and my grandfather, Abuelito Antonio, were as fascinated as Papi was by his improbable but ever-increasing successes, eager to hear from friends and confidants who had listened with their own ears to the reports from *Radio Revelde*, the clandestine rebel broadcasts with which Castro recounted his victories and repeatedly proclaimed the certainty of his triumph.

Papi's businesses continued to thrive despite the myriad political uncertainties and the constant threat that the fighting would come to Camagüey. Casa Vidal had become solvent again by the time the insurgents encamped in the Sierra Maestra, and my father was proud that the appliance store now generated enough capital that he and Antoñico could begin to initiate other ventures. First they bought a series of houses they renovated and made rental properties; next they added two floors of apartments to the building that housed Casa Vidal; they purchased a Fiat dealership, and because my grandfather's hotel always had been an excellent business, they planned to construct and operate their own hotel as well. We lived comfortably at La Villita Candado, often visited the beach house at Santa Lucia, and by the time Castro's victory began to seem a real possibility, Papi also had purchased a lot in a high-profile new subdivision dubbed Montecarlo, which its developers planned to fill with palatial homes for the wealthy of Camagüey. The grand new home my father looked forward to building would be proof both to him and everyone in his sphere that he had achieved his goal and now was indisputably one of his city's elite.

Under Castro's shrewd leadership, the revolutionary army—comprised almost exclusively of the poor and idealistic who had virtually nothing to lose—began to score a series of impressive and strategically important victories over Batista's forces, and by December 1958, Castro was confident enough of his soldiers' prowess that he launched a major offensive on the city of Santa Clara, with *Comandante* Che Guevara in command. Guevara's forces deftly captured an armorplated train Batista had sent to re-supply his troops defending the city and—fighting now with the weapons and munitions meant for their foes—Guevara's men seized control of the city. Santiago de Cuba was next to fall, and although the government still blithely contended via radio, television, and the press that the insurgents never could win, Fulgencio Batista understood, in fact, that his soldiers were deserting in droves by now, and that Castro had taken the upper hand. For some time, Batista secretly and systematically had shipped massive amounts of gold out of Cuba to Spain, and also had made a series of contingency plans to ensure his personal survival. Then, just prior to midnight at a lavish New Year's Eve party at which he was the host, a buoyant and surprisingly high-spirited Batista announced to his resplendently attired guests that he too was embarking for Spain by way of the Dominican Republic, his declaration sending shockwaves throughout Cuba and indeed much of the world.

Fidel Castro—no doubt as astonished as anyone—assumed power the following day, and never in all the history of Cuba was a New Year's Day more riotously celebrated. Fidel gave his first speech as the provisional head of state from a second-story balcony in Santiago, the city where his initial military sortie had failed so spectacularly five years before, and in every village and town throughout the country people flooded the streets and rejoiced with wild abandon. The mood in Camagüey was ecstatic, and although my brothers and I were too young to truly understand the dimensions of what had occurred, we could feel the crackling energy in the air that seemed to attest that something extraordinarily important had happened to our country. Bells tolled, car-horns blared, the telephone at our house rang incessantly, and friends and relatives knocked at the door, everyone embracing jubilantly and toasting a wondrous beginning to the New Year.

Then something odd occurred. Papi retreated into the bedroom he shared with my mother and returned to the living room wearing a broad-brimmed, pinch-front fedora I'd never seen him wear before and—to my amazement—he also had strapped to his waist a leather holster cradling a heavy pistol. Neither Kiko, Toto, nor I had the slightest notion that our father owned a weapon, nor did we have a clue where he might be headed as he marched out of the house.

Although he never explained his plan, I suspect that—like hundreds of civilians that day—Papi wanted to help ensure that soldiers in Batista's army who were stationed at small *cuarteles*, or forts, located throughout the country surrendered their weapons and accepted their defeat. One such cuartel was located a few blocks from our house, and a few minutes following Papi's departure it may have been the source of a sudden and frightening round of machine-gun fire. None of us could be sure whether the blasts from the gun had been fired in celebration, warning, or as an attack, but seemingly within seconds of hearing them Papi burst back into the house, nearly knocking over both Romelia and Mami as he rushed to the bedroom. After a time, he emerged again, this time without his hat, the pistol no longer dramatically poised on his right hip. He checked to be sure the two doors to the house were locked, then planted himself in front of the television, chain-smoking and monitoring the news of the astonishing day but offering none of us information about his brief brush with the revolution.

The first days of 1959 were filled with extraordinary excitement. Fidel and his troops seized control of Havana, securing all the government facilities located there, then the new leader began a victory march, traveling the whole length of the island, from Pinar del Rio in the west to Guantánamo in the east, a celebratory procession that would have rivaled any Caesar's triumphal entry into Rome. For days, offices and shops everywhere were shut down. Throngs of people spilled out into the streets, and virtually every Cuban tried to find a way to see and cheer our revolutionary hero as he made his way across the welcoming nation. In our particular case, we knew we were enormously lucky that as Fidel marched through Camagüey, he would pass immediately in front of my grandfather Ramos's home and medical clinic.

I remember that it seemed to take forever to drive to my grandparents' house on that august January day; everyone in Camagüey, it appeared, had the same plans the five of us did, yet at last we arrived and found my grandparents, Nene, Felix, and Juan, and joined them in amazement at the remarkable scene. The tank on which Castro—still wearing his army fatigues—was riding had stopped directly in front of the house, and Fidel himself was standing atop it, smiling broadly and waving, shaking hands, and kissing the babies parents lifted up to him with pride and adulation. People threw flowers, confetti, freed doves into the festive air, and I remember that Papi, proffering cigarettes to friends and strangers alike, seemed happier than

I ever had seen him before. His family's future had grown brighter for some time, and now his country's prospects were resoundingly optimistic as well. Finally everything in our lives had come together, and even Mami was radiantly joyful that day. She and Papi lifted each of their young sons high, and I touched Fidel's broad and sun-darkened hand, and it was a wonderful time to be alive.

Tres

The Bearded Ones

As if to cement everyone's faith in the certainty that the revolution had engendered real democracy in Cuba, Fidel announced that Manuel Urrutia, a widely respected judge, would become the nation's interim president, and José Miró Cardoña, dean of the Havana bar, would assume the post of prime minister. The sole role Castro wanted for himself, he proclaimed, was to be commander-in-chief of the nation's armed forces—and Fidel continued to appear publicly only in olive-drab fatigues. He was a simple soldier, he seemed to want to assure people, and he also appeared reluctant to surrender a romantic image of himself that first had taken form during the years he was encamped in the Sierra Maestra. He wore a pistol around his waist; he declined to trim his dark and unruly beard, and those closest to him maintained a similar personal style. His brother Raul, Che Guevara, trusted comrade Camilo Cienfuegos, and many others continued to dress like guerilla soldiers as well, their hair and beards long, braces of bullets slung across their chests, their rifles hung on their shoulders. And very soon, hundreds, even thousands, who hadn't lifted an arm during the war adopted the paramilitary look as well, as if to help keep memories fresh of the struggles and sacrifices Fidel and his *compañeros* had endured in order to win our collective freedom.

Legends surrounding the *revolucionarios* spread quickly across the island; they became folk heroes and celebrities, and in the popular imagination, Fidel grew larger than life. He appeared constantly on television, delivering long and fulminating speeches, catching more and bigger fish than anyone else on a widely touted deep-sea fishing excursion, pitching for a baseball team made up of revolutionary soldiers who dubbed themselves *Los Barbudos*, the Bearded Ones, in exhibition games against professional Cuban players. Yet the more the lower classes took delight in the escalating image of Fidel as a multifaceted man of the people, the more nervous the upper classes grew about who, in fact, now controlled the country. Although Fidel and Che were a lawyer and physician respectively, Cuba's old elite increasingly worried that unwashed illiterates now held tight to the reins of power, and their fears grew greater as Fidel ever more securely consolidated power and set about ridding the country of those whom he believed might attempt to mount a counter-revolution—employing precisely the same kinds of brutality Batista had used against his enemies.

With Che Guevara heading up the process as chief prosecutor, hundreds of policemen and soldiers from Batista's regime were arrested and tried for human-rights abuses and war crimes, and the cry *¡paredón!*, to the wall!, became commonplace, as the vast majority of those who were convicted were executed by firing squads. Che used imprisonment, torture, and expulsion from the country to intimidate those whose crimes did not merit death, and more and more, governments around the world began to look toward Cuba with alarm. In mid-April, cheering crowds greeted Fidel when he visited the United States at the invitation of the American Society of Newspaper Editors, and he assured the editors that neither he nor any of his inner circle were communists. But in Washington, a suspicious President Dwight Eisenhower snubbed the Cuban leader by refusing to meet with him—sending Vice-President Richard Nixon to confer with Fidel instead—and once back at home, Castro openly began to court the increasingly influential Cuban Communist Party.

On July 26, in celebration of the sixth anniversary of his initial, ill-fated attack on Batista's army in 1952—and only half a year since he and his soldiers ultimately had been victorious—Fidel announced with great fanfare an "agrarian reform" program at an enormous rally in Havana. More than a million *campesinos* had been bused to the capital city for the occasion, and as part of his long and passionate oration, he declared that all of the nation's sugar plantations immediately were being confiscated by the government and that their lands would be divided among the plantations' thousands of workers. In the months leading up to that moment, Papi had become increasingly concerned about whether Fidel would begin to nationalize businesses and private property; I remember him watching intently every moment of Castro's seemingly endless speeches, and Papi would marvel aloud at the brilliance of the man. He would listen closely for assurances that Fidel would not condemn the country's private holdings and would maintain a free-market economy, but on that sweltering July afternoon his hopes were dashed.

The color now blanched from his face, Papi explained to us that my grandfather's sugar plantation—the place where Mami and Nene had spent their happiest times as children—was lost as of that moment, and he was astonished too to think that Fidel had exhibited no qualms about seizing his own father's plantation and redistributing it to his workers. Like virtually every businessman in Cuba—as well as their counterparts in the United States—Papi was caught up in the terrible fear of communism that had been exemplified early in the 1950s by U.S. Senator Joseph McCarthy's "red scare" hearings, and, just two years before, by shock and dismay at the Soviet launch into earth orbit of the satellite Sputnik, signaling, it seemed terribly apparent, the ideology's might and the breadth of its worldwide reach. Like millions of people in the Americas and Europe, Papi was convinced that communists stood in virulent opposition to God, family, free enterprise, and the holding of private property, and he was horrified to think that the man he had thrilled to greet with his wife and sons only six months before now had introduced communist theory and practice into his homeland.

From that day forward, the political upheaval the revolution set in motion seemed to advance with ever-increasing speed, and thousands—even hundreds of thousands—of people like my parents began to grow frightened by the idea that they would live in a communist nation, and they viewed each new event with swelling suspicion. In October, Huber Matos, a Camagüey native whom everyone we knew greatly admired—and who had served alongside Fidel since his early days in the mountains—openly announced his concern that Castro was allowing communists in his ranks to unduly influence him, and warned that he would resign from his government post if that situation did not change. Fidel journeyed to Camagüey to attempt to persuade his old friend and ally to remain loyal, but when he failed to win that assurance, Castro accused Matos of being a traitor to the revolution and arrested him. At almost precisely the same time, *Comandante* Camilo Cienfuegos—beloved by many and believed to be a strong voice for moderation among Fidel's inner circle—died when his small plane quite mysteriously disappeared at sea, fueling rampant rumors that Fidel, Che, or someone close to the two had ordered his death, and further diminishing the hope that a constitutional democracy would be the legacy of the revolution.

José Miró Cardona had resigned as prime minister early on—Fidel naming himself to succeed him—then in November, Manuel Urrutia resigned as president, the whole of his cabinet departing with him. I still remember the looks of disbelief on my parents' faces when they saw on television the news that Urrutia was gone, and I remember being perplexed: Fidel *was* the revolution, as far as I could tell—at least he was the only person the news media paid any attention to-and I couldn't understand why the departure of someone I'd never heard of could dismay my parents so deeply. In December, Huber Matos was found guilty of treason and sentenced to twenty years in prison, and by New Year's Day, the first anniversary of the triumph of the revolution, only nine of the twenty-one members of the initial revolutionary government remained in office. A few weeks later—as if to solidify fears of Fidel's true goals—he formed his first pact with the Soviet Union, Premier Nikita Khrushchev agreeing to buy five million tons of Cuban sugar and to supply the country with oil, grain, and credit.

Throughout the country, and certainly in Camagüey as well, the Cuban people seemed to be losing all sense of civil order. Not a day passed during 1960 when we didn't hear shots being fired at all times of the day and night, and sometimes my brothers and I even watched from the relative safety of our walled garden as men shot at each other with rifles and pistols. We would panic at the sight of people in olive-drab uniforms roaming the rooftops of neighboring houses, and would run into the house and hide in the closets. Electrical blackouts became common, food was scarce, and the fights between Mami and Papi grew more intense, most of them initiated at the dinner table as they discussed Cuba's fate and our own. When Fidel finally declared in a broadcast speech that he was a "Marxist-Leninist and will be so until the day I die," his words exploded like a bomb out of the television set in our living room. Friends and family members rushed to our house—just as they had full of joy on the day little more than a year before when Castro claimed power—but this time everyone was in utter panic. By now the United States had severed diplomatic relations with the Cuban government and had set in place economic sanctions blocking the shipment of food, medical supplies, and other goods between the two countries, and I remember Papi declaring to those assembled that day that everyone would have to fight to preserve his properties and his businesses. People vowed yes, they would fight, but their options for doing so clearly were very limited, and the air in the room was thick and smoky with dread.

The first time I remember anyone talking openly about getting out of Cuba came only after Fidel announced that henceforth everyone in the nation would serve in the military to help defend our island against *los yanquis imperialistas*, the imperialist Yankees to the north. And the conversations about fleeing only escalated when the government instituted neighborhood surveillance teams, known as the "G-2," which were intended to empower the citizenry to defend the revolution, but which emerged instead as a kind of Cuban McCarthyism in reverse. Instead of alerting the government to reputed "communists" on the basis of unsubstantiated evidence and false accusations, as had occurred a decade before in the U.S., the Cuban G-2 began to attack "anti-communists" and "anti-revolutionaries" with the same kind of innuendo, hearsay, and fabricated evidence. And in our case, it became clear that local members of the G-2 were capable of zealously persecuting their neighbors out of little more than their hope for personal gain.

Memo Castellano and his family had been our friends since we had become their next-door neighbors more twelve years before. Memo—after whom I'd been named—babied our car in return for extra income, and his son Pillin, about ten years our senior, was someone Kiko, Toto, and I liked and admired. But by 1960, twenty-one year-old Pillin had joined Fidel's militia and had been named head of the neighborhood surveillance team. Pillin quickly began to take his new responsibilities seriously—so much so, in fact, that I once overheard Mirella Marín, mother of our buddies Kiko and Oriol and our neighbors as well, warning Mami and Papi to be wary of Pillin, who, she said, plainly wanted to move into our house. It seemed that on several occasions Pillin had shared with her his plans for our house once we were gone, clearly implying that he would see to it that my parents were jailed as counter-revolutionaries. Sometimes Pillin would suddenly appear at our house, then officiously and with grave disgust in his voice announce that we were violating some new curfew or regulation, and even at only nine, I was sophisticated enough to sense that their accusations had much to do with their confidence that Roberto Vidal *y toda su familia* would not remain at La Villita Candado for long.

To make matters worse, one of my father's most trusted employees at Casa Vidal had joined the militia as well. Papi had seen something special in Ernesto LaRua soon after he'd hired him half a decade before; the two became close as my father mentored him, and Papi said he could imagine making Ernesto a minority partner in the business one day. He was devastated therefore when Ernesto announced early in 1960 that he was joining what Papi now saw as Fidel's repugnant communist cause, then was outraged when Ernesto openly turned against him. On three separate occasions, Ernesto appeared at the store wearing a pistol and accompanied by other armed militiamen, the group of intense young *Fidelistas* attempting to make the case to Papi that he should accompany them to a local tribunal where he would answer for his supposed crimes. Each time Papi stood his ground, and for reasons that perhaps actually had something to do with Ernesto's early rapport with him, the men left without forcibly taking my father with them.

I'll never forget, however, the night LaRua and his gang of toughs descended on our house. My parents were out for the evening; Kiko, Toto, and I were watching television with Emilita, and, quite unusually, Gladis was seated in the living room with us as well. At about 9:30, the doorbell rang. It was considered courteous in those days to ring from the gate rather than to do so from outside the front door, and I remember all of us going toward the door to see who was waiting out on the sidewalk. Gladis reached the door first, opened it, and was shocked to see Ernesto and other men, their guns drawn, already on the porch and standing only inches away. Instinctively, she slammed the door shut and locked it, and we—like the young fools we were—rushed to a nearby window to try to make some sense of why these men had arrived. When Ernesto saw three wide-eyed and quizzical faces peering out at him, he shouted gravely that he was searching for "that thief Roberto Vidal on behalf of the people of Cuba." He demanded to be let inside, but, of course, none of us now would have considered opening the door. Gladis explained that my parents were out, yet despite his further demands, would not tell him where they were. After conferring with his fellow patriots for a few moments, he insisted again that we open the door; he and his comrades would wait for my parents inside, but when Gladis refused once more, they finally left. In retrospect, I'm not sure I understand why they didn't simply force their way into the house, which surely they could have done, but whatever their reasons for departing, we were temporarily safe, and the three of us insisted on waiting up for our parents to help explain to them what had occurred—quite incredibly—in their absence.

No one slept at La Villita Candado that night, all of us waiting warily for LaRua and his tormentors to return, and I remember fearing most of all during those endless hours the possibility that if they did, Papi once more would take his pistol from the bedroom and attempt to fight them rather than agree to being taken to jail. Then, not long after dawn, Papi and Mami came into the bedroom where the three of us slept to tell us the only safe thing for us to do was to go into hiding. We each would pack only a few things—as if we were just off to the beach for a day or two—but our destination would be one of the apartments above the Casa Vidal, which we would make our home until, well, they said, it wasn't at all clear how long we would be away from La Villita Candado.

As Mami, Emilita and Romelia were busy packing the car a short time later, somehow it had seemed to Kiko and me like the perfect moment for a sword-fight with sticks we found in the garden. But as Mami called us to come to the car, I let down my guard and Kiko scored with a direct hit to my eye. Whatever hopes my parents had that we could secretly leave that morning were shattered by my squeals of pain. Within seconds, Pillin Castellano was at his window, trying to assess the cause of all the commotion. His eyes met my father's; neither man made a gesture or changed his expression, and Papi returned his attention to me, yet he was certain that within minutes Pillin would find a way to inform Ernesto that all of us had left our home.

No doubt I continued to cry as we all bundled ourselves into the car, and Papi was silent as he drove us to the apartment in the Plaza de las Mercedes. We quickly unloaded the car, then Mami remained there with Kiko and Toto while Papi escorted me to a nearby hospital. My wound wasn't serious—and I got to wear a pirate's patch over my eye for a couple of weeks—and I think the patch added something to my sense of the drama of those days as time slowly unfolded and we sat huddled together above the store. Before the week was out, however, Papi said he believed it was safe for us to return home; yet he didn't explain what circumstances, if any, had changed, and, of course, Ernesto LaRua was far from finished with Papi.

The year 1960 seemed to progress inexorably from bad to worse. No longer could any of us feel safe in our homes, and the U.S. embargo against our country meant that absolutely everything was in bitterly short supply. Gladis, Romelia, Emilita—and even Mami—had to wait in endless queues for what little food was available. All restaurants and markets were closed, and we simply made do with what little we could scrounge: once I remember Gladis making soup from nothing more than the paper the meat we'd received earlier that week had been wrapped in. Medicines too were almost impossible to come by—a situation I became personally aware of when one day I fell from the great mango tree and landed on a metal grate, piercing my ankle. At the hospital emergency room, Dr. Viamonte, the physician who treated me, could spare a needle and eight sutures but he sewed me up without any anesthetic to block the pain nor even iodine or any other disinfectant with which to clean the wound. A tetanus shot too was out of the question, my mother was told: given the desperate shortages, my injury wasn't serious enough to merit the use of those precious medicines.

Cuba was returning to the Stone Age, Papi regularly proclaimed. He watched in horror as Fidel's government began confiscating and nationalizing foreign-owned businesses, and it wasn't surprising that

American companies were the first to be seized. The embargo effectively ended foreign investment in Cuba, and countries that once had been our important allies began to dramatically curtail direct economic aid, fearful of reprisals from the United States. As factories, farms, companies, and shops shut down, hundreds of thousands of people lost their sole source of income, and the "people's" government itself was far too financially strapped to offer them any assistance.

Then, in an effort to end the once-stark distinctions between Cuba's economic classes in a single astonishing move, Fidel announced that the nation's longstanding currency henceforth would have no value, meaning that stocks, bonds, savings, and financial instruments of every kind suddenly were worthless. In place of the old currency, every Cuban now would receive a one-time payment of two hundred new Cuban pesos—no more and no less. Every one of us—*dueños* and workers, servants and those they served—suddenly were economic equals, but in the process, people like my parents believed they had been robbed of the rewards of their life's work. Papi was beside himself with anger, loss, and the deepest kind of desperation. Everything he strived for—and the very work that had proved his worth as a man—now were gone. Fidel was insane, my father daily announced in disgust, yet sane or not, he possessed absolute power and at a whim could pull strings as if we were *marionetas*, making us ridiculously dance for perverse pleasures of his own.

Then, without warning, without a hint of his plan or so much as a single word to his children, without kissing his adoring grandchildren goodbye, Papi's father, Don Antonio, the family patriarch, disappeared in the early days of January 1961.

For two years, Cuban citizens had been deserting the island in enormous numbers. People tied to the Batista regime were the first to depart, of course, and they began to do so in the first days after Fidel assumed power on New Year's Day 1959. As the nature of the government and society Castro sought to create began to be more clear, and as people in Cuba's professional and business classes grew ever more convinced that not only were their wealth and prosperity threatened in the new Cuba but so were their very lives, they too chose to abandon their homeland rather than wait to see whether their fears proved correct. That my grandfather chose to be one of them wasn't difficult to understand, but what no one could make sense of—least of all his two sons to whom he left the precarious task of protecting the family's businesses—was why he trusted none of us with his decision, nor why he would leave my dear grandmother, Abuelita Cachita, behind, particularly because her health had begun to fail and medical services in Cuba had become problematic at best.

Yet although none of us understood why Abuelito Antonio had abandoned us so suddenly, there was no mistaking the way in which his departure became a watershed event, one setting in motion the exodus that followed. Soon after my grandfather was gone, Papi's best friend and college roommate José Ramón Zayasbazan, his wife Georgina, and their children left for Florida. Then at my grandfather's urging, Papi's older sister Elda and her husband, Aquiles Riverón, and their three boys joined him where he had settled in south Miami and had already begun to purchase properties in hopes he could rebuild his wealth and find ways to funnel dollars to those of us in his family still in Cuba. Next to go were Nenita, uncle Antoñico's wife, and their four children—Antoñico himself choosing to stay behind for the time being to help Papi in the struggle to keep the several businesses from being expropriated by Fidel.

We were far from alone; thousands of Cuban families similarly were torn apart, people immigrating to the United States, Mexico, and Spain foremost among many destinations, yet my brothers and I—too young to have insight into the ways in which large political events often so dramatically play themselves out in individual lives—simply felt deep loss and abandonment. All our cousins were gone, the cousins with whom we had raced through the halls of the Hotel Residencial for years and with whom we had gathered on holidays and at the beach. And I worried—privately much more than in shared conversations with Kiko and Toto—that our parents too were planning to take us away from everything we knew and loved. They never shared their thoughts with us, of course, no doubt out of fear that we would blurt out what we knew to people who meant us ill, yet I regularly overheard snippets of conversations in which it seemed sure that Mami and Papi were talking about leaving Cuba in hushed and anguished tones, their words becoming tense, almost certainly, then swelling into anger.

On April 17, 1961, fifteen hundred counter-revolutionary Cuban exiles supplied by the American CIA came ashore at Playa Girón and Playa Larga at the Bahia de Cochinos, the Bay of Pigs. Fortified by the United States, the invaders believed they quickly could win the support of thousands of Cuban citizens, then advance to Havana and forcefully remove Fidel from power. Yet when the plan, authorized by U.S. President John F. Kennedy, immediately proved disastrous—Fidel's air force sinking two of the invaders' ships and strafing the soldiers stranded on the open beaches—Kennedy hastily called off U.S. air strikes in support of the incursion, fearing they would trigger war with the Soviet Union, and Fidel and his regime never were threatened by the incursion. Ninety exiles were killed; 1,189 were captured, tried, and ultimately sentenced to prison for treason, and the absolute failure of the *yanqui* invasion was celebrated wildly throughout the island as further proof of Fidel's military genius and of the justice of his proletarian revolution.

The trials of the counter-revolutionaries were carried live on television for long hours every day, so the whole of the Cuban populace could witness the humiliation and fore-ordained fate of anyone who would dare oppose the revolution. We watched with fascination as man after beaten, exhausted man—all of them Cubans who had gone into exile before their disastrous return—admitted his guilt, perfunctorily denounced *los yanquis imperialistas*, then pleaded for the mercy of the court. It was obvious, even to us kids, that the men had been under great duress since their capture, and Papi told us he was sure they'd been tortured. All of us understood that the United States had betrayed these men—and had done so at the worst possible moment—and we felt very sorry for them. It was a solemn time inside our home, our parents watching the spectacle of the tribunals almost in utter silence, then Papi concluding, as at last he turned off the television, that war with the United States was certain to begin before long and that no one in Cuba would be safe from the American bombs.

If political symbolism was difficult for a nine-year old to understand, religious images were not, particularly because I was schooled in them every day. And I think it was in the context of the church that I understood most viscerally and emotionally how different Cuba had become in these two cataclysmic years, and how in a very real way, the violence I'd always know in my own home somehow had spread out of my house, run down the Carretera Central and throughout Camagüey, then, high and low, across all of poor Cuba.

We had never been the most pious family in Camagüey. We were Roman Catholics, of course, but Papi was seldom interested in attending mass. Most often, we went with Mami, either to the large, ornate, and beautiful church at the center of the Plaza de las Mercedes or to the simple Capilla del Asilo del Padre Valencia, the stark little chapel at the asylum across the road from our house. At either location, I remember, it was important when we went to mass for Kiko, Toto, and me, to take a ticket from the priest at the service's end, one which we would present at school the following day as proof of our Sunday devotion and the fact that our souls were not in the jeopardy that, no doubt, they sometimes seemed to be.

For many Cubans—prior to the revolution and in its aftermath—the church was a personal refuge from suffering and an enduring source of hope. But as Fidel's government became ever more clearly communist, leaders of the Cuban church, in turn, grew bold in their opposition, priests urging loyalty only to the Blessed Virgin, and warning that a political ideology that denied God was one to which devout Cuban Catholics never could offer their allegiance. Finally, however, Fidel—an avowed atheist—had enough of the clerics' insolence. He summarily closed all of the nation's parochial and private schools, and demanded that all priests and nuns—save the handful who were his open supporters—leave the country at once.

It was simply one more agonizing exodus, the next in a lengthening line of departures from the island that so recently had seemed to me to be the center of the universe. Yet it was particularly crushing to hear that our beloved teachers were being forced to go away as well. Kiko, Toto, and I attended an impromptu farewell gathering at the *colegio* for the Marist Brothers with whom we had spent our school lives, and who now were bound for Spain. We helped Hermano Pedro and Hermano Joaquin, whom we loved, pack books, paperweights, and mementos into boxes. We tightly embraced each dear man, then tearfully said goodbye, and at home later on that deeply sad day, my brothers and I cried inconsolably as we watched on television as those same men climbed up the steps of a Madrid-bound plane.

From that day forward, my brothers and I never returned to school in Cuba, a clear sign even to us that our parents by now had given up on investing in any kind of future for us in our own country. Fidel's confiscation of the churches and schools was an action that sliced through every segment of Cuban society. For some, it was cause for riotous celebration and was proof that the revolution had freed the Cuban people from all the oppressions of the past. Thousands of others however—privileged, destitute, or somewhere in between, people who theretofore had held fast to their faith—now were empty, bereft, and broken.

And then the churches were ransacked. Everywhere, atrocities were committed against sacred sites, and although some certainly giddily cheered the violence, many people were as outraged by it as they were powerless to do anything in response. I remember how traumatic it was for me to see for myself the plundered remains of La Iglesia de las Mercedes. The church of God's mercies, it was called, yet in the name of the revolution, hoodlums and saboteurs had not been merciful to our church in any way. Statues, stained-glass windows, and doors were broken and tossed aside; golden chalices and candlesticks were looted; walls and columns were scrawled with graffiti; human waste lay on the ancient stone floors, and everywhere crosses were defiled. Rumors about who the true vandals were raced through the city, and the loud gossip indicted virtually everyone, including the priests and nuns who, some said, had trashed the church themselves in final act of defiance against Fidel. But ultimately, more people blamed Castro's minions for the crimes than any other possible culprit.

I had been taught as a child that a church was a physical symbol of the spiritual body of all believers, and that in the hushed sepulcher of each church, Christ was literally present in the form of the consecrated Host. But as I looked in disbelief at the savagery I saw, it seemed clear to my nine-year-old eyes that no one would pray or say mass here ever again. Christ no longer resided in the center of the Plaza de las Mercedes, and Papi, Mami, Kiko, Toto, and I agreed that God had exited our land.

Our beloved Casa Rojugui at Santa Lucia Beach, wher we spent many hours boxing with Papi.

Cuatro

La Pescera

During the sweltering and always uneasy summer of 1961, we began to spend most of our time at the cottage in Santa Lucia. Strangely, weeks would go by without Papi expressing the need to return to Camagüey to look after his businesses, and although Kiko, Toto, and I loved being at the beach as always, something new now hung in the seaside air. Fear, uncertainty, and a numbing kind of helplessness had blown in off the Caribbean, it seemed—or perhaps down from the high Sierra Maestra like the wind that had swept Fidel into power three years before—and although we still were very young, at the beach we Lost Boys breathed into our lungs something that made us aware that our lives were quite different now.

When summer waned and our parents made no attempt to enroll us in school, we paid close attention, yet asked no questions. And neither were we brave enough to enquire when Mami began to sew exotic new clothes for each of us—including leather hats with ear-warmers and heavy winter jackets, apparel we never would need in Camagüey. Then one day late in August, Papi told us with as much gusto as he could muster that the five of us were taking a two-week family vacation to Havana. The world we knew at the time was no larger than Camagüey and Santa Lucia, and my brothers and I were thrilled by the prospect of visiting our country's great capital city, but as soon as we found ourselves at the feet of more towering buildings than I believed could possibly exist, Papi mysteriously announced that our vacation would have to be cut short. We drove home to Camagüey, but then, in only a couple of weeks, Papi said it was time to begin our vacation again, and this time, my brothers and I were wise enough to understand that we would likely be traveling far beyond Havana.

On our final day in Camagüey, Mami called the three of us in from our garden adventures. She had something "really important" to tell us, she said, tears welling in her dark eyes. She enveloped the three of us in her arms, then softly and painfully spoke. *"No existe Santi Clos,"* she said. "There is no Santa Claus."

I was stunned. This was not news. I had presumed we were about to learn some shameful family secret, or perhaps hear an awkward explanation of the birds and the bees, but that was all she wanted us to know. Like most children, my brothers and I had learned that Santa Claus was a fiction far sooner than our mother imagined, but I've wondered ever since why she believed it was important for us to have that particular information as we set out on what would become an extraordinary journey. Was this the only way in which Mami could share with us something far more profound—the certainty that the world we were about to enter was a place of dashed dreams and a mountain of hurt?

That night, Papi came into our bedroom, not to break more news but simply to play with us. He had bought each of us a bolero, a bell-shaped piece of wood connected to a short wooden stick by a string. Papi, Kiko, Toto, and I competed to see who could impale the bell with stick the most times in a row, and this is the final memory I have of La Villita Candado and my life in Camagüey. It was the final time I ever played with my father, in fact, and the last time I had a sense that I belonged somewhere for a very long time to come.

It had been a hurricane of rumors that foremost had set our journey in motion—the kind of gossip and fear-mongering that I suspect would almost certainly drive any two parents to act on their children's behalf in ways previously incomprehensible to them. And the worst of the rumors that swirled through the streets of Camagüey in the preceding months had been that Fidel and his *communistas* were intent on tearing all Cuban children from their homes and sending them to residential government schools where they would be rigorously and permanently brainwashed. The first thing my parents heard—and on the most reliable authority—was that the new government would allow children to return to their parents only one weekend each month. Before long, other people they spoke with knew for a fact that brainwashed youngsters still would return home each month, but only in order to turn their parents over to government authorities when the children heard them speaking negatively about Fidel and his policies. Then word on the streets had it that difficult and incompliant kids were being sent deep into the sugar-cane fields and never were seen again, or worse, to Moscow for training by the feared Soviets. The bodies of the Cuban children who could not survive the harsh Russian winters were made into dog food, the stories insisted, so that all traces of them simply would disappear.

Mami was particularly horrified, I remember, by the constantly repeated story of a Cuban boy who had asked his new teacher, who had replaced an exiled priest, if he could pray at his desk as he formerly had at his Catholic school. "Close your eyes and pray to God that in his divine omnipotence he will give you a bag of candy," the vile teacher, dressed in army fatigues, responded. The boy did as the teacher suggested, praying as ardently as he could, but when he opened his eyes, he discovered his prayer hadn't been answered. Next the teacher said, "Now, close your eyes and pray to Fidel that he, in his divine omnipotence, will grant you the same wish you asked of your god." Once again the boy dutifully did what was asked of him, and while his eyes were shut, the teacher placed a bag of candy on the boy's desk. "See," the teacher announced to the whole of the class when the boy opened his eyes, "The god you believe in does not exist. The only god for you is Fidel and only he, through us, can provide for the things you want and need." Who knew whether the story was true? Perhaps it was, perhaps it was only apocryphal. But Mami believed in its veracity—that much was certain—and dozens of stories like it fueled in my parents the dread that if their sons remained in Cuba, they would be stripped of their faith and would learn only what Fidel allowed them to learn. And when Castro announced that as part of his "Year of Education," high-school seniors immediately would leave their classrooms and go out into the countryside to teach *campesinos* to read and write, their fears appeared to them to be confirmed.

The rumors and stories grew ever more horrifying, and if radio, television, and the newspapers didn't literally bear the stories out, the government-controlled news did seem to certify that children in Cuba henceforth would be puppets and the de facto property of Fidel, a prospect that engendered a strange kind of madness in Mami. The more terrified she became that the communists would destroy us, the more she beat us herself. As usual, she chose to attack Kiko more often than Toto and me, and increasingly, Mami tore at us in response to the most minor offenses. She would beat Kiko because his hair was uncombed; she would bitterly whip Toto because he had dirtied his shirt; I suffered at her hands too, but more frightening than the beatings was my suspicion that Mami had no control over her burning fury.

My mother's emotional equilibrium became increasingly unsteady as people she knew disappeared. Somehow, the fact that friends and acquaintances kept their plans for leaving Cuba as secret as they could in the weeks prior to their departures exacerbated for Mami her swelling sense that each day would bring new horrors and that absolutely nothing could be counted on any longer. One day, a dear friend simply would no longer seem to exist—she, her husband, and their children vanishing as if into the air. On another day, a dentist, a shopkeeper, a neighbor would disappear, leaving no trace, no evidence that they ever had been part of her life. Children who once played for hours each day on our street suddenly were gone, and Mami was desperate for explanations. Were they in Russia already? Had they been turned into dog-food? Had Fidel imprisoned them, just as Ernesto LaRua had attempted to imprison Papi? Were they trapped in indoctrination camps? Had they escaped to Mexico, to Spain? Were they safe in the United States?

Although Papi paid close attention to the rumors that reached his ears, and although he too was troubled when a colleague simply vanished, it was his belief in the inevitability of war with the United States that foremost drove his desire to see his sons safely out of the country. Papi was convinced that the U.S. would not allow Castro to remain in power much longer—it was simply a national security risk of too huge proportions to permit the communists to permanently establish themselves ninety miles from Miami, he contended—and he feared that a U.S. assault would mortally endanger everyone on the island, whether *Fidelista* or not. In the months following the failed Bay of Pigs invasion, Papi fervently expected to see American bombers lace the skies over Camagüey, and although we had no idea of what was happening at the time, for him, the only logical option was to find a way to send his sons safely away from the island while he and Mami remained behind to do whatever they could to defend their businesses and properties. I'm certain that the moment they first heard in 1961 of *Operación Pedro Pan*—a hopeful story for once of Cuban children reaching loving, and surely very temporary, foster homes in Florida—they immediately resolved, somehow, to get us safely to the United States. Soon they would find the means, they swore to themselves, to get us aboard one of those dozens of children-filled flights from Havana to Miami; then my grandfather, Don Antonio, my aunts, Tia Elda and Tia Nenita, and my uncle, Tio Aquiles, would care for us until the Americans had won a brief war and we returned home.

Papi took numerous short trips alone that fateful summer, and I now know that he made them in hopes of securing three of the thousands of visa waivers the U.S. state department had made available beginning earlier in the year to assist Cubans desiring to send their children to safety. When the Eisenhower administration severed its diplomatic relations with Fidel's regime in January 1961, no longer was there a way for people like my parents to apply for necessary visas for entry into the United States. But through the exhaustive efforts of Father Brian O. Walsh, the Spanish-speaking director of the Catholic Welfare Bureau of the United States—and the man who almost single-handedly had set Operation Peter Pan in motion a few months before—U.S. officials did ultimately agree to waive visa requirements for a virtually unlimited number of Cuban children between the ages of six and sixteen. Yet in order for each child to legally reach the United States, he or she had to personally possess a visa waiver, and repeatedly, Papi would arrive at a safe-house in Havana where he had been assured the waivers were available, only to find he had come too late and that none of them remained.

Like many thousands of his countrymen, Papi also had to purchase tickets for our one-way flight to Miami through an elaborate black-market system. In December, Fidel suddenly had made it illegal to use Cuban pesos to buy airline tickets for American destinations, and so people quickly became creative in finding ways to pay for the short journey. In our family's case, Papi began the involved process by giving furniture and appliances from Casa Vidal to families in Camagüey who already had relatives in Miami; when those new immigrants into the U.S. received word that the complex transaction had commenced, they paid my grandfather for the goods in American dollars, and Don Antonio, in turn, purchased the necessary airline tickets from a Miami travel agency that still maintained an office in Havana, where proof of their purchase was easy to verify. It was a process that ultimately worked to secure passage out of Cuba not only for my brothers and me, but for seven of our cousins as well, and I suspect none of us would have left Cuba, in the end, if my grandfather hadn't so suddenly chosen to lead the way a year before.

It was one more failure to find visa waivers that abruptly had ended our first trip to Havana in August, but by mid-September, Papi at last had secured them, and although our parents continued to tell us nothing about the plans they were making—my brothers and I, for our parts, never daring to ask the questions we might have—this time we knew somewhere deep in our hearts that a trip to Havana would only begin our journey, and, just as so many of Mami's friends had done, we left our hometown in secret. I was exited to travel again—eager and apprehensive, edgy and more than a little afraid—and it wasn't until we were ensconced in the backseat of my father's car en route to the capital that I realized that we hadn't said goodbye to our buddies Kiko and Oriol. We hadn't even said the simplest of farewells to our grandparents or Tio Nene or the aunts, uncles, and cousins who remained behind. We simply slipped out of Camagüey and found our way onto the wide new highway that linked it with distant Havana, and it was impossible for me to know in those moments that many of those people I never would see again.

It's poignant for me to remember that during the two weeks we spent in Havana that September, Papi and Mami did not fight a single time. Never before in my life had I seen them so apparently at ease with each other, so willing to suspend their warfare for a reach of days. It was a truce they never had been able to maintain before, one that came only on the eve of losing their sons for an unknown time, and as I think back on it, I believe they were able to get along on those counting-down days simply because at last they truly shared something in common: both were severely wounded adults who—despite their many faults—deeply loved their children, and both were about to say the most anguished kind of goodbye.

Yet even now, none of us spoke openly about what we collectively knew soon would happen, Mami and Papi choosing never to explain to Kiko, Toto, and me why we were leaving Cuba without them, or when we could expect to see them again, or what they believed we would encounter when we reached Miami. It was a profoundly new future toward which each of us inevitably was moving, but one about which we, as a family, offered no discussion, no conjecture, no shared or simple words. Instead, what we chose to do was to make a remarkable holiday out of those days, delighting in the great city and its myriad pleasures, and celebrating an internal peace that our family otherwise never knew.

We shared a room on the top floor of the opulent Hotel Riviera, one that made my grandfather's Hotel Residencial in Camagüey seem rather plain and Spartan in comparison. The views of the city from its windows were breathtaking—the grand and towering buildings, the streets clogged with carefully polished American cars, the mile-long seawall and promenade called the Malecón reaching in the far distance to the sixteenth-century Spanish fortress of El Moro, waves ceaselessly crashing against the wall where thousands of people made their daily *paseos*, or after-dinner strolls, the waves sending fine spray high into the fragrant tropical air. By day we would explore the city in which we all took such patriotic pride—despite the fact that Havana too now bore at each new vista the unmistakable mark of the revolution that was sending us far away from home—and shopping for toys our parents were eager to buy for us even though all of us understood we would have to leave them behind. Each night we would eat in the hotel's wonderful restaurant, a place apparently unaffected by the embargo and the shortages that by now had made me far more appreciative of food than I otherwise would have been. The foreigners who shared the dining room with us were *Russians*, my parents whispered to us, and although it was hard to know what a Russian was, on those evenings I was delighted to be in their company, and in the precious company too of my parents, Mami and Papi smiling as we ate, even laughing, the five of us the best kind of family—if only at that focused time and place—the revolution, *communismo*, and the otherwise omnipresent figure of Fidel far away from us on those sultry September nights, my mind racing as I tried to sleep, my thoughts inevitably turning toward my crescendoing fears.

I was awakened by my mother's crying on the morning of September 29, 1961. Instinctively, I understood that I was not overhearing the dénouement of one of her battles with Papi; his genuine attempt to console her, and the sadness that hung in the air like fog made it clear to me before I was out of bed that the unnamed and never-spoken-of day had arrived, and that neither Mami nor Papi really wanted to be putting us on an airplane without them. I don't remember eating breakfast that morning, or even dressing. All I remember is holding tightly to each of them as they helped me prepare for a day whose end none of us could quite envision. I was numb and I cried continually, and every sweet pleasure of the preceding days already had vanished, replaced by a sense that I was about to die.

Mami carefully weighed each of our three duffle bags with a bathroom scale—we were allowed only sixty pounds each of luggage—then we made the short journey to the Havana airport. Locally known as *La Pescera*, the aquarium, the passenger waiting-area at the airport's terminal was an all-glass enclosure that swept up to a high and brightly lit ceiling. Kiko, Toto, and I, we were told, would be required to enter La Pescera quite soon, and wait there alone for our flight. We were stunned to learn that we would have to say our goodbyes so quickly, but Mami explained that she and Papi could watch us through the glass until we were safely on our way. Then, silently, the two of them tenderly hugged each one of their sons, holding each of us as tightly as they could, kissing our faces, our heads, our necks, my skin soon wet with our blended tears. My heart was breaking, but, like the others, I had no idea what I could possibly say. It all seemed so impossible to understand; we were strangely acquiescing to such an unimaginable event, and then Papi sensed that perhaps a few words could offer us comfort. "We'll all be back together in two or three months at the most," he assured us. "The United States is not going to allow this to go on much longer and will get rid of Fidel." We nodded in response and he said nothing more. We hugged Mami and Papi a final time, then, crying bitterly, Kiko, Toto, and I made our way into the glass aquarium.

The hours we waited in La Pescera were torture. The enclosure was filled with dozens of children who were every bit as frightened as we were, and the sounds of their crying echoed off the glass walls that now entrapped us. The people who processed our paperwork—

dressed in army fatigues and draped with rifles and bullets—were offi-
cious and brusque and utterly uninterested in trying to calm anyone's
fears. They searched each of us, tore into our duffle bags, spilled their
contents across an ocean of tables, then left us to try to sort out our
belongings from everyone else's and repack them. I had turned ten only
two months before and had little experience of life, but these were the
most ruthless people I'd ever encountered, and I remember thinking
as well—with perhaps the first spark of compassion of my brief years—
that I would be sure to convince Papi to free the fish in his aquarium
once we returned home: if this place were a glimpse of how those fish
were forced to live, we would have to let them go.

At last we found a place where we could see Mami and Papi through
the glass. We pressed against it, and they came close on the other side,
and the three of us were comforted to be close to them again, the
glass wall separating us but allowing us almost to touch, the three
of us moving our open palms to the glass where their palms already
were pressed hard, repeatedly mouthing *te quiero*, I love you, none
of us able to take our eyes off each other until the moment when we
could wait no longer and were forced to walk to the plane.

We walked backward as we boarded the Pan American DC-7 so
we could continue to keep our eyes locked on our parents, and the
pain I felt in my heart as I watched them recede made it seem certain
that I was about to die. Mami and Papi moved to the terminal's roof-
top observation deck, and when we were seated, we could see them
again as the plane turned toward the runway. The cabin was filled
with the cries of children, and I remember thinking that if I closed
my eyes, perhaps God would come to take me away. But with my
eyes shut, the crying and whimpering only seemed to grow louder,
and God chose to show me no mercy. I looked at Kiko, at Toto, and
none of us could utter a word, but we could see the shared expres-
sions of fear and overwhelming sadness on each other's face, and then
we could see Mami and Papi on the terminal roof. In the seat beside
the window, I kept my eyes utterly fixed on them as the plane taxied
down the runway, gathered speed, then finally lifted into the air. We
were leaving them, and I watched my mother and father as my heart
split in half, seeing each of them grow smaller and smaller until at
last they were indistinguishable from the island of Cuba itself.

My brother Kiko and me playing on the beaches of Santa Lucia for the last time.

Cinco

Lost Boys

J.M. BARRIE's *Peter Pan*, which premiered onstage in London in 1902, is the story of a boy in magical place called Never-Neverland, who refused to grow up. It was a story my brothers and I did not know when we left Cuba in 1961, and as we became aware of it in the succeeding years, it always seemed odd to us that Father Walsh had chosen to name his child-refugee program after Barrie's fictional character. The first child Father Walsh helped reach safety in the U.S. was a fifteen-year-old named Pedro—Peter—and the flights that ultimately carried more than 14,000 Cuban children out of the country almost always were Pan American, so the name was logical enough, and no doubt Walsh hoped "Operation Peter Pan" would carry with it for many of the children it served a sense that their flights out of Cuba were magical journeys themselves, the sort that never would engender foreboding, fear, or a terror so deep you believed you were going to die.

Yet for my brothers and me, Operation Peter Pan demanded, in point of fact, that we grow up in a single day. We simply were offered no other choice, and I know I never called them Kiko and Toto again once we had banked away from Havana en route to the United States. From that day forward, we were solely and exclusively Rojugui—Roberto, Juan, and Guillermo—three brothers bound into a single destiny, and our childhoods suddenly slipped away from us in the way that sand would fall from our hands on the beach at Santa Lucia.

Father Walsh, based in Miami, first became involved in the exodus of children from Castro's Cuba when the boy named Pedro was brought to the Catholic Welfare Bureau in hopes he could help place the young immigrant in a foster home since his U.S. relatives were too poor to care for him. Walsh succeeded in finding a home for Pedro, then assisted a Cuban mother in placing her two children in what she hoped was temporary foster care before she returned to Cuba, where she and her husband were involved in dangerous clandestine anti-Castro activities. Those three placements quickly convinced the priest that many thousands more would be needed in the coming months—a mass exodus of children from the island was brewing, he came to believe—and by December 1960, Walsh had obtained a million dollars from the Eisenhower administration to partially fund his child-refugee program.

Father Walsh began to work closely with James Baker, headmaster of the prestigious Ruston Academy in Havana, which, prior to the revolution and Fidel's closing of private schools, had served the children of U.S. residents and Cuba's affluent class. Many Cuban parents already had begun pleading with Baker for help in getting their children safely to the United States, and Baker had begun to look into the possibility of establishing a large boarding school in Miami for Cuban children. Father Walsh ultimately was able to convince him however that because so many of the arriving children would be quite young, families in foster homes could care far better for them than could a school, and the two subsequently became an effective team—Baker overseeing arrangements for hundreds, then thousands of children's departure from Havana, and Walsh accepting responsibility for them once they reached Miami, ultimately finding them homes with relatives, family friends, and empathetic Floridians.

It was a dangerous mission, particularly for Baker, but Castro's government appeared to be paying no attention to the operation, and by the end of 1960, he and Walsh successfully had coordinated the relocation of 125 children. When Fidel summarily forbade using Cuban currency to purchase airline tickets to the U.S. early in the new year, it was Baker, Walsh, and the Catholic Welfare Bureau that devised the system of purchasing them via family members already in Florida and routing the tickets through Miami's W. Henry Smith Travel Agency, which maintained an office in Havana. And, of course, it was Walsh who successfully persuaded the Eisenhower administration to waive visa requirements for the children seeking asylum. By the early spring of 1961, many hundreds of children had reached the United

States, and the program's biggest hurdle became finding homes for each of the hundreds of children who now arrived every week.

First Walsh converted buildings at Camp Kendall, an abandoned army base, into temporary housing; then he found a large house in Miami proper; next he employed a group-home operated by nuns, a summer youth camp, and the homes of hundreds of Miami Cubans, but still more children arrived, some of whom were utterly unexpected and who Walsh and his assistants would find wandering alone—and often terrified—in the Miami airport. Soon Walsh was forced to place children far from Miami, and before the program ended youngsters in the care of the Catholic Welfare Bureau were assigned to homes—and orphanages—in thirty-five U.S. states.

Was Fidel aware of Operation Peter Pan? It's hard to imagine how he could not have been. Could he have staunched the flow of children out of Cuba at any time? He unquestionably had the power to do so, yet my father and many others believed that Castro did not see any value in those who opposed him and his policies continuing to live in Cuba when, in fact, they were eager to leave. My family and the thousands more like us were simply *gusanos*, worms, the revolutionary government loudly and everywhere proclaimed, and if many hundreds of children were allowed to leave the island, then surely their anti-revolutionary parents soon would follow.

What was harder to know were the true motives of the administrators of the exodus. Was Operation Peter Pan simply a humanitarian effort by a kind and compassionate nation to provide refuge for the children of a neighboring country spinning chaotically out of control? Or was an imperialist U.S. government working diligently to terrify people in Cuba's business and professional ranks into sending their children far from home, thereby ensuring that they would follow in time, and that their exodus would work to undermine the future of the revolution? My own opinion is that Father Walsh, James Baker, and hundreds more like them cared very deeply for the lives of the Cuban children themselves, but as the embargo, the Bay of Pigs invasion, and what later would be a series of failed attempts to assassinate Fidel made plain, the United States did without question undertake repeated and sometimes unorthodox measures in opposition to the revolution. Whether my brothers and I were lured out of

Cuba by an insidious American propaganda machine, or were sent away only in the verifiable face of untenable futures in our homeland, what remains clear to me is that for people like my parents, Operation Peter Pan emerged as a blessed life-raft, and if the prospect of our separation from them was horrific in many ways, at least it offered them an opportunity to *act* on their family's behalf at a time when action of any kind otherwise seemed impossible.

On the short first leg of my journey with Peter Pan, the Miami-bound DC-7 pitched and rolled dramatically in the air above the Straits of Florida. Under other circumstances, Roberto, Juan, and I surely would have considered our first ride in an airplane a great adventure, but on that impossible day, all I could do during the short flight was grip my seat's armrests as tightly as I could and pray that my grandfather, uncle, aunts, and cousins would meet us in a few minutes and assure us we were still loved and wanted.

Looking out the plane's window, I could see we were approaching a strange and unusual land. Florida's keys stretched southwesterly from the tip of the mainland, and I was astonished to spot the causeway connecting them. What an amazing thing, I remember thinking: they can build highways on top of the sea in America, then next I saw the enormous city of Miami spreading below—larger by far than Havana—and the apprehension that had been mounting in me all day now only increased.

When the plane landed and pulled to its gate, we made our way with dozens of other children and scattered adults down a portable staircase to the tarmac, where our duffle bags lay among other luggage. Every sign we observed was in English; the people surrounding us spoke words we could not understand, and my first impression with my feet on its ground was that the United States was a cold and hostile place. As we walked toward the terminal, we searched in every direction for our grandfather Don Antonio, but he was nowhere to be found. Surely Tia Nenita and her kids were waiting for us inside, we told ourselves, but once we entered the terminal our hopes were dashed. Were Tio Aquiles and Tia Elda and their boys late? Would they turn the corner with their arms spread wide in only a few more minutes? We waited, then waited longer still, but no one came. In time, each of the other children on the Peter Pan flight was greeted enthusiastically and whisked away, but still we waited, then at last the three of us agreed that for reasons we couldn't understand our family simply wasn't coming. Perhaps there had been a mix up; perhaps no one had been able to reach them to tell them when we would arrive. We were devastated and utterly confused and tried as best we could to determine what in the world we should do next.

Finally, in our wandering we encountered someone else who apparently had met the same fate. He was a sixteen-year old Cuban boy who walked with a cane as a result of having suffered polio, and since he was a virtual adult in our much-younger eyes, we were delighted when he readily took us under his wing and suggested that we go look for help together. Roberto, Juan, and I roamed the terminal with the boy we soon called Bat Masterson—after the gambler in the television Western we liked who also carried a cane—looking for the kind of assistance that we weren't at all sure how to find. At last we encountered a guard who spoke Spanish. He mentioned Operation Peter Pan, and we eagerly said, yes, that's us, and then he explained that at the end of the day someone would come from the Catholic Welfare Bureau offices to sweep the airport for unescorted and unclaimed Cuban children.

So we waited once more, and after many hours, a man approached us with a list of names in his hand. Our three names—and Bat Masterson's too—were on his list, we were very relieved to discover, so we followed him to a waiting van that took us in the dark Miami night to Camp Kendall, where we would be temporarily housed. After what seemed like an endless drive, we found everyone asleep at the camp except for an older couple who were awaiting our arrival. Fernando Pruna and his wife led us to an enormous dormitory filled with bunk-beds in tightly spaced rows, and we could see that two boys were asleep in virtually every bed. I was happy when the Prunas assigned me to sleep with Roberto, but although I was exhausted I couldn't sleep, longing for my parents and my own bed at faraway La Villita Candado and trying to imagine where my beloved grandfather could be and why he had not come to save us.

In the morning we discovered that Camp Kendall was overflowing with what appeared to be hundreds of boys and girls, and that the place was absolutely bursting at its seams. After a breakfast that included an inedible food called oatmeal—which looked all-too-much like dog vomit, the three of us agreed—we were led into Fernando Pruna's office where we were each presented with a model-airplane kit and a dollar bill, the administrator handing them to us without any kind of explanation—in English *or* Spanish. Would we be tested on how well we could glue the models together? Would they be sold to supply the camp with income? Was the money the kind of allowance our parents had given us in Camagüey? Later, someone told us that *every* new arrival at Camp Kendall received an airplane kit and a dollar bill, evidently simply in hopes that the gifts would help ease the pain of these first days away from our parents.

Señor Pruna then explained that we would remain at the camp only temporarily. A few kids were waiting for family members to come collect them, but virtually all the rest of us would go to foster homes, he said. We did our best to explain that we had many family members who already were in Miami, but the camp had no listing of them, no paperwork from our parents explaining who those family members were or how to contact them, and, no, he told us, he and his staff had no way to try to find them. Rumors circulated among the tense and apprehensive children that Operation Peter Pan had, in fact, run out of foster homes and was placing children in orphanages instead. Then we heard—in much the same way my parents had heard stories in Camagüey that terrified them—the rumor that America's orphanages were so full as well that siblings were being separated and sent to states far away from each other.

The rumor proved true after we had been at the camp for a week. Señor Pruna called us into his office, this time for an important discussion. He wanted us to know that an orphanage in New York had openings for two children, and another in Oregon could take a single child. He didn't ask us whether we would agree to fill those slots and was maddeningly indirect about what he did want to know: how would we choose to split ourselves? The twins together, or one of the twins with me? We were shocked and all the more terrified about the future, but as I think back on it, I know too that as eleven- and ten-year olds just days into life in a foreign land, we did a rather remarkable job in the following moments of stubbornly standing our Rojugui ground. Prior to that moment, Mami and Papi had made virtually every decision pertaining to each aspect of our lives, and we had no experience whatsoever in successfully countering the wishes or plans of an authority figure. Yet what we wanted, we said, and even demanded, was to live together with our grandfather, who we knew had a home only a few miles away. We would wait at Camp Kendall for as long as it took to find him, and, most importantly, we would stick together.

We left the meeting literally clinging to each other's shirts for comfort and reassurance, even though Señor Pruna promised us before he escorted us out of his office that he would find a way not to separate us. He did not pledge to find our grandfather or aunts and uncle however, and I think it was likely for that reason that I suffered the worst asthma attack of my life that night. I remember dreaming that I was dying, then awakening unable to breathe. I struggled so hard to suck in air that I couldn't speak, making only frantic deep-throated gasps, and I careened wildly around the enormous room waking dorm-mates as I could, but because I couldn't speak, none of the children I roused had any notion of what was wrong. Finally, one of the supervising adults heard me, instantly recognized my plight and rushed to drive me to the hospital. I labored increasingly hard for each successive breath and was certain I was going to lose the battle. For more than a week, I thought I was going to die, and now I knew I finally had reached that moment. But just as I began to lose consciousness, we reached the hospital's emergency room and someone was quick to inject me with adrenaline and quite soon I was breathing again.

After observing me for an hour or so, the emergency-room doctor allowed me to return to Camp Kendall, and I remember wondering as I struggled to find a way to sleep how many times I had to suffer before I was allowed to die. Yet the next day, an angel appeared at crowded Camp Kendall in the form of Rigoberto DeLeon, a good friend of my father's, who had only just arrived in Miami himself. In the days before we departed from Camagüey, Papi had confided to Rigoberto that he and Mami would be putting us on an Operation Peter Pan flight in the final days of September, and Rigoberto could not have been more correct when he thought perhaps we might enjoy seeing a friendly face. He found us by calling the offices of the Catholic Welfare Bureau, where he was pointed toward Camp Kendall, and I treasure even to this day our moments with him. He brought sugar-coated doughnuts for us, which were delicious and reminded me of the *churros* I loved at home—the first American, food, in fact, that I had truly enjoyed since our arrival. Rigoberto ate doughnuts with us, and I noticed that he looked weary and was clearly very distressed about something—who knew what troubles he had endured in reaching the U.S. or whether his hard times were only just beginning, yet he was incredibly gentle, as he always had been, and simply being held in his strong, cologne-scented embrace warmed my heart and reassured me of my chances for survival in a way that nothing else has done so profoundly ever again in my life. I hadn't felt good since leaving Cuba, but I felt *wonderful* in the brief minutes we spent with him, the four of us smiling broadly and speaking warmly of Camagüey, and although he had no news from Mami and Papi, I remember we even found ways to laugh together before my brothers and I reluctantly let him go.

Ten days into our new lives in America, the camp administrator informed us that he had found an opening for three children in a foster home in Pueblo, Colorado. We had no idea how close to Miami this place was, but both "Pueblo" and "Colorado" were Spanish words, so we hoped it might be close enough that from there we could conduct our own search for our family. We desperately wanted to live with our grandfather and aunts, our uncle and cousins, but even more importantly, we *had* to remain together, and after some brief discussion, Roberto, Juan, and I accepted the placement, fearing that, if we said no, Operation Peter Pan might attempt to separate us once more. We announced to the administrator that, yes, we would join the *muy amable* family in Pueblo, Colorado, and he, in turn, told us we would leave the following morning.

As instructed, we were ready to go by sunrise. But we were surprised and more than a little concerned to discover that six other kids were joining us on the journey. Ada and Hector Diaz stood ready with their bags; so did Juan, Alina, and Bilo Bautista, and Olga Pichardo. Did this American family have such a huge American house that we all would fit?, we wondered. Or, as my brothers and I eventually concluded, were the other children bound for other homes in this place called Colorado? Joining us as well on that trip was the second angel God sent our way: short and warm and affectionate Father John Sierra spoke with a pronounced Castilian accent, one that made him sound rather worldly and important, we thought, and he proved in time to be incredibly important to us-not simply ensuring our safe arrival in Colorado but continuing to offer us shoulders to cry on, true concern for our welfare, and the enveloping *abrazos*, hugs, that we otherwise never would have had during the long years we would come to be without our parents. All we knew of him early that morning, however, was that he would be our adult Spanish- and English-speaking escort, and that alone was enormously reassuring.

The ten of us began our trek westward with a long flight to Chicago—this one far less stressful than the flight ten days before—and as we commenced a long layover prior to boarding a flight to Denver, we were met by several men dressed in suits. With Father Sierra's consent, the men whisked us into a room inside the terminal full of bright lights, a forest of microphones, several television cameras, and what appeared to be dozens of reporters as well. Our escorts, as it turned out, had been Secret Service agents, and we were astounded when, after we were seated in chairs placed prominently before the cameras, into the room walked U.S. Attorney General Robert F. Kennedy. Even at our ages and despite the fact that we were such recent arrivals, we certainly knew who he was because we had seen President Kennedy and his brother on television, and we were utterly flabbergasted to be shaking his hand and hearing him say to each one of us with a wide smile, "Welcome to United States." *Señor Kennedy dice bienvenidos a los estados unidos*, Father Sierra said, translating the attorney general's words before he briefly spoke to the assembled reporters and Father Sierra moved us along to go meet our Denver flight.

Years later, in what would seem an amazing coincidence, I would work for Joe Dolan, the former Kennedy staffer who set up that impromptu meeting between the attorney general and nine shell-shocked Cuban kids, an encounter Kennedy himself had insisted upon when word somehow reached him as he waited for his own flight that a group of young Cuban refugees were in the airport as well. Barely ten, by now I had shaken hands with both the already-legendary leader of the Cuban revolution and perhaps his most embittered counterpart in the U.S. government, two separately celebrated men whose lives would take very different paths, yet whose political actions would profoundly affect my brothers and me and all the citizens of both nations.

A few hours later, as we walked from the plane in Denver to the bus on which we would make the two-hour trip south to Pueblo, I was shocked by the bitterly cold night air. It was early the twentieth of October, and I suppose in retrospect that the temperature hovered around forty degrees, but to my tropical bones the weather seemed arctic, and I longed anew for my home, my parents—my life. Once underway in the bus, however, I was warmed by the thought that very soon Roberto, Juan, and I would join a nice new family, and I imagined what it would be like to receive my first hug from my kind and affectionate American parents. Would they have children themselves, and might I have a sister or two for the first time? I worried about our new family having to wait up so late for our arrival; I anticipated falling into my own new bed, and I fell asleep as the bus droned on, awakened at last at about two a.m. when the bus slowed and jerked to a stop, Father Sierra announcing with tired pleasure in his voice that we had reached our destination.

After we found our bags, we made our way with Father Sierra through the cold, coal-dark night toward what appeared to be a large and imposing stone structure, and we were stunned when we saw the words "Sacred Heart Orphanage" carved into the stone bricks above its massive wooden doors. None of the nine of us spoke or read English yet, but I suspect only five-year old Bilo Bautista failed to instantly understand: an orphanage in Spanish is an *orfelinato*, and our hearts sank to our shoes. I thought instantly of the Asylum Padre Valencia across the street from our house in Camagüey and of the sad and desperate people it housed, afraid suddenly that our future would be much like theirs. My brothers and I had been betrayed by the people of Operation Peter Pan; we had been told a family awaited us, that a family *wanted* us, but the truth that terrible night appeared to be that we were doomed—Lost Boys without parents, without a home, without even a country we could claim.

Sacred Heart Orphanage—The Asylum

Seis

Boxing for Cuba

I cried myself to sleep on my first night in Colorado. A few hours before, as we made the bus journey to Pueblo, I had been so hopeful envisioning my American mother and father, and so sure that I would be loved and protected in their home. But instead of a home, what I encountered was a place that appeared to my young eyes like a big American prison for children. The lights were very dim as we made our way inside and up to the building's third floor, where a dormitory I was assigned to appeared to be home to perhaps three-dozen boys. A tired nun showed me my bed, indistinguishable from the others in sea of beds, then quickly took Roberto and Juan somewhere else, and I was all alone except for three dozen sleeping strangers. I wondered as I lay whimpering in the dark what terrible sin I had committed to deserve this sort of punishment, this banishment to the coldest place on earth, and I regretted terribly everything I had ever done to engender Mami and Papi's anger, everything I'd ever willingly done that had made me less than a perfect boy.

I was awakened the following morning by the sound of someone's heavy footsteps on the tiled hallway floor. I heard him stop, then yell something I couldn't make sense of. His loud steps continued and grew closer before at last he came into the large room where I lay. The man was wearing cowboy boots, denim blue-jeans, and a denim snap-button shirt, and he carried a leather belt with a big buckle in his hand. He snapped his belt on the floor and shouted, "Wake up sleeping beauties," although I had no idea what the words meant. Yet as soon as they heard them, the dozens of boys in the dorm scrambled out of their beds and fell to their knees on the floor. "Our father, Who art in heaven . . ." the man continued, and the boys loudly joined him in the prayer. He continued to recite what I guessed was the "Our Father" as he stomped out of the room, but he then turned suddenly, scowled, and marched to a bed where a boy still lay. He tore back the bedcovers and began whipping the boy with his belt, the youngster trying as best he could to escape the blows by sinking to his knees like the others. Then a second kid suffered a similar belt whipping for a reason I couldn't make sense of before the bowlegged man moved on, like some sort of movie cowboy whose work for the day was done.

I still lay in bed, and I was grateful that the man had spared me, yet it was easy enough to presume that this fellow wouldn't go easy on the new kid for more than a day or so. I had to wait for a turn at a urinal in the enormous and disgustingly dirty bathroom, and when I returned to my bed and opened my bag to remove something to wear, I found that a number of my clothes were missing. Did one of the boys steal them from me in the minutes I was away? Had one of the nuns thought we had too much and redistributed our clothing soon after we arrived the night before? My clothes were everything I owned, everything that connected me to the only life I knew, and their loss made me even more desperate than I had been before.

But I did find Juan and Roberto in the hall soon after I went searching for them; I was greatly relieved to see them, and together we made our way downstairs to breakfast. While we waited in line, the cowboy got up from a table where he was eating and marched toward us. He didn't welcome us to what we learned was euphemistically called "Sacred Heart Home," didn't introduce himself, and didn't seem to give any thought to the possibility that we might not understand what he said. We would hear nothing directly from him until the third day when, after hearing us speaking in Spanish to one another, he came over toward the three of us, and planted his feet widely before he announced, "I don't want to hear any of you speaking Spanish ever again. You will speak only English from now on." Then he added, "Your names are no longer Roberto, Juan, and

Guillermo. You are now Bob, John, and Bill." With that he stomped away in his high-heeled boots, and, by chance, the only non-Cuban resident of the place who spoke Spanish, a boy named William Casados, was waiting in line beside us. He translated what the cowboy had said, told us the cowboy's name, Jim McCoy, and explained as well that he was the home's custodian and the person who punished children, the man in charge of making sure that the place was kept clean and orderly by the boys themselves, that schedules were met and rules were obeyed—many of which, we learned, were rules of his own design.

Yet on that first day, before we sat down to what we had come to believe was the universally bland and often inedible food Americans ate, it began to appear that the queue in which we were standing wasn't based on a first-come, first-served sort of system. A few boys simply marched to the head of the line for this buffet-style breakfast without objection from anyone else already waiting. Others chose a place in mid-line as they arrived, as if they were joining friends or assuming a pre-assigned spot, and at last we realized that *no one* was falling in line behind us. And that evening at dinner, what began to appear to be a pronounced pecking order among the boys became very clear. Dinners were served family style, and I simply helped myself to a platter of food nearest my plate soon after I sat down. I didn't speak to anyone—because I still could say nothing more in English than "Set up a roadblock"—and because none of the five other boys at the table seemed the slightest bit interested in me. Yet after the meal, just as soon as we all had moved out of sight of the nuns and the cowboy McCoy, who were monitoring the dining room, my table-mates pinned me down and proceeded to take turns punching me in the face and belly. All the while they shouted admonitions at me, and ultimately succeeded in making it clear that I had done something wrong at dinner, and by now I had a good sense of what that intolerable breach of etiquette was. The next time I sat down to eat, I waited and simply watched the others, paying careful attention to the order in which they helped themselves to food and making sure I served myself last. That evening, I avoided a beating, but fighting, however, would nonetheless become an almost daily part of life for my brothers and me at the Sacred Heart asylum.

What Roberto, Juan, and I discovered almost immediately was that a culture of violence thrived—and was encouraged to thrive—at the orphanage. Outlaw Jim McCoy ruled mercilessly with his wide leather belt, striking boys constantly for infractions both real and imagined. He was all-too-eager to strike with his fists as well, and one of his favorite group punishments whenever some of us were guilty of a collective mischievous prank was to demand that we kneel on the hard-tiled floor of the central hallway with our spines erect and our arms held out in front of us parallel to the floor. We were required to hold this position for fifteen minutes without slouching or dropping our arms, and when one of us faltered, the offender would receive a fierce kick in the ass from McCoy's pointed-toed boot, and then the sadistic cowboy would begin the count over again. Sometimes we would be on our knees with our arms outstretched for an hour or more, and we always were in agony by the time McCoy relented and allowed us to stand.

When one of us occasionally would run away—desperate to escape, even for a day—McCoy would ritually employ his belt's big buckle. It was a punishment he reserved for that specific offense, and I'll never forget watching in horror as he lacerated Jimmy Aragon's head with blow after blow from the metal buckle when the boy, hungry and defeated, returned to Sacred Heart—Jimmy screaming in pain during the beating, then enduring the further humiliation of McCoy shaving his head so the rest of us could read a cautionary tale in the cuts and welts he suffered.

And who could be surprised when the boys themselves used violence to maintain the rigorously enforced pecking order whose importance already had been beaten into me? The toughest, meanest, most intimidating kids claimed the highest ranks, and the place beneath them each of us claimed was determined rather simply: you held absolute power over everyone you could beat up, and everyone who could crush you in a fight had dominion over you. The only way to move up in the ranks was to challenge the boy ahead of you and beat the hell out of him, and all-too-often, it seemed, boys we never dared to challenge went out of their way to keep the new Cuban kids in line. Our biggest nemeses were the Roldan brothers, Tim and Danny, who were eighth graders, and a seventh-grader, Robert Duran. Almost daily, the three of them would smash Roberto, Juan, or me into a locker, or steal something from us, or pop one of us in the back of the head as we stood in one of the endless lines that occupied our days. Once Danny Roldan kicked Roberto in the face so violently that his left eye swelled shut; it was swollen so badly that Juan and I worried that he might not be able to see from it again, and we weren't surprised when Jim McCoy refused to punish Danny from what he had done—Roldan was one of McCoy's handful of "favorite boys," kids who could get away with almost anything because McCoy liked and coddled them for reasons none of the rest of us could understand. When Danny's brother punched me in the face a few days later, we decided we had no recourse but to take retribution as a team—the Lost Boys of Camagüey against these American tormentors.

Danny Roldan—a big, strong, mean-tempered son of a bitch—was, without question, the most powerful kid in the place. No one else dared to mess with him, and his place at the top of the pecking order only fueled his need to constantly terrorize anyone he disliked, and, evidently, he harbored longstanding ill-will toward immigrant Cubans kids whose last names were Vidal. But when Roberto spotted Danny lying alone on his bed in an otherwise empty upstairs dormitory one day, an idea flashed into his head. He quickly found Juan and me, enlisted us in his plan, and, making sure that neither McCoy nor any nuns were nearby, we pounced on the unsuspecting Danny—Roberto and I holding him fast to his mattress while Juan—blessed Juan, the carport champ of Santa Lucia—landed punch after punch to the kid's mid-section. It was beautiful: Juan hadn't lost a step since the last time we'd boxed with Papi at the beach, and, for a time thereafter, at least, we were free from the torments of Danny Roldan.

Soon we retaliated also against Robert Duran and achieved similarly satisfying results, and our three-Vidals-on-one plan continued to work brilliantly whenever one of us got picked on: if one of us was in danger, the other two would come running. We called it the Rojugui defense, but after a time the American kids figured a way to counter our family-style approach to fighting. Now, when one of them had to face the combined force of the three of us after having dared to single one of us out for abuse, ten or twenty American toughs would swarm in and over-power us. All we could do was position ourselves in a kind of triangle, our three backs protected at least, but their numbers were just too great, and they tore at us with fists, feet, belts, and sticks, beating us badly sometimes but virtually never being punished, in turn. Each time we went to McCoy, one of the nuns, or a priest with a complaint, we were blithely ignored.

Sacred Heart "Home"—yet every bit the asylum that Padre Valencia's was in Camagüey—was established in 1928 as part of the Pueblo archdiocese of the Catholic church, which supplied most of its funding. During the 1960s, however, the costs of housing and schooling my brothers and me, the five others who had arrived with us in early October, and eventually dozens of other Cuban children were borne in largest part by Catholic Social Services. An imposing four-story, red-stone building surrounded by Pueblo's Mountain View Cemetery on three sides and a low-income housing project on the fourth, the asylum housed about seventy boys and eighty girls when we arrived—the genders rigidly separated by a succession of locked steel doors to ensure that we could not do any number of things the church would have terribly frowned on. In addition to dining rooms, dormitories, and "living areas" equipped with a few tables and sofas and old black-and-white TVs, the facility included a massive industrial kitchen, an infirmary, a church, baseball and football fields, and a school attended by resident children the first through sixth grades. Kids in the seventh and eighth grades were bused to Catholic secondary schools scattered throughout the grimy, steel-mill-centered city, all the residents "graduating" to another institution when they reached their first year of high school.

Most Sacred Heart kids were either Mexican-American or African-American and many had lived at the asylum since birth, often having been abandoned by their natural parents—the nuns and priests and assorted sociopaths like Jim McCoy the only family they had ever known. The nuns, principally charged with providing motherly influences in our lives—nuns like Sister Alex, Sister Arthur, and Sister Doris—seemed to share a common trait: they were always exasperated, no doubt because they had the impossible job of looking after so many boys, aware that at any time a dozen or more of us likely were either getting into mischief somewhere in the huge building or out on the four-acre grounds or committing mortal sins with gleeful abandon. It was their job to see that we completed our chores (which we always were loath to do), that we maintained our personal hygiene (which meant bathing once a month or so, whether we needed to or not), and that we maintained the home's loving and mutually supportive decorum (which we did between sudden battles and protracted wars.) We called the nuns vultures, not only because of the way they appeared in their all-black habits, but also because of the uncanny way they would swoop down on us without warning, apparently eager to steal from us our moments of unbridled fun.

The nuns who did the cooking, dishwashing, and laundry we virtually never saw, and I presume their earthly reward for lives of back-breaking work was simply not to be required to interact more directly with those of us who were imprisoned in the place. And it was the nuns who were our teachers with whom we developed important bonds and personal rapport. My brothers and I and the other Cuban kids got to know Sister Gloria early on, specifically because she spoke Spanish and therefore had been assigned to teach us English. With nothing more than *Dick and Jane* readers as curriculum materials, she threw herself into the task, and before long— and in largest part because of the miraculous way in which children acquire language—we were able to make sense of what we heard in the classrooms, where only English was spoken.

It was Sister Gloria who censored the letters we were required to write to our parents once each month—the asylum staff hoping, I always presumed, that *they* would be better served if their charges described only visits from Santa Claus and springtime Easter-egg hunts rather than blood feuds with the Roldan brothers or Jim McCoy's terrible belt. And Sister Gloria was our dedicated choral instructor as well. It's still easy for me to picture her ardently pounding the keys of our battered classroom piano, and I know I was well into my adulthood before I realized that the lyrics to her favorite Christmas carol did not actually begin, *"Silver bells, silver bells, sing children, sing!, it's Christmastime in the city."*

Like Father Sierra, who had escorted us from Miami to Pueblo, and who maintained a caring connection to my brothers and me over the years, Father Friel, the pastor of the parish with which the asylum was associated, was an easy man to both admire and love. He was gentle and attentive and he cared enough about the Cuban children who came into his care that soon after our arrival he began studying Spanish. At first he could direct only a few words in our direction, then a few sentences, but in time he began to deliver his Sunday homily in both Spanish and English so all of us could understand his words, an effort that I know inspired us in our own struggles with English, and which proved to us he believed we were the equals of the other children, if perhaps no one else did. When one of us was in the infirmary for a few days, Father Friel would visit and bring a small gift, and I know that for me, at least, it was the good Father who briefly convinced me to become devout for the first time in my life.

I loved the visits from the archbishop, midnight masses, and other great celebrations of the liturgical year, and I even began to rise early enough each morning to make it to the 6:00 a.m. mass, something that Father Friel convinced me and many of the other Cuban kids we could do for our faraway parents and our beloved country. Months after arriving in Colorado, I still couldn't bear the cold. It seemed to find its way to the core of my bones, and I often worried that my fingers and toes would grow so numb that, like icicles, they would simply snap off. I literally rolled myself in my blankets like a kind of *cubano* burrito each night as I went to bed, and falling on the tile floor at Jim McCoy's shouted command felt like journeying naked onto the Arctic wastes. Like most Catholic clergy, Father Friel was well-schooled as a guide on extended guilt trips, and I remember as if it were yesterday the first time he gathered all of us Cuban kids and, in a voice both gentle and stern, told us how lucky we were to be in the United States—safe and well-fed (if not always entirely warm.) He asked us to consider the persecution and suffering our parents likely were enduring in Cuba at that moment, then suggested that our link to God, through our prayers, might be the only hope our parents had. Quietly he whispered, "Are you really willing to give up the only hope for your mothers and fathers just so you can sleep for a few more minutes each morning?" With that he walked away.

Every Cuban child in Pueblo, Colorado was seated early for mass the following morning, and most of us continued to attend faithfully each day for many months thereafter. And although over time, my daily attendance dwindled, and then virtually ended—as was the case with the others—I did feel for a time that I was doing something on Mami and Papi's behalf, and praying for them, whether in

mass or rolled in my blankets in bed, was a way to remain connected to them, to Romelia and Emilita as well, to Gladis, Felix and Juan,
and everyone in faraway Camagüey, people I loved and prayed were
still alive.

Despite his many kindnesses and the positive role he played, Father
Friel never stood up for us in the face of the many outrages we suffered at the hands of the asylum's bullies or the hated cowboy McCoy.
When one of us would visit him after a beating, our cheeks stained
with tears, he would hug us and dry our faces, ask us to bow our
heads as he said a brief prayer, closing it with a blessing made with the
sign of a cross, yet never did he intercede on our behalf, and I always
wondered whether he simply chose not to exercise any authority over
Jim McCoy or whether, in fact, he was powerless to do so.

McCoy had been at Sacred Heart since he himself was a baby. For
him, the place that was an asylum—a virtual prison to us—was everything he knew by way of heritage, home, and family. He clearly loved
the place in his own warped sort of way, and it astonished me that
he chose for his own two daughters to attend school with us, as if he
wanted them to share in the special, life-shaping experience that had
so successfully molded him. McCoy often spoke wistfully about the
characters he had grown up with at the orphanage, and would outline
for us in great detail the many disciplinary methods whose legacy he
was preserving. He believed—and made sure we understood the depth
of his conviction—that the arrival of every-more numbers of Cuban
kids, did not serve the asylum and its traditions well, and it was McCoy
who imagined creatively one evening that he might succeed in ending
the daily warfare between us and the American kids.

It started early one morning while I waited in line for breakfast.
For reasons I couldn't make sense of, a kid named Tyrone Ortega
kept egging me on to sing a song. "Sing, sing," he implored me, as if
daring me to do so. But "sing," to my ears, sounded very much like
singar, a Cuban slang term synonymous with "fuck." When I determined that Tyrone was taunting me and telling me to fuck off, it
seemed to me that I had little choice but to punch him in the mouth.
The kids surrounding us were outraged by my quick strike, and they
attacked me; my brothers dove to my defense, and we fought for half

an hour before Jim McCoy finally pulled us all apart. For days, the
tension between the loutish Americans and the longsuffering Cubans
continued, culminating on the winter night when Timmy Roldan
pinched his eyes and repeatedly mouthed the word "after" at us as
we ate dinner—a word we would come to understand meant *I'll
kick the shit out of you after we're free to get up from this table*. Juan followed Timmy to settle the score once and for all, a dozen kids trail-
ing behind them, but only two of us were intent on defending Juan,
and by the time the encounter ended the boys from Camagüey had,
in fact, gotten the shit kicked out of them. When we went to McCoy
and implored him to do something about this injustice, he exploded.
He had had it, he shouted at my brothers and me, with this constant
fighting between the Cuban and American kids, and now was the
time to stop it, and he would do so by staging a spectacular fight.

McCoy wanted tough-guy Robert Duran to box for the United
States of America, and although we suspected that he would select
older and bigger Juan Bautista to fight for the island nation of Cuba,
our hearts soared when he tabbed my brother Juan instead. Juan,
Papi's accomplished protégé, could out-box *any* kid in this place called
Colorado, we were certain, and it went without saying that he could
kick Robert Duran's sorry American ass. We were thrilled. Duran,
fourteen, was two years older than Juan, and was taller and heavier
as well, but Juan was a *boxer*, we knew, and all our troubles, it seemed,
were about to come to an end.

McCoy instructed a few kids to move all the furniture to the walls
in the large TV room, and the place was packed with every boy in
the asylum as soon as word spread that something truly entertaining was about to happen. The cowboy produced two pairs of boxing gloves, which he personally laced up for the two fighters, and in
the minutes before the bout was underway, Juan was transformed
in my eyes from big brother to a hero of historic dimensions, one
who was boxing for me and all of us refugees, for our beloved Cuba,
and in the sacred name of *justicia*. My chest swelled with pride as I
remembered his prowess in the carport of the cottage in Santa Lucia,
and I knew that at last we Cubans were about to earn the respect
we deserved, the cycle of unfair beatings ended once and for all by
Juan's pugilistic skills and his towering courage.

Juan was beautiful in the opening moments of the bout; he was sharp, well-balanced, and he landed his punches with perfect accuracy. The American, on the other hand, was a brawler at best. Duran's punches were wild, and they grew wilder still as he became infuriated by Juan's stinging jabs. He hoped to take Juan out with single heavy blow, but Juan easily side-stepped his haymaker swings. I was ecstatic, and I wanted to shout at Duran, "Take that, asshole! Now you don't have all your *yanqui* tough-guy friends to help you." But then I slowly began to see that this was not at all the kind of boxing match that Papi meticulously produced in Cuba. Here there were no rounds, no minutes to rest between them, and no rules of any kind governed the fighting. If McCoy knew anything about boxing, he wasn't showing it, and when Duran began to hold Juan and try to wrestle him to the ground, McCoy, the "referee," didn't object, as Papi certainly would have. When Juan tried to retreat from one of Duran's wild swinging barrages, the American kids rushed out and pushed him forward again into his opponent's path. *"Eso no es justo, no es justo!"* Roberto and I shouted, and it *wasn't* fair, of course, but McCoy was unconcerned.

Without any time to rest, Duran's greater strength began to wear Juan down, yet he fought on valiantly, my brother continuing as best he could in the face of the American's furious swings and dirty moves. I became ever more concerned for Juan and the fight seemed to drag on for hours; it was far more akin to an alley brawl than any boxing match I had ever seen. Then finally, Duran caught Juan hard on the face and sent him reeling backward. He lost his footing and fell hard, striking his head against the metal lockers that were fixed to the wall. The blow knocked him unconscious. The fight was over.

Everyone watching was stunned. Duran, exhausted, sat down on a chair and the American kids began to cheer his victory. The shouts further fueled my brother Roberto's rage, and he rushed at Duran and desperately began to hit him, the brawler too tired to do anything but take by brother's punches. Then at last McCoy took the only action he would take on that horrific night: he brusquely pulled Roberto away from Duran and ordered him to go to the hallway to kneel with his arms out. Roberto broke into tears, refusing McCoy's ordered punishment, and when he did so, the cowboy relented and left him alone. McCoy and every other kid in the asylum simply walked away, leaving only Roberto and me to tend to Juan, who was regaining consciousness but not yet able to get to his feet.

I was still incredibly proud of my brother—and of Roberto as well, of course—as we helped Juan up and did our best to ensure that he was okay, yet I was more defeated than I ever had been before. I had been overwhelmingly anguished that day half a year before when we were trapped in the Havana airport's aquarium waiting for the flight that would take us to exile. Yet even more than on that awful September day, now the terrible reality of our situation had grown starkly clear. We had no parents to protect us any longer, no community of like-minded friends and relations, no adult willing to demand simple justice for us. The beatings would continue in the months to come, and we would have no choice but to endure them. On the night of Juan's fight, Robert Duran beat a message into all three as completely as he knocked Juan unconscious, and that was the truth that our lives now counted for nothing. We remained Rojugui—at least we three were still united against the world, fighting for Cuba as best we could—but it was a grim and unforgiving world ruled by Jim McCoy and a pack of ruthless American kids. We might once have been the princes of our own little realm at La Villita Candado, but no one cared about that any more. Now we lived in a foreign land and were at the brutal mercy of beasts.

Tio Antoñico, Alfredo Perez, and Papi (from left to right) during better days at Casa Vidal.

Siete

Betrayals

When at last Mami received a letter from us after five agonizing months during which she heard not a word about where we were, she was ecstatic to hold the soiled envelope in her hands, and was destroyed moments later as she read the letter's contents. Both she and my father had presumed since the day we boarded the Pan Am plane that we were safely with Papi's father and sisters in Miami. They were shocked to discover that Father Brian Walsh ultimately had contended with the deluge of Cuban children arriving from Havana by sending his charges all over the United States, to foster homes and—unbelievably to them—to orphanages as well. And where in God's name was Pueblo, Colorado? When Mami finally found it on a map, she was horrified. It was so far from Camagüey, and even Miami, that it might as well have been on the moon.

Just as we had reacted on that cold night in October when we arrived at Sacred Heart, when my parents first read the word *orfelinato*, they imagined us captive in a place very much like the Asylum Padre Valencia, which—as if God were punishing them for the sin of sending us away—they clearly could see from their living-room window, and which they were forced to confront visually each time they traveled to or from home. Over the years, Mami had taken us to mass at the asylum when it was more convenient than driving us to the parish in the Plaza de las Mercedes, and the miserable conditions in which people lived there—which once she had paid scant attention to—now haunted her and her guilt began to overwhelm her.

I would learn from Mami years later that her remorse and misgivings about the decision to send us away had been severe even when they believed we were safe and sound in south Florida. As they returned to La Villita Candado the day following our departure, she was virtually inconsolable. The sight of our room, empty except for our clothes and our toys, filled her with towering grief, and soon the house grew quieter still when she and Papi were forced to release beloved Romelia, Emilita, and Gladis; in our absence their services were no longer needed, nor was there money any longer with which to pay them.

Our departure rooted in Mami new emotional monsters she was ill-equipped to face. Had she willingly betrayed her own children? The answer now seemed to be yes, and she ceaselessly berated herself for not journeying with us to America, as Tia Nenita had done when she left Tio Antoñico behind and journeyed with her four kids to Miami. She wanted to believe my father was correct in insisting that the U.S. soon would invade the country and overthrow Fidel and his jackals—it was Papi's love of her she so long had doubted, seldom his judgment or his resolve—but I know too she was ashamed to admit to herself that she might have stayed behind most particularly because she feared she couldn't survive without her husband, that she didn't have the skills or the courage to care for her sons in a strange and unfamiliar land. Now she shamed herself for not securing a clear promise from our family members in Florida that they would take us in before she allowed us to board our flight, and for long hours each day she had little to do but long for the three boys who till now had consumed her life with a complex stew of responsibility and exasperation, daily anger and joy. She often invited neighbors Kiko and Oriol over to play inside the walls of La Villita Candado, offering them our toys for their enjoyment as well, but sometimes the presence of other children at her house made the pain of our absence even more severe, and her life now seemed achingly empty except for that piercing pain, the guilt that bore it along, and the rage she aimed outward in every direction.

Papi, I know, was similarly devastated by the hole he now found in his life. Yet it was his nature to respond to enormous stress by planning for what would come next, rather than allowing himself to consider what-might-have-beens, and it was this coping mechanism, I believe, that was enormously helpful in allowing all five of us to survive the ordeals we had suffered till now as well as those that would visit us in the years to come. All Papi believed he could do from that point forward was to continue to rely on the United States to rescue Cuba from the grip of the communists, and to endeavor as best he could to protect the family's properties and businesses, ensuring that we would thrive again once the madness ended and everyone returned safely home. Eventually, everything would be fine, he believed resolutely, or at least as confidently as his anxious mind would allow. To think otherwise, to imagine his life and all our lives destroyed in the end, was more than my father could bear.

When Mami and Papi went to Santa Lucia these days, they sometimes invited Kiko and Oriol to go with them. The beach was a place for children, it seemed to them, and they were cheered to see the two boys take the same delight in the simple pleasures it had offered us. Tio Antoñico regularly joined them too, and more and more, he became their constant companion. With his wife and children away in Miami, Antoñico's latent paranoia and depression had re-awakened; his mood swings and suicidal thoughts descended around him like storm clouds, inevitably often enveloping my parents as well. And then, even the bit of joy he took from the beach and the relative ease of life there was gone when the trips to Santa Lucia ended completely. Gasoline was in scarce supply and was terribly expensive as well, and parts for Papi's beloved 1956 Rambler American no longer were available. When its engine finally failed, Papi sold, a piece at a time, every scrap of the car he could, and the last he knew of it, the Rambler's metal carcass was being pulled behind mules as a plow on a sugar plantation in the countryside near Camagüey.

By the spring of 1962, Cuba's economy was in shambles, and the Vidal family's financial world had collapsed as well. With the change in currency, virtually no one had money with which to buy anything, and when people did manage to put a few pesos aside, they had to spend them on food, medicines, and essential supplies rather than new refrigerators or ranges, and appliances, furniture, bicycles, and the other goods at Casa Vidal, which now simply gathered dust in a showroom that customers no longer even entered. People who had bought items on credit from the Vidal brothers stopped paying their bills, and the business withered and all-but died.

The rental properties fared little better because tenants had no more money than anyone else. When rumors that Fidel soon would confiscate all private property began to circulate wildly, the renters grew even less inclined to find the means to pay, and most tenants now expected the government to allow them to live in their rented homes at no cost. The Hotel Residencial seldom had paying guests any more, since both tourism and business-related travel had virtually ceased. Yet the employees at the hotel and the store, as well as those who maintained the rental properties continued to come to work. No longer was there much work to be done; no longer did my father offer his employees motivational speeches or suggest sales quotas to strive for, and neither could he pay their wages. Virtually everyone stayed on, however, simply because no one had anything else to do, and, like him, most continued to hope that things would be set right soon enough—either by the power of Fidel's intellect and will, or the rather different sort of power the Americans wielded.

In addition to the stress of contending with moribund businesses and a wife with a history of emotional instability who had become even more unbalanced in our absence, Papi also had to attend to his brother's deepening psychological crisis, which had grown severe. Antoñico's now-paralyzing depression made it impossible for my father to rely on him for day-to-day help in protecting what assets remained to them, and my uncle was trapped by black moods that made it a challenge for him even to get out of bed. Antoñico wasn't an upper-middle class playboy any longer because Camaqüey's upper-middle class no longer existed. Women didn't clamor for him anymore, and the respect his financial good fortune once offered him now was lost. If Papi was determined to survive despite the enormous obstacles Fidel had set in his way, Antoñico, on the other hand, believed it was only a matter of time before everything the family owned was utterly lost, and from his dark perspective, Papi's determined efforts and stubborn resolve were nothing more than naïve tilting at windmills, an outlook made even more bleak by Antoñico's uneasy mind.

When he at last agreed to battle his depression with electric-shock treatments—considered a promising therapy in the early 1960s—it fell to Papi to accompany him to the hospital where the procedures were performed. Watching his long-adored older brother writhe violently and foam at the mouth as jolts of electrical current coursed through his brain forced my father to come to terms with who his brother had become. Blinded throughout his life by his belief in his brother's prowess, and still thwarted by what he saw as his own severe limitations, Papi at long last began to understand that he, in fact, was much the more stable and capable of the two. Beloved Antoñico's future might be as desperate as Cuba's was, he now had to consider, and he increasingly sensed that he was entirely alone. His wife and his brother had become psychologically compromised; his mother suffered increasing senile dementia—what in later years would become known as Alzheimer's disease—and Papi found it impossible to offer any of them empathy or meaningful emotional support. It simply wasn't in his nature, or in the set of skills he chose to develop. All he was capable of was concentrating his resources on the family's collective financial and physical survival, and the latter, like the former, appeared to grow more vulnerable every day.

Once neighbor Pillin Castellano discovered that my parents had sent my brothers and I away, he became newly convinced that Roberto Vidal and his wife Marta were enemies of the revolution, and his sudden appearances in my parents' garden—and even inside their house—became commonplace. His rantings about the certainty that they would be brought to justice unnerved them terribly and only sharpened the emotional knife-edge on which Mami endured her days. Neither one was willing to stand up to Pillin and order him out of their home, afraid that if they did anything to protest the invasions, the neighborhood G-2 squad would march them away, and so they cloistered themselves, even from dear friends and the family members that remained close at hand. They could trust no one, they vowed, and even the spirited clandestine gatherings at which they had argued about Cuba's future and collectively devised intricate plans for survival, which had been so important to them during the preceding three years, they shunned now, afraid to say anything to anyone out of mounting fear for their personal safety. My father increasingly sensed that representatives of the revolution had cornered him and that they bore formidable weapons, while all he had with which to defend himself was the equivalent of one of the toy rubber knives that lay in a box in our bedroom, and his trepidation proved justified when Ernesto LaRua returned to terrorize him again.

One of the things Papi always had admired in his former employee was his determination to get ahead, and now he had to presume that, true to form, LaRua was attempting to move himself up the revolutionary ladder by successfully capturing a "traitor," and that he had chosen my father as his focused target. I suspect, too, that LaRua harbored a deep grudge over some injustice on Papi's part—whether real or imagined—back in the time when they worked together, but for whatever the mix of motivations, LaRua succeeded in May 1962 in having my father arrested and jailed.

What once was a very bad dream had become an unimaginable nightmare. Papi now was trapped in a tiny and hideous jail cell, one without light or a even a cooling breeze. He was offered little to eat, but worse, no one would explain the exact nature of the charges against him, and his efforts to find a lawyer to represent him were futile. Thousands of lawyers already had fled the county, and those who remained were afraid to take cases like his, fearful that if their client were judged guilty of crimes against the revolution, they might be charged themselves for having defended a member of the contra-revolutionary insurgency. Mami now was virtually imprisoned herself inside La Villita Candado, afraid to go out or to say anything to anyone, afraid to search for help for her husband because a presumed friend or a once-trusted professional might well be a G-2 member, in fact, my mother's mounting horrors compounded by the uncertainty of whether she would ever see her husband again.

Years later, Papi would describe his eventual trial to us as a circus, a charade, a ridiculous cross between a military tribunal and a kangaroo court. He had no choice but to defend himself, and his sole ally was Alfredo Perez, a longtime friend who had been Casa Vidal's accountant for many years. At no small risk to his own safety, Alfredo had succeeded in passing the store's ledger books to my father in jail, and as the trial commenced, Papi could do little but hope that he would be allowed to use the ledgers to prove that he had never cheated his employees, his patrons, or the government, and that the charges against him were false. Yet that thin optimism was dashed as the judge entered the dimly lit room at the jail where his trial was held, wearing army fatigues and a wild beard much like Fidel's and pounding the butt of his pistol on a table to gavel the proceedings to order.

First, the judge called Ernesto LaRua to testify, and my father's former employee quickly began to seethe, screaming about Papi's allegedly heinous crimes, lacing his speech with obscenities, insults, and threats of death, LaRua pointing his pistol at my father, and appearing barely able to contain himself from pulling the trigger. Three more men followed, each one making similarly fictitious accusations, insulting Papi, threatening him, and pointing their pistols at him as well. He was forbidden to object to any of their statements or allegations or to question them in any way, and as he sat passively listening, it began to be clear to him that LaRua and his cohorts' tactic had been to get my father to lose his temper. Papi suspected they were trying to goad him into bursting into a rage, hoping his anger would prove his guilt in the judge's mind. He also imagined that had he risen from his chair and shaken his fist in fury, one of them might well have felt justified in summarily shooting him dead.

Papi contended each time he recounted the story for us that his ability to keep his cool had saved his life that day and ultimately had earned him his freedom. He remained courteous and respectful at each stage of the proceedings, and never raised his voice. When at last he was allowed to begin his own defense, each time LaRua interrupted him with a new rant, Papi simply stopped speaking, puffed patiently on his cigarette, and waited for his accuser to finish and for the judge to give him permission to begin again. Carefully, methodically, and always in the calmest voice he could muster, Papi made his best case, using the ledgers to corroborate his statements. When it became clear that the judge actually was paying attention to him, he did his best to focus solely on the judge and to persuade him with the simplest truths he could offer. When at last the judge had heard enough, he announced that Roberto Emiliano Vidal Pares was innocent of the charges brought against him. LaRua was outraged, but for the moment could do nothing more, and my father immediately was allowed to leave the jail and walk home to La Villita Candado, where Mami was elated to see him—an emotion, I suspect, she never truly had experienced before.

Papi understood that being acquitted offered no guarantee that LaRua would not conspire to have him arrested again, or that subsequent imprisonments would lead, like this one had, to his exoneration. His days of freedom likely were numbered, he knew, and so, in August, Mami, Papi, and Antoñico made their way in a borrowed car to a farmhouse outside the city of Santa Clara, where they were scheduled to meet five others, the eight of them planning to board a twin-engine plane that—flying below radar detection—would secret them out of Cuba. Clandestine flights like this one were far from rare and often were successful, and on the heels of his imprisonment, this escape plan's significant risks now were dangers they were willing to face. But when the three of them were less than a kilometer from the farmhouse, the car's radiator over-heated and began to spray boiling water from under its hood. The plane's departure wasn't planned for a few hours, so Papi decided it was best to pull over and walk to the farmhouse for water. He knocked on the door and was let in, discovering inside the panicked faces of the five who hoped to travel with them. But their plot had been discovered, they frantically explained to Papi; government militiamen already surrounded the farm, and they begged my father to leave. He took a can of water with him as he left, walked as nonchalantly as he could back, filled the car's radiator, then drove away with his wife and brother.

The three of them heard on the news the following day the story of the dramatic arrest and jailing of five *gusanos* attempting to desert the island. Papi had barely escaped imprisonment for a second time, but his luck wouldn't hold. Three more times he was arrested, each time being hauled away in the middle of the night by LaRua and his thugs, my mother convinced in each instance that she never would see him again. Yet miraculously, my father repeatedly was freed after dismal weeks in a jail cell, calmly and respectfully making the case for his innocence at each subsequent trial, just as he initially had, and being declared innocent each time of the charges against him.

Antoñico also was jailed the fifth time Papi was arrested, the two of them charged with operating businesses that were not legally theirs.

The new government claimed that all enterprises and real estate became property of the state when their owners fled into exile—as my grandfather had done nearly three years before—and his name plainly remained on the deeds to everything the family owned. This time, Papi could see no way to escape the charge—my grandfather was still the titular owner of everything—until by chance he discovered that a pre-revolution law declaring every spouse a co-owner of her husband's property had not yet been repealed. With the help of their sister Mella, who continued to care for their increasingly infirm mother—Papi and Antoñico now claimed that their mother remained the properties' and businesses' owner and that they operated them as her legally appointed surrogates. The two of them were blessed by another miracle on the day frail and demented Abuelita Cachita came to the court and lucidly announced that, yes, her sons labored on her behalf and with her complete permission, yet Papi knew too that he could not count on divine intervention forever. Somehow, and by whatever means, he, Mami, and Antoñico would have to find a way to leave their homeland.

My father was an intelligent man, and it remains difficult for me to understand his deep and sustained conviction during the preceding days and months that the United States would come to Cuba and save the day, much like the American cavalry dependably did in the Western movies we watched. Was the U.S. intent, in fact, on overthrowing Fidel, at least until events on a global scale made an American invasion diplomatically impossible? Or did Papi simply delude himself during those critical years into believing in the certainty of an American rescue? Given his years of hard work and the commensurate financial rewards he had reaped, did my father grow blind to larger realities in order to continue to justify his single-minded fight for his businesses and his stubborn refusal to leave Cuba while it remained relatively simple to do so? It wasn't until the crisis of that October—during which the attention of the whole world was focused on the island—that Papi at last surrendered his faith in the great American invasion. And in the aftermath of the near-catastrophe, he felt utterly and shamefully betrayed.

On October 14, 1962, U.S. spy planes flying reconnaissance mis-sions over Cuba spotted unmistakable evidence of four medium-range ballistic-missile sites nearing completion on the island. No longer was American President John F. Kennedy faced solely with the threat that Cuba would become a strategic outpost for the spread of communism throughout the Americas; unbelievably, Cuba also was about to become the base from which Soviet nuclear weapons could reach New York, Chicago, and Washington within only a few minutes of being launched. Kennedy had warned Soviet leader Nikita Khrushchev that there would be grave consequences if the USSR were to install offensive weapons in Cuba, but now it was clear that Khrushchev had scoffed at the threat, and the American president faced the very real possibility that forcibly removing the missiles from the island could trigger a world war of horrific, even cataclysmic dimensions.

For nearly two weeks, tensions intensively mounted and millions of people around the world were transfixed by the possibility that the planet was on the brink of destruction. If the two super-powers did go to war, Cuba almost certainly would be at the epicenter of the conflagration, and when, on October 22, President Kennedy announced a U.S. Naval blockade of the island, intended to prevent Soviet missile-bearing ships from reaching Cuban ports, it appeared to Mami and Papi in Camagüey and to millions of others in Cuba that their lives soon would end in a nuclear nightmare. And for three brothers in faraway Pueblo, Colorado, that possibility seemed astonishingly real as well.

It was clear to us and all the other Cuban kids at Sacred Heart, whose numbers at the orphanage now grew by the day that our country was about to be blown to bits. I found it impossible to sleep during those terribly anxious nights, and as we watched the news during each day I thought constantly about my parents, wondering how their actual deaths would occur when the nuclear bombs began to explode. And even if the three of us survived the nuclear war, it was hard to imagine the future: with our parents dead, our status as orphans would be cemented and we would be forced to live at Sacred Heart until we were old enough to be shipped to another asylum. We would have no homeland to return to; we would be forced to live in Pueblo America forever, and it was hard to fathom how all of the world could have gone so mad in the four years since Fidel had marched victorious through Camagüey and I had shaken his hand.

Then, incredibly, there was hope. The president announced on October 27 that the Soviets had agreed to the removal of nuclear weapons from Cuba in return for the United States' promise, in turn, to dismantle U.S. Jupiter missiles in Turkey aimed at the Soviet Union. Critically for Fidel and his government—and catastrophically for people like my mother and father—the U.S. also pledged not to subsequently invade Castro's Cuba, nor to support an invasion led by any other nation or anti-revolutionary group.

Around the world, people rejoiced, and all of us at the asylum were thrilled to think that our parents would survive and we would have a country to go home to, yet Papi, Mami, Antoñico and millions more immediately believed that they had been brutally betrayed by John Kennedy. The president and his administration had sold out the people of Cuba as a means of ending the crisis, it appeared obvious to them. Without the threat of invasion from the U.S., Fidel and his henchmen would reign terror with impunity from now on; without a threat of invasion, the communists' hold on power would become inviolate. No one could check Castro now, and Papi was certain that nothing would prevent him from completing the systematic destruction of the lives of all those he once had vowed to make free.

In the aftermath of the missile crisis, the United States summarily severed every remaining tie with the Cuban nation. The embargo was quickly tightened and U.S. borders were sealed against immigration by Cuban citizens, abruptly ending Operation Peter Pan, and throwing the lives of the families of the more than 14,000 children the program had helped reach the U.S. into even more chaos. Estimates were that as many as 50,000 children with visa waivers also were stranded in Cuba when commercial flights between the two countries abruptly ended, and I was sad to think that our friends Kiko and Oriol and our cousin Gonzalito would have to remain in a place the American nuns increasingly assured us was evil. And although Mami and Papi were still alive, if planes no longer flew between Cuba and the U.S., it was impossible for me to imagine how I could ever see them again.

From my father's perspective, his life and the lives of his family had been shattered by the most contemptible kinds of betrayals. Fidel, foremost, had betrayed the promise of the revolution, destroying the democratic dreams of people like Papi and replacing them with the yoke of communism. Ernesto LaRua, whose life Papi had helped set on a prosperous course, repeatedly had betrayed his mentoring with the kinds of harassment that might well have led to his lifelong imprisonment or death. And now, cowardly John F. Kennedy had bitterly betrayed whatever thin hope remained that Castro could be brought to his knees and that millions of Cubans could return home and begin rebuilding their lives. Kennedy's decisions in the midst of the missile crisis shattered forever Papi's dreams of remaining in Cuba, sustaining his businesses, and bringing his sons home to proudly grow up in their homeland, and this betrayal, most of all, opened a deep psychic wound in my father that never would heal.

In the aftermath of the missile crisis, Mami panicked, convinced that she never would see her sons again. Her fear filled her anew with rage, and she aimed her fury in every direction she could—at Fidel and his counterfeit revolution, at her fellow Cubans who had so easily escaped and left her behind to suffer, at Kennedy and all the idiot Americans who were blithely oblivious to her terrible plight, and to God, who had allowed her life to so utterly crumble to nothing. Yet most of all, she directed her rage toward my father. It was her husband, *her husband*, who had chosen stubbornly to hold onto his businesses rather than his own precious children. *That* was a true betrayal, she screamed almost incessantly at him, and the more desperately she raged, the closer my mother came to the cliff-edge of losing her mind.

Ocho

An American World

T here wasn't a single morning in my years at Sacred Heart Home that didn't begin with outlaw Jim McCoy shouting out of the darkness, "Wake up, sleeping beauties," followed in seconds by each of us bleary eyed boys falling out of bed and onto our knees on the freezing-cold floor to recite the Our Father, our breaths steaming into the air. Nothing about my imprisonment at the asylum was more predictable, and there was nothing I hated more than McCoy's sadistic dawn revile.

Yet life, nonetheless, had begun to improve in palpable ways by the last months of 1962. When a final group of Cuban kids arrived in Pueblo soon after the October missile crisis—and combined with the other three groups who had come in the months following our arrival a year before—we now totaled a hundred Cuban boys and girls and we had become a slim, and even powerful majority.

I remember being thrilled each time news spread that more Cuban kids were on their way, hoping that a few of them, at least, would hail from Camagüey, even that one would be among my former classmates at El Colegio Champagna and that I would have a close friend. I would flood him with questions, I fantasized, about our beloved hometown, and perhaps he even would bring me news about Mami and Papi. The reality, however, was that none of the Cuban kids who joined us in Pueblo were *camagüeyaños*—or *agramonteros* as we actually preferred to be called, in honor of Ignacio Agramonte, a native son who had fought heroically for Cuban independence from Spain in the late 1880s. Yet even so, it was wonderful to have recent refugees from our island arrive in our midst. They always arrived late at night, just as we had, and I would rush to their beds immediately after McCoy had roused us the following morning, studying each face for one I recognized, defiantly speaking Spanish with the new boys to help them feel a bit less terrified than I at first had been, eager to hear their perspectives on Fidel, the revolution, and when we might be able to go home again, warning them as quickly as I could to steer clear of the evil McCoy.

It seemed to me that all the new boys were wonderful baseball players—and of course, they were; they were *Cubans* and Cubans played *beisbol* better than anyone else, we knew—and some also brought phonograph records with them that we listened to constantly: salsas, merengues, rumbas, and far more often than anything else, the popular and melancholic "Cuando Salí de Cuba," songs that made our hearts swell with pride when we heard them, and that also often filled me with *morriña*, homesickness, in the way that music so powerfully can. Yet by the time the final group arrived in the days after the missile crisis came to its dramatic end—these wards of Peter Pan already having reached Camp Kendall by the time the flights suddenly were suspended—something odd had occurred: I had become American enough that these latest arrivals seemed nothing less than exotic to me. The new boys were big and quite mature, and they were still steeped in Cuban culture, of course. To my Americanized eye, their mannerisms and ways of speaking were loud, peculiar, and etched with a kind of pride and self-possession that I both envied and disliked. They retained an attractive *tropicalismo* that had been stripped from me in only a year in the asylum, and this recognition engendered in me more rage toward McCoy and the other culprits who ruled my life than I already possessed.

I paid particular attention to thirteen-year-old Juan Del Águila, who was far more passionate in his nationalism than anyone else, and who plainly viewed American kids as inferior to him and his fellow Cubans. He was a gifted athlete, strong and brave; and he simply wouldn't let bullies like Danny Roldan intimidate him. Juan and his brother Miguel were brash and undaunted, and their refusal to be cowed by the American toughs, as well as their immediate demand that they too were part of the ruling class, gave me a self-confidence I couldn't have claimed without them, one that filled me with patriotic delight. José Alvarez also seemed to me to be wonderfully larger than life, yet he aimed *his* passion in what was, to me, a fascinating and very compelling new direction. Although still only a seventh-grader, José immediately began to boast to the rest of us of his extraordinary exploits with girls prior to coming to America, and he vowed that the strict separation of the sexes at the asylum would not impede him from similarly continuing his conquests here. I was spellbound by the stories he would tell—they were fascinating whether they were true or not—because by the time I was twelve, it had become quite clear to me that girls possessed an importance I hadn't entirely understood until now.

Early in my captivity at the asylum, it had become obvious that one of the few benefits of being an altar boy at those desperately early morning masses was the rare opportunity to actually get near girls and study them for a few seconds. Charged with holding the paten, a small gold plate designed to keep the body of Christ from accidentally falling onto the floor as Father Friel moved it to the communicant's tongue, I stood within inches of every girl attending that particular morning's mass. It was a delicious opportunity to see for myself that they were very interesting creatures, and although I was slow to catch on, finally I noticed that whenever I was assigned to serve at mass, Olga Pichardo—who had arrived with us from Camp Kendall—was in attendance as well.

It was obvious, my older and far more worldly brothers explained: Olga had a crush on me, and that was why she went out of her way to attend mass each time she knew I would be serving. Olga was blonde and older than me, although we were in the same grade in school. I certainly thought she was cute, but never imagined that she would select me as an object of any sort of affection, at least not with my dashing brother Juan on the premises. Yet in time, I began to notice the rather unmistakable evidence for myself, and eventually I mustered the requisite courage to ask Olga directly if she liked me. Her answer—quite stupendously—was yes, and we became girlfriend and boyfriend, although other than in the application of those titles, our relationship hadn't had the chance to grow deep by the time Olga's parents succeeded in reaching Miami and she simply disappeared from my life when she joined them one day in April.

I barely had the opportunity to hold hands with Olga before she departed for Florida—and only once had we stolen a quick and awkward kiss inside a broom closet—and so those tales of what José Alvarez already had accomplished in his short but evidently very eventful life awed me. And when he soon began to plot a romantic, no, a *sexual* tryst with beautiful and already bosomy fourteen year-old Connie Vasquéz, I knew instinctively that José could succeed at his plan if anyone could. He would regale us with the particulars of what he would do with Connie, what he would do *to* her when they found a way to be alone—more vital information than I could have dreamed, the kind that made me think that José, just two years older than me, was indeed a man among men.

No one could be quite sure how it happened, since boys and girls virtually never had a chance even to casually talk together, but sure enough, before long José and Connie clearly were "going together." Then they began to succeed at stealing kisses without getting caught, which was truly inspiring to me. Yet José increasingly complained that he needed extended time and privacy, and at last he found a way to obtain them. On Saturday afternoons, all of us had several hours of unstructured time, and although we weren't supposed to have access to the asylum's classroom area, we all knew it normally was deserted during that time. José and Connie meticulously planned their rendezvous there on a Saturday in December, alerting only a few friends who, they hoped, would help them secure the intimate moments that any relationship depends on if it is to mature. But by the appointed hour, fully thirty boys and thirty girls, each of us giddy with interest in what was about to happen, had descended on the classroom area's hallway, desperate to see, if we could, a bit of what was about to transpire.

Although true privacy now was out of the question, Connie and José insisted that no one would be allowed in the classroom they selected as their love chamber, yet in return for our willingness to serve as lookouts and to alert them if McCoy or one of the nuns should appear, they ultimately agreed that we could watch them through the classroom's windows. And what we saw was, without question, the most erotic spectacle Sacred Heart Home had ever produced—José exploring wantonly with his hands under Connie's blouse and under her skirt as well, her hand finding his crotch and the two of them pressing eager, if awkward tongues into each others' mouths.

"Oh, my God, what's he going to do now?" one of the girls gasped. Another asked in wonderment, "When are they going to come up for air?" And it *was* astonishing, every one of us in the hallway who had managed to squeeze near the windows agreed as we stared, wide-eyed and enthralled and thoroughly aroused ourselves. Connie was clearly nervous at first, and she obviously lacked the finely honed skills José had acquired back in the sensual climate of Cuba, but she more than made up for her inexperience with a kind of enthusiasm that thrilled me. From that day forward, José became an utterly legendary figure at Sacred Heart Home, and having a girlfriend and exploring the wonderful world of sex with her—at least to the very limited degree we could—became something of a badge of honor among us boys in the months and years to come, and I was convinced as I watched them that day that life held promise for me—even in a foreign country, and perhaps even while I remained captive inside the asylum.

By the time I spent my second Christmas at the asylum, I still wasn't faring well in my attempt to follow in José Alvarez's amorous footsteps, yet I was growing strangely more at ease in the United States. Life with Mami and Papi at La Villita Candado now was only a memory, one that grew ever dimmer, and despite the fact that I hadn't chosen to live at Sacred Heart Home, my days unfolded in ways that offered a kind of dependability I thrived on. I still desperately missed being enfolded regularly in the loving arms of an adult, one who could assure me that all would be well, but I had formed important supportive bonds with many of the kids who shared my fate, and as I grew older I found dozens of things I was fascinated by—baseball, football, basketball, Elvis Presley, and the enduring image of a girl something like Connie Vasquéz whom I could someday call my own.

Because I had reached the seventh grade and the asylum's own school didn't extend beyond the sixth, I now boarded a bus each day to attend St. Patrick's Catholic School. I loved escaping the asylum, loved venturing out to a real school where there were no locked and bolted doors, loved spending my days with kids who lived in houses and had parents and knew lots about the actual world. Back at the asylum after school, unless we were at benediction, or eating a meal, we were free to go outside and play ball, even in the most severe weather, and I discovered in playing thousands of games of sandlot baseball, touch football, basketball, and horse that I was an athlete—regardless of Papi's earlier proclamations—and that there was something about physical competition that deeply appealed to me. And although McCoy and the nuns exercised an erratic and illogical kind of censorship over what we watched on television, they never objected when we watched televised sports, and I became a passionate fan of the Naval Academy, the Green Bay Packers and Boston Celtics and New York Yankees, players like Bart Starr, Roger Staubach, John Havlicek, Bill Russell, and Mickey Mantle—all but the last of whom were virtually unknown in Cuba—becoming American gods as far as this no-longer-pudgy kid from Camagüey was concerned.

The Americans at the asylum had been enthralled with the music of Chubby Checker at the moment when Roberto, Juan, and I arrived in fall of 1961—and although we certainly learned the twist, it was Cuban music that still captivated our imaginations. But when The King began to ever more constantly command the top of the record charts, we were astounded by the raw sexual energy of his music, and I was hooked forevermore. Elvis ruled among all of us as the unchallenged sovereign of popular sound; we did our best to dress like him and to imitate the silky and muscular voice that could so demonstrably make girls weak in the knees. We dreamed of *being* Elvis, or at least I did, and when the Beatles began to usurp The King in the minds of most of the girls at the asylum, I chose to hold my ground, joining a coterie of male music sophisticates who refused to allow other boys to play Beatles records in our midst—loyalty to The King mattering even more to me than securing the affections of girls, something that, in retrospect, I find a bit hard to believe.

It was easy enough to accept that I had become enamored of American sports and American music—I was almost a teenager, after all—but further proof of how suspiciously persuadable I'd become was the fact that now I liked American food and even American weather. Hamburgers, which I had thought were the most ridiculous food ever imagined two years before, I now devoured on the special occasions when I was offered one, and even the cold wasn't the scourge it once had been. When I first stepped off an airplane in Colorado in October 1961, I felt as if someone had thrown a bucket of ice-water on my naked body, and in the months that followed I often worried that my frozen fingers and toes would simply snap off in the arctic weather, but by now the cold seemed as natural to me as the sunrise, and I had discovered I was enchanted by snow.

My brothers and I first saw it fall from the sky on an evening less than a month after our arrival. The asylum's yard lights gave the darkness an amber glow, and when flakes began to descend we raced out into the night in wonder. Snow was wetter than I had expected it to be; I loved the tingle each flake brought to my up-turned face in the seconds before it melted, loved seeing the flake's intricate shapes before they quickly disappeared in my open hands. The snow settling onto the ground, then blanketing it, seemed to set the world in slow-motion and induce a silence that was the richest stillness I ever had heard. Then I thought of Cuba, of course—of the Christmas carols we sang about snow in that place where it never snowed—and I understood at last why the magic of Christmas and miracle of snow for so long had been linked together.

On one of the last days before Christmas each year, soldiers at nearby Fort Carson hosted a holiday celebration for us that was the highlight of the whole year. Army buses arrived early in the morning and escorted every boy and girl at Sacred Heart Home thirty miles north to the base, where each of us spent an astonishing day with our personally assigned soldier escort—a kind of individual attention we otherwise seldom received. Together with dozens of kids from other orphanages around the region, the army treated all of us to striking displays of Cold War weaponry and even staged a mock-battle, complete with thunderous and spectacularly fiery explosions, the perfect kind of Christmas treat for America's orphans, the army must have presumed—and indeed it was. Perhaps they knew that it was kids like us, filled with admiration, who would join their ranks. But an even greater pleasure was the holiday dinner that followed in a cavernous army mess hall, one that culminated with a visit from a surprisingly authentic-looking Santa, who—somehow very impressively—knew every one of our names when he presented each of us with a present, a gift the strict nuns insisted we had to wait until Christmas morning to open.

Yet if the asylum's staff often seemed harsher in its treatment of us than it needed to be—and, in McCoy's case, just a trifle more venomous—people in the Pueblo community who volunteered at the home were universally wonderful to us, particularly the Spanish-speaking women who helped us learn English, patiently slogging with us through our Dick-and-Jane readers and, at lesson's end, regularly offering us shoulders to cry on when we confessed our troubles to them in a language neither the nuns nor McCoy could understand. And then there was James Eddy, tall and slender and perhaps the blondest, fairest-skinned man my brothers and I had ever seen—someone we truly gave our hearts to for the first time since we had left Camagüey.

Mr. Eddy, as we always called him, was director of the Colorado Boys Ranch in nearby La Junta, a residential facility for emotionally troubled youth, and one of those particular sorts of American men who had found something compelling in Boy Scouting throughout his life—both as a scout himself and as a dedicated scout leader. Roberto and Juan first met Mr. Eddy at a large Colorado scout jamboree in the summer of 1963, my brothers attending as members of a troop the Sacred Heart parishioners recently had organized. At the end of that week, Roberto and Juan were quick to find me when they returned to the asylum to tell me that they had met a cool scout leader who was interested in "taking us out," the phrase asylum kids always used when we were invited to spend the weekend with people out in the community. They had explained to kind and soft-spoken Mr. Eddy that there was a third Vidal boy at the asylum, and he readily welcomed me as well, and before long we began to see Mr. Eddy, his wife Yvonne—as dramatically broad as Mr. Eddy was thin—and their son Jimmy roughly one weekend a month, the Eddys making the hour drive to Pueblo to take us out to dinner at a Denny's restaurant or, if the occasion were particularly special, to a movie, experiences that felt like winning the lottery to us.

On holidays, Mr. Eddy would ferry us back to his home, where Yvonne always had mountains of delicious food at the ready as well as big, enveloping hugs—huge treats for boys starved for affection of every sort. Their son Jimmy was much younger than we were and we thought he was a pain-in-the-ass, but he liked us too and seemed to

look up to us, and around their dining table the six of us were something of a scene from a Norman Rockwell painting—reproductions
of which I'd seen in a Pueblo drugstore that made America seem like
a place where everyone except us was wonderfully fed and secure
and quietly joyful—our conversations always shaped by their que-
ries about school, our circumstances at the asylum, and our aspirations for our lives. Sometimes Mr. Eddy simply would take the three
of us to one of Pueblo's parks, where it was certain that he would
say yes to touch football, complimenting our passing skills during
the course of our two-on-two games, letting us beat him on a pass
or elude him on a long run, all three of us believing at the end of the
game that one day we would play for the Green Bay Packers.

We were English speakers by now, and we shared with the Eddys
the particulars of our former lives, our parents' predicament, and our
suspicion that we never would see them again. And then one Saturday near the close of 1963, Mr. Eddy startled us by asking whether we
might be interested in being adopted by him and Yvonne. Roberto,
Juan, and I flashed glances at each other before we spoke, telegraph-
ing our quick agreement that each of us liked the idea *a lot!*, then—
as calmly as we could, and in an American manner we'd learned
from The King—we said, yeah, that might be good. As Mr. Eddy
began to look into whether adopting us would, in fact, be possible,
joining his family increasingly seemed to us to be the answer to a
dilemma for which we hadn't yet found a Rojugui sort of solution.
In half a year, Roberto and Juan were going to complete the eighth
grade and would have to leave the asylum—and me—behind. Their
likely destination was the Cañon City Abbey, a Catholic prep school
an hour away that, to our minds, at least, sounded a lot like being
transferred from one Catholic penal institution to another. But if
the Eddys adopted us, we understood on the other hand, we could
remain together, move to the country, live with a family whom we
had begun to love, and attend *public* schools—clearly the coolest of
schools—for the first time. But then, as already had happened several times in our young lives, a momentous event occurred far away,
one that seemed to profoundly affect us in ways we knew we couldn't
yet completely understand.

On November 22, 1963, I was on the playground at St. Patrick's
School in Pueblo when four ashen-faced nuns rushed out of the build-

ing, gathered us as quickly as they could, and explained to us through their tears that President Kennedy had been shot and killed.

Like everyone else in a nation where I had begun to feel tentatively at home, I spent the following three days watching the aftermath of Kennedy's assassination unfold on television, yet my twelve-year-old take on what I observed—most particularly the televised murder of Lee Harvey Oswald—was deeply, and quite traumatically, colored by my memories of the post-revolution years in Cuba. It was impossible for me not to presume that the chaos that had occurred there now had traveled to the United States and that many more murders would follow, that the streets of Pueblo and every American town soon would be filled with rioters, looters, and mob-crazed soldiers—people bent on destroying the place that had begun to feel like a safe haven to me, their mayhem's success ensured by the fact that an American world I wanted to be part of was spiraling out of control.

For every child at the asylum, the president's assassination was a grave event of enormous proportion, but for those hundred of us who hailed from Cuba, it immediately seemed to bear a broad and sinister context as well, one that we instinctively believed was connected directly to us. Was Kennedy murdered in retaliation for his administration's attempts to overthrow Fidel? That seemed very possible. Or had Kennedy's betrayal of the anti-Castro cause at the close of the missile crisis been the terrible catalyst for his killing? That too could have been its cause. It seemed impossible to know the true answer as dozens of us sat silently on the floor of the television room watching those somber events unfold in Dallas and Washington, yet it seemed utterly certain that the person who shot the president was allied to one side of the Cuban struggle or the other, and once more it seemed to us that we had personally been selected to suffer for our island nation's sins.

On television, I watched Robert F. Kennedy walk behind his brother's coffin, his face etched with terrible pain as he escorted the president's widow, and I couldn't help but remember how broad and warm his smile had been two years before when he offered it to me as he shook my hand. At twelve, I was old enough to understand that every life was entwined with both good and bad, and that sometimes it was difficult at first to know one from the other—and that particular kind of confusion was my first response when, just four days after President Kennedy's assassination, my brothers and I received a telegram from Mami and Papi, informing us that they and Tio Antoñico had safely reached Mexico City, and that as soon as they could secure the proper visas, they would journey to the United States and we would become a family again.

Their telegram spoke in celebratory terms about our pending reunion—they loved us dearly, the words in Spanish affirmed, and everything soon would be alright, and they were counting the days until they could hold us in their arms. But for Roberto, Juan, and me, the telegram's arrival was deeply disturbing. The news it carried was as shocking as the assassination, and it demanded that we begin to think of our parents again in ways that now it was easier not to, and to imagine them again as part of our lives.

In the time since we last had seen them—their tear-streaked faces so terribly anguished as we watched them recede from view at La Pescera—we had learned the vital trick that dismissing them from our lives as best we could made our days and months at the asylum far more easy to bear. In the time before we received the telegram, we dimly presumed that our parents were alive, but we seldom spoke of them or spent time imagining how they fared, and I know I didn't believe I ever would see them again. Given all the upheaval in our young lives, it was enormously difficult to live with slim hopes or unlikely dreams. I much preferred my secure and confident vision of my life unfolding without them—however grim that life sometimes could be—to the uncertainty of a future in which they *might* reappear. The only dream I dared entertain was of joining the Eddys in La Junta—Mr. Eddy and Yvonne and little Jimmy, whom we would box into submission, Roberto and Juan and I forming a true family in rural Colorado—but now, it seemed, that dream was dashed.

He was excited for us, Mr. Eddy assured us, as soon as he heard the news. It was great—we would live with our parents again, even if we would not live with him and Yvonne and Jimmy—but no matter how hard Mr. Eddy tried to convince me that all would be well, I remember that as November gave way to December and the holidays arrived, I responded to this new turmoil the only way I knew how: Mami and Papi would never leave Mexico City, I determinedly convinced myself, and I would not wonder about them or worry about them ever again.

After more than two years of failure—and at the vain expense of thousands of dollars in the Cuban black market—at last Papi had been able to obtain visas that allowed him, Mami, and my troubled uncle Antoñico to legally emigrate from Cuba to Mexico, and in a final act of defiance before their departure, Papi signed over owner-ship of La Villita Candado to an army officer who had helped them secure passage out of the country, thwarting in the process the envi-ous intentions of our neighbor Pillin Castellano, the G2 member whose harassment of Mami and Papi had been so relentless for so long. The other properties—Casa Vidal and the Hotel Residencial, the rental houses and apartment buildings, the warehouses and the lot in "Monte Carlo" where they hoped to build their dream home, and the beloved beach cottage at Santa Lucia—they simply aban-doned as they boarded a plane in Havana and flew away from the island each of them had loved as deeply as they knew how.

Ten days after they settled into a small apartment in Mexico City, Mami was devastated by the telegraphed news that my grandfather, Dr. Ramos, had suddenly died. Returning for his funeral, even very briefly, was out of the question, and it was that impossibility—yet another way in which circumstances seemed to conspire both to con-trol and crush her life—that made the loss of her father particular-ly hard to bear, my mother's depression and now her grief robbing her of any new hope that might have accompanied her first days in exile. As they would describe them to us later, our parents' months in Mexico were filled with a kind of numbness, loss of equilibrium, and a profound exhaustion that no amount of sleep seemed able to cure. Occasionally, they would muster enough energy to go see one of the celebrated sights in the Mexican capital, but otherwise they simply endured a long string of listless days, sustained in their tiny quarters by the $40 a month they received from my grandfather in Miami, Papi attending doggedly to the seemingly interminable pro-cedures that ultimately would lead, they trusted, to visas allowing them to enter the Unites States, Mami's rage the sole release she reg-ularly had from her stupor, Tio Antoñico still adrift and terribly com-promised by his psychological storms.

Then, five months after their departure from Cuba, the three received word from *La Torre de Libertad*, the Tower of Liberty—an organization established by the U.S. Immigration and Naturalization Service specifically to assist Cuban exiles hoping to secure residency in the United States—that their path was clear at last, and they flew to Miami, where La Torre officials greeted them at their offices, gave each of them a coat and twenty-five dollars in cash, then wished them well. Antoñico was enormously eager, of course, to see his wife Nenita and four children, and Mami and Papi wanted to move as quickly as they could to claim their sons in distant Colorado and bring them back to Florida. But during the few days they spent with my father's extended family they discovered that they had done nothing to help us two and a half years before. Papi was outraged over what he believed was their willing abandonment of us, and he vowed to never live near his father, sister, brother-in-law, and sister-in-law again, despite the fact that my grandfather Don Antonio had been faithfully sending desperately needed money since his own arrival in Miami in January 1961. No, Papi announced in answer to Antoñico's implorations, he was not interested in hearing their explanations— their pathetic excuses—for why they had failed to come to our aid. My parents focused their attentions entirely on how they could free us from the asylum, and when they had found a way—one that necessitated a move to Colorado—they and Antoñico simply said a brief and awkward goodbye, Papi presuming he might never again see the brother with whom he was closer than anyone else in his life.

A minister from Colorado was visiting the La Torre offices in Miami on the early April day my parents received their coats and cash. Reverend Elizabeth Knott, associate-pastor of the First Presbyterian Church of Littleton, a Denver suburb, had come to Miami in hopes of finding a Cuban immigrant with excellent carpentry skills, one whom her congregation might sponsor, trading his work on construction projects at the church for room, board, and financial assistance. But what she encountered instead were a weary and surprisingly sorrowful couple spending their first day in the United States. The husband spoke a bit of English, and she was interested to learn from him that the couple's three young sons already lived in Colorado and had for some time—in an orphanage in Pueblo. When my father explained that he and my mother would travel to her state soon to reunite with their sons as soon as they had earned enough money, Reverend Knott suggested that perhaps she and her congregation could be of help. It was far from easy to accept her largess, yet what other choice did they have? He and my mother quickly agreed. Yes, they would be deeply thankful if she could help them get to Colorado, Papi replied in the best English he could manage, his gratitude for the moment surmounting his fierce Cuban pride. And then the following day, Father Friel called Juan, Roberto, and me into his study to give us unbelievable news.

I was stunned. I was angry as well, and terribly confused. I had convinced myself in the preceding months that nothing substantive had changed in my life. Mami and Papi lived in Mexico now—that much was easy enough to accept—yet I still firmly believed I would never see them again. I wanted to explain to Father Friel how distraught I was at this news, but he was the person who most of all had asked me and the other Cuban kids never to surrender hope that we would live with our parents again one day, and I realized that my honest response to the news that Mami and Papi would arrive in a few days was surely a terrible sin. I said nothing to him, opting instead to try to appear excited, and I didn't even dare share my true feelings with my brothers. The only time I spent with them anymore was on our outings with the Eddys; we had separate friends nowadays, and it was important for them to make clear how much older than me they were, and somehow the asylum at last had broken our Rojugui spirit. I couldn't be sure my brothers shared my apprehension or my melancholy, and so I kept my feelings stuffed deep inside, and I remember crying in my bed late into that night. I was distressed by the new turn my life now would be forced to take, saddened by the certainty that I was about to lose my friends and the stability the asylum—the home, *my* home—had offered, unhappy at the prospect of being asked to bond with my brothers again, and deeply afraid that I could no longer love my parents.

Saturday morning, April 11, 1964, passed in a blur, my stomach wound into knots, my brain disconnected from the rest of my body. I couldn't eat, couldn't even think, and by the time Sister Doris at last came to take us to the tutoring room where our parents were waiting,

I was close to jumping out of my skin. As we reached the door of the small room, I closed my eyes for a moment, afraid of what I might see inside it, yet neither could I help but look. And as soon as Roberto, Juan, and I caught a glimpse of them, we flew into Mami and Papi's arms.

This man and this woman were our *parents*, we instantly knew—something ineffable, some silent genetic information made that truth immediately and wonderfully clear—yet I was simultaneously shocked by how much they had changed, both of them grown so small and so old. Papi, then only forty-five, had turned entirely gray; his face had wrinkled, and no longer was he the proud, tall man I remembered. His shoulders were hunched forward, his skin seemed to hang from his bones, and he wore the stress of the past five years like an ill-fitting suit of clothes. Mami, too, was old, although she was barely forty. Our beautiful mother—whose photograph the kids at the home had begged us to show them again and again—apparently had remained behind in Camagüey, and in her place was her weary shadow. Her eyes were sad and tired, and her skin was pasty and white, as if she hadn't seen the sun in a very long time. Her hair had grayed and wasn't perfectly coiffed like it always had been before, and the trim figure she always had been so proud of she now no longer owned.

We, in turn, astonished them. The desperate, tear-flooded boys they last had seen in September 1961 now had become rather self-assured young men, and they needed a few moments of study to determine which one of us was who. They confessed later that they had been terribly afraid as they made the drive south from Denver with Betty Knott that they would find us living in destitution, and that we would be unforgivably angry with them for everything we had suffered, yet both fears already were allayed. Sacred Heart Home wasn't as bad as they had feared it would be, and as we smothered each of them with our hugs and kisses they knew we instantly forgave them, my brothers and I soaking them with grown-up tears and two-and-a-half years of buried and often-denied emotions, expressing our love to them again as if none of us ever had left our home in Camagüey.

It wasn't long before we began to pepper them with questions: how were our dog Lucky and our cat Rififi, and where were they now that Mami and Papi were here? Who was looking after our house in their absence and had they lately seen our aunts and uncles and cousins?—their answers often interrupted when one of us suddenly was desperate to hug and kiss them once more. Kind Reverend Knott suggested we leave the home and go to a restaurant after a time, and it was fun to offer Mami and Papi advice about the food they might find to their liking. As we ate we were often silent, the continuing shock of the reunion and our shared struggles to believe we were truly together again stealing the words from our mouths. Yet I *wasn't* dreaming, I continually reassured myself, and Mami and Papi explained before we left the restaurant that they would return to Denver that evening to find a home for all of us there.

Denver? We weren't moving to Miami, as had all the Cuban kids we knew at the home when their parents had reached the U.S. and claimed them? This was fine news for me. I would be safely a hundred miles away from McCoy, but surely close enough that we also could invite my friends to come visit from time to time, and my brothers and I returned to the orphanage that night with an utterly new sense of our destinies. We *did* have parents, and we still were connected to them in ways that bridged the years, the two nations, and the separate experiences none of us could ever completely describe. I did my best to put my foreboding behind me and simply accept the fact that I was the youngest son of Roberto and Marta Vidal, formerly of Camagüey and soon to be of Denver, Colorado. I would live with my parents because that was what twelve-year olds did, and there seemed to be little else to consider.

In the following days, Father Friel, Reverend Knott, and our parents collectively agreed that it made sense for us to spend six more weeks at Sacred Heart Home so we could complete the school-year, time that would allow Mami and Papi to get settled into a house in Denver prior to filling it with three rambunctious boys, and allow us to pay our farewells to our schoolmates at St. Patrick's, the kids at the home we were close to, Father Friel, Father Sierra, and to Mr. Eddy, Yvonne, and Jimmy, whose lives we would no longer be joining, no matter how much we recently had longed to, and, of course, still did in ways we couldn't confess. At the park playing football one afternoon, I was teamed with Mr. Eddy against Roberto and Juan; I misjudged a pass from him, and the football hit me in the face, a blow that wasn't serious but that loosed a flood of my tears. I couldn't stop crying, and Mr. Eddy comforted me until I could play again, understanding, even if I immediately did not, that I had been wounded by something other than the ball. "I know you're worried and confused about being with your parents again. But it will be okay. You'll see," he assured me, pledging on the ball field that all would be well in a way I presumed the best fathers did to their sons.

On the last day of school, Betty Knott again drove my parents to Pueblo to pick us up, and for the first time, I allowed myself to feel enormous relief at the reality that we were leaving Sacred Heart. Never again would I have to endure McCoy's discipline, never again would the son of a bitch wake me up in the darkness and the cold. Over time, my brother Roberto had forged a true bond with Jim McCoy—perhaps because he had been so bonded to Papi in ways I never had—and I wasn't surprised when McCoy said a kind goodbye to my two brothers, yet pointedly ignored me. But when our parents arrived and my passage out of Pueblo, Colorado was safely assured, I decided I would have a word with McCoy in any case. I wanted to tell him what a piece of shit I thought he was, and how happy I was to have escaped his abuse. I felt bold and defiant and free in that moment, and I walked up to the cowboy in the seconds after the car was loaded and we were ready to leave and announced, "Someday, I'll come back and kill you." They weren't the words I'd intended, but I had spoken them nonetheless. I was astounded and scared and proud all at once, but McCoy simply smirked, saying nothing in return before I left his asylum forever.

A Desperate Man's Eyes

The first evening we spent together in our rented house in Littleton was a magical one, the five of us not simply reunited but together for the first time as a *family*, the kind we had never had been before that moment, a family in the way each of us always had longed to be—even Papi, who forever had found it so hard to physically express his affections, often hugging me so tightly that night he took my breath away. Squeezed together on a careworn sofa in the living room of the tiny, two-story house rented to us by a member of Littleton's First Presbyterian Church, we shared a thousand stories spanning the thirty-two months we had been apart. We cried, we laughed, and we clung to each other constantly to be certain the moment was real. With one of us seated in each of their laps throughout the hours we spent and the third son's arms wrapped around one of their shoulders, we heard how terribly empty La Villita Candado had seemed without us and how Mami and Papi had been so sad to let Romelia, Emilita, and Gladis go when there was no money with which to pay them. They told us about Papi's arrests and trials, their struggles to get to Mexico, and the long months of waiting in Mexico City. We, in turn, described the shapes of our lives at Sacred Heart Home, and what we described often brought tears to their eyes. We rejoiced in what a godsend Betty Knott had been, and I was quick to express my delight in moving to a big city like Denver, and even with Roberto and Juan I could feel the rekindling of an old and deep connection. They were my brothers and I was theirs and Papi assured us that we all had returned to the planet of Rojugui—and I overflowed with joy.

Every day on the beach at Santa Lucia had been a good day, and the morning when Fidel passed triumphantly through Camagüey had been etched with enormous euphoria; the days we spent with Mami and Papi in Havana had offered us many collective pleasures before we were forced to part, and the staged Christmas combat and real Christmas meals at Fort Carson had highlighted days I would always remember, but never before in my life had I been *this* happy, I knew. Never before had pain, and sorrow, and aching uncertainty lifted so quickly, like clouds at the close of a Colorado summer storm, and I was sure that our family's many travails had run their course and that we were free from suffering at last. It was impossible to imagine how anything bad could happen—to any of us ever again—and at the close of that incredible night I offered heartfelt prayers of thanksgiving to God before I finally fell deliciously and deeply asleep.

Yet life as I more accurately understood it returned as soon as the following morning. I was barely out of bed, hadn't eaten breakfast yet and had just descended the stairs when I realized with sudden, breathtaking terror that the previous night had been one of those blessings that arrives only very infrequently in anyone's life, and that the larger truth was that my life remained anchored, as it always had, to violence and chaos that were completely beyond my control. Simply moving from Pueblo to Denver could not make that life perfect, it now was shockingly clear, and Mami and Papi were my parents in ways that far more often would entrap me rather than support me, in ways I very seldom would celebrate and simply had no choice but to accept.

Mami was waiting at the base of the stairs when she called us down to breakfast. Juan and I were moving down them toward her as she called up to Roberto, asking him to close an open window at the top of the stairs, when suddenly she raced past us, forcing us out of her way, and reached Roberto, still on the upstairs landing, in only a second or two. She grabbed him by the neck, threw him down, and began to ferociously punch and slap him, Roberto doing his best to shield himself from her blows but otherwise not fighting back. Juan and I were too stunned, too disbelieving to do anything in his defense except glance in horror at each other and watch from the bottom of the stairs until finally her rage subsided and stilled. Then Mami stood, collected herself and smoothed her hair, and explained to Juan and me that Roberto had been insubordinate when he scowled at her as she asked him to close the window. For his part, Roberto said nothing and evidenced no emotion, determined to emerge the victor by proving to her that she no longer could hurt him, a skill he had learned not when he suffered Mami's blows in another time and country, but from the ways in which he had learned to survive Danny Roldan and a dozen other bullies during our years in the asylum.

I hadn't once considered Mami's temper in nearly three years—hadn't run from it, hadn't whimpered in bed in fear, hadn't been paralyzed by my mother's rages—yet who Mami was and how readily she could explode flooded back to me in that moment, and I realized that no longer were Romelia, Emilita, or Gladis at hand to help her quell her furies or pull her away from one of us. Mami could *hurt* someone, I viscerally understood, in ways more brutal perhaps than even the odious Jim McCoy could, and he crossed my mind in that moment, and I thought of Sacred Heart Home, and I wondered whether there *was* a place in the world where I could be both happy and free.

Mami's attack on Roberto that morning triggered within minutes a fight with my father as well, the two of them soon screaming vile epithets at each other, Mami scratching and clawing at him, Papi egging her on, doing whatever he could to fuel her explosion, taunting her and laughing sadistically in ways that seemed to me to make his violence as brutal as hers. For the first month we were in Denver, not a day passed during which my mother didn't rage against Roberto, Juan, or me—or the three of us combined—and almost always her outbursts led to a pitched battle with Papi. Each of them used their sons as weapons against the other, hoping to win our unilateral loyalty, hoping we would join their bitter attacks, and most often, Juan and Roberto chose to side with Papi, running to him for protection and always seeking his consolation. But for me, it was almost impossible to take Papi's side—as if this were a boxing match and he was sparring with the storied Kid Gavilan and expected me to be in his corner cheering him on with filial pride. I could see—in ways perhaps my brothers could not—how he took perverse delight in Mami's crescendoing anger, how his pushing her into rage offered him a release as well, a tactic he never took responsibility for, one I couldn't respect. Yet neither could I sympathize with my mother; she was too volatile, too unpredictable in ways that made me long for the clockwork sting of Jim McCoy's belt, and so I distanced myself from each of them as much as I could, vowing that I would flee from their home as soon as I could find a way.

Every day during that first month, my parents grew increasingly aware of how mature and independent their sons had grown in their absence—and how American—both of which transformations dramatically heightened the tension in the small house that seemed to offer none of us room even to breathe. We were young men now, and testosterone and teenage angst shaped our responses to virtually everything, and we balked at our parents' insistence that we comport ourselves in a Cuban manner and accept their Cuban idea of discipline. They were wounded that we had become so American so quickly, that we seldom spoke respectfully or even wistfully of our island heritage—that we never expressed what it meant to us to be *Vidals*—and rather than evidence pride in the fact that their sons had learned to speak English so well and so swiftly, that too was an injury to them. Not only had they lost everything they once had set their hearts on, not only had they been forced to abandon lives and work in which they had taken great pride, now their sons, their flesh and blood, seemed to blithely dismiss those losses and to reject the worth and the valor of their Cuban lives.

Nothing cut them more deeply than their lingering, festering considerations of the fact that Juan, Roberto, and I had been very open and eager to being adopted by the Eddys. There was no way to explain to them why we felt we had to erase any hope for a reunion with them from our lives in order to simply survive, yet how we nonetheless still longed for the daily sustenance and larger meaning of a family life, one the Eddys had offered without any strings attached. When they briefly met Mr. Eddy when he paid us a brief and uncomfortable visit in Littleton, they could sense for themselves the deep affection each of us felt for him, and the fact that we could love this tall and angular and bed-sheet white American man was a stab to their hearts—one they could attend to only in ways we might have predicted: James Eddy surely was a pedophile, they whispered to us—they were far older than us and understood these things—and what good fortune it was that they reached Colorado before we actually joined the Eddys and were forced to live in family where we would suffer awful abuse. Of course, these insinuations, we knew, were not based on any reality—Mr. Eddy had been a very supportive and loving force in our lives at a time when we really needed it—but their insistence on their belief only added to our growing resentment of them.

One day in mid-summer, Reverend Betty Knott, whom we continued to see often, came to the house to invite us to a special Sunday service at the First Presbyterian Church. We would be the congregation's special guests and they would be honored by our presence, she said, words we eagerly translated for Mami and Papi to be sure they understood. Members of the church had been so moved by our plight and so pleased to help us, she explained, that she wanted to ensure that everyone in the church had an opportunity to meet us and offer us their personal welcomes to America and the assurance that they would remain steadfast in their assistance to us as long as we needed it.

In the time since she had met Mami and Papi in Miami, Betty Knott had arranged—and, of course, paid for—their flights to Colorado; she had repeatedly driven them from Denver to Pueblo to visit us and most recently to bring us to our new home, a house one of her parishioners agreed to rent to us for only a few dollars a month, and she and other church members had ensured in the time since that the refrigerator never was empty of food. Papi had immediately begun to search for a job—one he was desperate to find both to provide for his family in the way his self-esteem demanded and to end his indebtedness to the Presbyterians as soon as he possibly could. The more help we received, the more he longed to entirely cut it off. Yet his English was very poor, he didn't have a car, didn't know the city of Denver, and he had had no choice but to accept the generous offers of church members to drive him to job interviews, to act as his translators on occasions, these wonderful people from Littleton cheerfully offering every sort of assistance they could simply because doing so seemed right to them.

It was a blow to Papi to discover that the state of Colorado would not honor his doctoral degree in pharmacy from the University of Havana; he simply wasn't a pharmacist as far as state regulators were concerned, and the kind of employment he would have been proud to have was simply out of the question. Given his struggle with English, so too were jobs managing a furniture or appliance store—or even working in one—and neither could he coach boxing, even if he had been able to find a gym or a club eager to have his seasoned experience. He would have to settle for manual labor, he soon understood, and by the time Juan, Roberto, and I joined them in Denver, Papi had taken a job nickel-plating instruments for the Colorado Serum Company, a manufacturer of veterinary products and medicines.

I could sense Papi swelling with pride on a bright Sunday morning in early July when, as she addressed her congregation, Reverend Knott repeatedly referred to him as Dr. Vidal, a title that rightfully he could claim but, of course, could not demand. We did our best to whisper translations to Mami and Papi throughout the service, one my brothers and I were awed by: these Presbyterians knew we were Catholics but clearly didn't care, and they showed no interest whatsoever in converting us, and in virtually every prayer and her remarks before each hymn, Reverend Knott made specific reference to us, expressing thanksgiving for our well-being, for the work of many church members on our behalf, asking God's blessing on the Vidal family's future in Colorado. The service was filled with flowers, bright robes, songs, and celebration—even a bell-choir performing especially for us, we were told, and as it closed, the pastor asked the five of us to move to the back of the church, where those in attendance could greet us as they departed.

We explained to Mami and Papi what we had been asked to do, then led them to a spot near the sanctuary's door and stood in amazement as everyone in attendance patiently waited to shake hands with each of us. And my brothers and I were dumbstruck when virtually everyone we met also pressed a few folded bills into our palms. At the asylum, we had received an allowance of just twenty-five cents a month, and I know I'd never seen a ten- or even a five-dollar bill before, and Juan, Roberto, and I periodically exchanged furtive and gleeful glances, acknowledging in our momentary eye contact that these Presbyterians were making us *wealthy*.

We were aware too as the church slowly emptied that Mami and

Papi were very uncomfortable. They shook every hand, accepted the cash, smiled warmly, gratefully, and said "thank you very much" in English two hundred times or more before we were alone. I was dizzy with anticipation; I couldn't wait to count all my money, our money, and surely this fortune would solve every one of our financial problems, it seemed sure. But then, to my astonishment, Papi collected the bills from each of us, and instead of counting them or tucking them into his suit coat, he stuffed all of them into a poor box that stood beside the door. Then he turned to us and sternly announced, *"Nosotros no recibimos limnosa ni caridad de nadie."* "We don't receive charity or handouts from anyone. I want you boys to remember something. We are Vidals, and Vidals make their own way in the world. Do I make myself clear?"

I couldn't answer him. I was stunned and angered and mystified by what he had done. For weeks our parents had spoken to us about how different our Denver lives would be from our lives in Camagüey. We no longer would enjoy two homes and the assistance of servants; each of us would soon have to find jobs to help pay our bills; and already there had been days when Mami prepared no lunch, as if she'd simply forgotten, and although all three of us had outgrown our worn-out shoes, we had been told there simply was no money with which to buy new ones. Yet in his idiocy, it seemed to me, Papi had chosen to take the money we very generously had been offered moments before—several hundred dollars, no doubt—and had given all of it back. And what was this about not receiving charity? What bullshit, what *mierda*, I wanted to shout at Papi. His sons had been sheltered and fed in an orphanage. He and Mami and three of us had been gratefully receiving vital assistance from Betty Knott and her parishioners for nearly three months now. Vidals *did* accept charity; I had seen us do so repeatedly with my own eyes, and now Papi had risked offending the very people who had kept us alive by turning away their latest gifts.

I was too young, of course—and too terribly disappointed by the loss of that fortune—to understand that it had been one thing for Papi to accept gifts when he simply had no other option. He had understood along the way that if he wanted to get to Colorado, if he wanted to secure his sons' release from the orphanage, if he wanted a home for his family and a job that paid him something at least, he had no choice but accept those separate charities and to be deeply thankful for them. But something very different had occurred that Sunday morning. From Papi's perspective—one he did not express and which it took me a long time to comprehend on my own—we had been asked to dress in our best tattered clothes and come to Littleton to play the roles of the indigent poor, to be characterized as helpless immigrants in front of hundreds of people and to receive their handouts of cash as a means of making them feel good about themselves. In his arrests and trials in Camagüey, Papi had been shamed in front of only very few people; there had been no throngs of observers at the trials, no bellowing crowds witnessing him being hauled away. But here, as he saw it, he and his family had been humiliated and profoundly shamed in front of a large and cloyingly compassionate audience, and they had made our shaming an Easter-like celebration, although that was never their intent. Papi's fierce Cuban pride had been emasculated by these empathetic Americans, and, as far as he was concerned, I'm sure, it was better to endure more hardship and go without dozens more meals than to acquiesce to a public disgrace of that proportion—and far preferable as well to forego their assistance than risk becoming comfortably accustomed to it, a hidden fear I would come to learn about my father. If he allowed himself a momentary lapse of accepting charity, he would lose his resolve to make it on his own.

Yet all I knew as Betty Knott drove us back to our house a few minutes later, each of us doing his best to continue expressing our gratitude to her, was that it appeared Papi was *choosing* a life of poverty for us, opting to continue our troubles and the wrecking of our lives, and I bitterly blamed him for what I believed didn't have to be.

It wasn't long before we moved again, this time into a two-bedroom apartment in central Denver. Papi was eager to distance us from the generosity of the Presbyterians, and as managers of the apartment building, we now would pay no rent, even if the battles my parents waged now would be all too easy for the people of Denver to hear. While Papi labored each day at the Colorado Serum Company, Mami showed vacant apartments to prospective renters, collected rents, oversaw evictions and maintenance, and resolved complaints—something she proved remarkably capable of despite her lack of English, her white-hot temper virtually never surfacing, even in moments it might have. In addition to regularly relying on my brothers and me to be her interpreters, she and Papi assigned to us the manual labor that the building required—vacuuming hallways, washing windows, mowing the lawn, shoveling snow, as well as cleaning, painting, repairing holes in apartment walls, unplugging toilets, and emptying ghastly refrigerators when they were vacated, work that demonstrated to my horror what pigs people could be.

We also became teenage entrepreneurs, borrowing money from Papi to buy three sturdy bicycles, then taking on paper routes in our neighborhood, delivering the afternoon *Denver Post*. The system required us to buy our papers directly from the *Post*, then collect from our customers ourselves, one that quickly taught us to pay wary attention to the numbers of papers we purchased and to our neighbors' comings and goings: if a family moved out and we didn't catch them before they departed, it fell to us to pay for the papers we had supplied them, and in that low-income neighborhood it was all-too-common for people to refuse to come to their door when they could see that one of the Vidal brothers had come to collect. The after-school job kept us from playing sports; we had to get up at two a.m. in order to get the Sunday paper delivered by six, and in snow storms the job was hell—pushing our bikes, weighed down with dozens of papers, through a foot of slush oftentimes, what was normally a two-hour job taking four or five to complete in the foul and freezing weather.

Yet we did make money—good money as far as we were concerned—and we earned a set of encyclopedias and a Super-8 movie camera as prizes from our diligent efforts to add new subscribers, rewards selected by Papi from an array of possibilities that seemed wonderful beyond belief to us, the Universal encyclopedias occupying a place of honor in our living room, if only occasionally being used. And as soon as our family acquired a telephone—a sure signal, it seemed, that we were making financial progress—we began to attach fliers to the papers we rolled and secured with rubber-bands, offering our lawn, snow-shoveling, and painting services, and even offering Mami's expertise at sewing and alterations, advertisements that proved remarkably successful in keeping all of us extremely busy and in keeping money coming our way as well.

For his part, Papi struggled to meet the physical demands of his job at the Colorado Serum Company, backbreaking work that would have been far better suited to the young boxer he once had been than to a middle-aged man who had smoked three packs of Chesterfields a day for nearly three decades by now. He would come home at the end of the day and fall into his chair utterly exhausted, physically spent by the thousands of pounds of equipment and chemicals he had hoisted all day, those same chemicals also often giving him terrible nausea and headaches. Yet he never missed work, never failed to do what was asked of him, and before too many months were out, the company transferred him to the department that produced serums and vaccines, a job his pharmacy background certainly prepared him for, but whose biggest challenge was that now he was required to wrestle with sheep—working with two other colleagues to capture, hold, and extract blood from powerful animals devoting every ounce of their strength to foiling the plans of the white-coated men who approached them.

Papi always had loved animals of every kind—often proclaiming loudly in front of my mother that his *only* true loves in life were dogs and cigarettes—and although he was utterly at ease with the sheep, dogs, rabbits, and mice he worked with, it was emotionally taxing for him when, as often happened, he and his colleagues would be forced to extract so much blood from an animal that it collapsed and died, and it was far from rare for Papi to come home and need to share with us the story of how he had been a party to the killing of a dog that day, his voice quivering and full of sorrow as he spoke, his eyes filled with tears.

He was far less emotional about the deaths of rabbits and often brought their carcasses home with him; in fact, touting as he came in the front door the feast we would have for dinner that night. Early on, a co-worker had offered him a recipe for roasted rabbit, and all of us enjoyed those meals, yet I remember wondering sometimes whether the emerging fact that I thought about sex incessantly and that my body seemed single-mindedly bent on actualizing only a single human activity had something to do with the fact that I had eaten so many rabbits that by now I was eager to fornicate every bit as often as they did.

We were surviving, even without the help of the First Presbyterian Church, yet it was obvious that the physical demands of their work and the constant financial stress were taking a further toll on my parents. They did daily battle with language and cultural barriers, arduous jobs, bills they couldn't find means to pay, and three teenagers increasingly intent on demonstrating their independence; and together with their undisguised dislike for each other, those stresses relentlessly boiled over into chaos and combat. Their constant wars would flare over what seemed to me the most insignificant issues, and they would continue to rage until both Mami and Papi were utterly exhausted, incapable finally of screaming another insult, yet it seemed they were propelled to fight again the following day by forces they couldn't control, and as I grew older I began to understand that terrorizing each other was perhaps the only way in which each of them could express how bitterly angry they were at the turns their lives had taken, how outrageous it seemed to them that their good lives now were gone.

Physically, at least, it was Papi who showed most disturbingly the effects of everything with which he contended. He grew ever thinner; his slouch had grown pronounced, his once-powerful frame small and bent and servile now to an enormously heavy if invisible load. His face had grown quite pale—his days of boxing at the beach house, scuba-diving, and fishing in the sun clearly were long gone—and in the place of his warm smile and good humor was little more than a visage of resigned indignation. With every animal whose death he was a party to, every enormous grocery bill, and every vicious round in the ring he endured with my mother, his life seemed to slip further away from him, and I began to worry on sleepless nights whether Papi would survive his introduction to life in the United States, and, if not, whether the four of us could continue without him.

Yet finally something occurred that seemed to cast a ray of light on Papi's beleaguered soul. He discovered that in several states exiled Cuban lawyers were being given the opportunity to teach Spanish in high schools—work that was less than ideal perhaps, yet which offered them more substantial jobs than waiting tables or clerking in liquor stores. In Cuba, Papi was well aware, schoolteachers were comparably well paid and held in esteem by the community, and he presumed that teachers were similarly recompensed and respected in the U.S. as well. Although the state of Colorado wasn't yet making this opportunity available—and although nowhere were pharmacists or businessmen being given similar options—he believed it nonetheless might be the way out of the dog- and sheep-wrestling business.

Colorado's Department of Education had never made an exception before to its requirement that all the state's teachers—in private as well as public schools—have a degree from an accredited U.S. college or university and full teaching certification, yet Papi chose not to let that precedent stop him, and he initiated a series of letters and daily telephone calls to the secretary of education's office. Low-level bureaucrats in the office repeatedly turned him away but the Old Man—an English sobriquet my brothers and I recently had begun to use when we were far from our father's ears—would not be deterred. And after months of insistence, at last he was able to meet with the secretary himself, a man who was sympathetic with Papi's plight, and who guaranteed him that if he could find a principal willing to hire him to teach Spanish, the state would waive its requirements, provided he enrolled in college and eventually obtained a degree in education and his teaching certificate within three years.

Papi was elated, never mind the fact that these requirements would make his goal all but impossible to achieve—a fact Mami haughtily reminded him of as he arrived home with the wonderful news, shattering the small celebration he believed was in order. How could he work at the Colorado Serum Company, or teach at a high school, for that matter, and go to college at the same time, she wanted to know? And where had he hidden the surplus funds that would pay for his tuition? But Papi was too excited, too filled with hope for the moment, to enter the ring with her, and within a month, he had contacted dozens of high schools—all of which flatly said no. Then, at last, Papi learned that St. Francis De Sales High School, a Denver parochial school just five blocks from our apartment, was in need of a Spanish teacher because of a sudden resignation.

Sister Mary George, the school's principal, was intrigued by the possibility that Dr. Roberto Vidal might quickly be suited to a job she was eager to fill, yet because of the unusual circumstances, she deferred to Monsignor Gregory Smith, pastor of the parish with which the church was allied. After no small amount of pleading on Papi's part, Monsignor Smith ultimately agreed to let him teach, but solely on the condition that he agree to accept only half a regular teacher's salary until he had received his certification. My father agreed, despite the offer's inherent unfairness—it wasn't as though the Old Man's *Spanish* were remedial, and he would be working full-time, after all—but we did celebrate at last. All of us were happy for my father; the new job would give his self-esteem an enormous boost, and I did my best to hide my mounting revulsion toward many aspects of the church. What really got my goat was remembering how enormously generous Betty Knott and the Presbyterians had been toward us, regardless of the fact we were Catholics and had to be considered unlikely prospects for conversion. The monsignor might have chosen to respond with similar Christian charity and to have paid my father—as nominally Catholic, let's face it, as St. Francis De Sales himself—what other new teachers at the school earned; he might have, but he chose not to, and henceforth, as far as I was concerned, the monsignor was a son of a bitch.

Yet it did seem to Papi and all of us that we finally had caught a small break. Although she wasn't effusive, Mami appreciated the prestige she believed my father's new career as a teacher would bring to our family, and she had just accepted a job in a dress shop—work her charm and sense of style suited her for despite her still-limited English—a job that would help off-set the cost of his tuition. The three of us vowed that we could find ways to bring in more money as well—increasingly happy about going our separate ways, our years as an indivisible threesome long gone, and eager to spend as much time as we could away from the war that raged in our home.

Soon the Old Man's much-anticipated first day at school arrived, and all of us eagerly awaited his arrival home that evening, but Papi walked in a beaten man. It was easier to jab long needles into terrified sheep, he said, than to face a succession of classes comprised of thirty hormone-crazed teenagers eager to drive this new teacher from their midst. He had been frightened by the sheer size of some of the high-school boys, and intimidated by the speed with which they spoke English, their incomprehensible slang, and the fact that they utterly ignored his directives. Worse, his apprehension had caused him to stutter—the same machine-gun stuttering that had made his life hell when he was these high-schoolers' age—and the students were all too quick to ridicule him, loudly imitating his Cuban-accented stutter each time he turned toward the blackboard. Yet my father returned to his classroom the next day, and the day after—his prestigious new position more a nightmare than a blessing, it initially seemed, and the stubbornness with which he had endured his travails throughout his five previous decades served him once more.

For the next two years, my father would return home briefly after a taxing day at St. Francis De Sales, have a quick bite to eat, then leave for night school, and he often studied till one or two a.m. on his return. Many of his courses were held at the University of Colorado's downtown Denver campus, but regularly he was forced to pilot his 1959 Studebaker on the hour's drive from our apartment to the university's main campus in Boulder, propping a sharpened pencil under his chin to ensure that he didn't nod off at the wheel. He had loved the Studebaker he owned and proudly drove during the good years in Camagüey, and it seemed to me that in purchasing another one—despite the fact that it was ugly as pug dog and deeply embarrassing to my brothers and me—Papi was doing what little he could to recreate the elements of his Cuban life in Colorado. This was *exilio*, exile, he constantly reminded us; and he wouldn't, he *couldn't* be at home again until he returned to the island.

Inevitably, whenever the Old Man needed to prepare for an upcoming exam or write a paper, that would be the moment Mami would choose to berate him for some perceived sin, her tongue-lashing giving way to sustained rage as he calmly rocked back and forth in his chair, ignoring her as utterly as if her words were simply a cooling breeze. Surely she was attempting to sabotage his efforts to earn his degree and double his income, my brothers and I agreed after repeatedly observing her timing, but it wasn't until a bitterly cold Saturday in November 1966 that I began to understand what emotions underlay his determined and silent rocking—refusing to spar with my mother in a way he otherwise always was eager to do. Papi, I realized in a rare moment we spent together that arctic morning, was desperately afraid he wasn't going to make it, that he would fail in this strange and difficult life in exile and we would be left with nothing at all.

The day was overcast and the temperature barely hovered above zero, yet despite the early onset of winter Mami and Papi announced after breakfast that it was a perfect Saturday for the five of us to visit the Salvation Army store. Since we had moved to Denver, my parents had become passionate thrift-store shoppers, taking both pleasure and pride in their abilities to pull true treasures from the densely packed racks of clothing and overflowing shelves of used goods of every kind. Buying what we needed—from shirts and socks and shoes to furniture, appliances, and pots—at the lowest possible price was as important to our survival as our collective income was, and prices weren't lower anywhere than they were at the stores operated by Goodwill Industries and the Salvation Army. Mami was a marvel at proving that *anything* could be washed, dyed, disinfected, repainted, or recovered and given a triumphant second life; she could alter any prized find to make it fit—or almost fit—one of us, and if we never could find at the thrift stores the tight white Levi's and penny loafers that were decidedly cool and we were desperate to wear, at least our lives in the orphanage long had made us accustomed to looking like the three least hip kids in Colorado, if not on the earth itself.

Papi too relished his trips to the thrift stores and the ways in which buying a good-quality sofa for just a few dollars, or a cherished black-and-white TV for ten could lift his spirits and convince him he was as shrewd financially as he always had been, yet on that particular November Saturday, nothing captured his attention as he perambulated the aisles, and so he ventured out into the cold to smoke a couple of the sixty cigarettes he would have that day. I soon had enough of the store myself, and followed him outside where I found him intently watching two derelict men lying nearby on the sidewalk, one lying on top of the other as if he were trying to keep his companion warm in the bitter weather.

"*Mira*, Guillermo," he said, motioning toward the men as I approached him. "Notice how strong the desire is in humans to act with goodness and kindness towards others. Even when men like these have absolutely nothing, one still finds it in his heart to help his friend stay warm."

Papi continued to watch with what seemed genuine admiration, but I watched as well, and before long it was apparent that Papi had been entirely wrong. The man on top was systematically rifling every pocket of every garment the unconscious man beneath him wore, then transferring to his own pockets the items he found of interest. Just as I whispered, "Look, Papi, he's not keeping him warm; he's stealing from him," the man on top ripped the winter coat from the arms of the unconscious man and ran away with it as fast as he could.

Papi was shocked by what he observed and disturbed by how dramatically mistaken he'd been, and I was entirely taken aback when he burst into tears. I had seen him cry before, but I'd never witnessed forlorn, bottomless, and irrepressible sobs like these, and I simply stood motionless beside him until at last he recovered enough to speak, but the words were not meant for me, and I knew Papi had inadvertently made me a part of an internal conversation that was ever-present in his mind. *"Dios mio,"* he cried, "that could be me. There have been so many times I have just wanted to give up. That could be me. That could be me," his sobs overtaking him again, his heaving breaths and his sorrow steaming into the icy air.

Still I said nothing; I didn't touch his arm, or place my palm on his back, or catch his eye to show him I heard him and understood how hard these years had been—because I couldn't understand, not completely, and because I was profoundly frightened by his vulnerability. I had worried before that Papi might die, and added to that concern now was the possibility that even if he lived, he might become terribly fragile, incapable of mustering any longer the courage and resolve of the boxing ring that always had been his hallmarks. I resolved as the wind stung my cheeks and froze the hairs in my nose that I never would do anything to add to his burden in any way, but commingled with that determination was my fear and my anger to learn that my father could even imagine surrender.

From that day forward, and for the rest of his life, Papi never encountered a homeless or derelict person without offering a bit of help. Yet he never did so directly; he would pass a few coins or a dollar bill to my one of my brothers or me and instruct us to pass his money to the person in need. It seemed to me that he used his sons as intermediaries because he was afraid to get too close, frightened that homelessness somehow might be contagious, fearful that he would see himself if he looked directly into a desperate man's eyes.

Cheering For Cassius Clay

I titled my speech "Without Optimism, failure," and felt certain that at last it was ready for delivery. I had had two months to prepare for the Optimist Club of America competition, and Papi had worked hard with me in those weeks to help me perfect it, patiently listening to me practice every day, offering suggestions about both content and delivery in ways I welcomed, but which were very unusual for him. In part, I know, he and Mami simply hoped the competition would help me overcome the shyness that had endured into my sophomore year in high school, and I'm sure he was honored as well by my public acknowledgment of my Cuban roots and my family's struggle in the years following the revolution. My speech's professed optimism about my future in the United States really was little more than a recitation of Papi's personal creed. He liked to refer to the speech as *"Optimismo o Muerte,"* "Optimism or Death," and he did define his life—our lives—in those stark and simple terms: we had no choice but to believe passionately in our abilities to triumph over the circumstances life had brought to us; we could succeed in exile or we could die.

Annabelle Martin, a speech and drama teacher at St. Francis De Sales High School who had been very supportive of my brothers and me, had tabbed me for entry into the competition—one of five students who would vie for the opportunity to represent the school at the district meet—and each of us practiced our speeches a final time in her class the day of the competition. My classmates scored my presentation as second best of the five, a showing that boosted my confidence a bit and helped me harness my anxiety in the hours before we delivered our speeches from the school's stage in front of an audience of a hundred or more. Papi was so nervous that he couldn't look at me as I spoke—the first of the five to do so—but by the time I concluded, I knew I'd absolutely nailed it. It was by far my best delivery ever, and Papi leapt to his feet, offering me a solitary standing ovation until Mami joined him as well. I was stunned to look out and see them on their feet and cheering; they virtually never offered me that kind of praise, and certainly not in public, and now I wanted to *win*—for them, for me, and in the hope for more of that kind of commendation, which I thirsted after as if it were water.

But the judges ultimately scored my presentation as the worst of the five, and the Old Man responded with disbelief and obvious anger. I was clearly the best of the group, he assured me—the other four did fine jobs, but my speech was superior by far, he said. I told him it was okay as we left the auditorium, and was trying to express too that being the winner in *his* eyes was victory enough for me when one of the judges stopped us as we reached the door. He wanted me to know what a wonderful job I'd done, but he wanted to tell us as well that I'd made a "fatal mistake" in discussing my life in Cuba and our journeys to Denver. When he saw the look of bafflement on my face, he further explained, "We're only interested in sending our home-grown boys on in the competition."

Papi was outraged, and for a moment I was sure he would hit this grinning American with a quick right hook. I had seen that same incendiary look in his eye only a single time before—in the seconds before Papi roundly punched a man in Camagüey who had had the audacity to take a pair of scissors and cut off the necktie he was wearing, which had been given to him by his mother. This time however, my father simply took Mami brusquely by the arm and escorted us out to our car. On the short drive home, my mother asked incredulously again and again, "What does a person have to do?" but neither of us answered her. At that moment both Papi and I understood all too well, even if perhaps she did not, that home-grown boys virtually always prevailed in America, and that this was just more of the same old shit.

By now, Papi had worked for paltry pay at the Colorado Serum Company because bureaucrats had deemed his Cuban degree in pharmacy worthless and had ruled his taking a Colorado licensing exam out of the question. And he had taught for two years at St. Francis De Sales, shouldering more courses than any other faculty member at half the school's base salary for reasons only Monsignor Smith understood. When Papi complained to Smith about that disparity, the cleric had only responded, "Don't worry, Mr. Vidal. Someday God will reward you," and, in much the same way that the comment offended and deeply angered my father, it helped drive me even farther away from the Catholic church than I already had traveled.

Because Papi was a faculty member at St. Francis De Sales, it had seemed to our parents to be the logical high school for Roberto, Juan, and I to attend. Before the revolution, they had been convinced that Cuban Catholic schools offered the best possible education, and they presumed the same would be true in the United States. But for our parts, we were as deeply out of our depths at a parochial school as we would have been at Denver's South High School, where we otherwise would have gone. None of the Catholic kids had the slightest interest in welcoming us into their midst, and each of us was frightened to death at first by the new environment and its particular nuances and demands. At the asylum, we had discovered that social status was determined by one's ability to kick the shit out of someone else, but at St. Francis De Sales, status appeared linked to far subtler sorts of skills that we could neither decipher nor put into practice. And because "fraternizing" with members of the opposite sex had been strictly forbidden at Sacred Heart Home, we were stunned to observe girls—who were in a huge majority at the Denver school—walking right up to boys to talk with them in the halls, and even *holding hands* with them, a sight that both fascinated and intimidated the hell out of the three of us.

Our thrift-store clothes continued to be so uncool they drew pointed fingers and derisive laughter, and although by now we spoke perfect English with only a trace of an accent, everyone knew we were the sons of Mr. Vidal, the Spanish teacher whose stutter-laced accent was thick and often difficult to understand, and so we were labeled "Mexicans" in the best of circumstances, and hardly a day went by when someone didn't call out to me, "Hey, spic," or "How's it going, greaser," and epithets like "pepper gut," and "beaner" were names I simply had to learn to ignore. I remember my Latin teacher, Sister Judith, explaining that she lowered my grade at the end of the term because she hated the way I pronounced Latin words with a Spanish accent, the two languages evidently having little in common as far as she was concerned. And Sister Adelma, who taught psychology, once insisted that I stand in front of the class and pronounce the word "elbow"—instead of my "*ahl*bow"—twenty times. As I stood there in horror, doing my best to get "elbow" right, the kids in the class whistled and hooted and pronounced me a "stupid spic," but Sister Adelma was utterly unconcerned. Roberto and Juan suffered similar kinds of harassment—the sort that internally knifes at a teenager's self-esteem—and the three of us virtually never mentioned the name-calling, teasing, and mean-spirited pranks to our parents, choosing instead simply to persevere.

Papi was with us at school every day; he could readily observe how we were treated—and he was often the brunt of similar kinds of taunting as well—and neither was Mami immune from abuse. Tenants sometimes complained to the apartment building's owner that the Mexican manager harassed them, threatening to move if any more beaners moved into the building, and clerks in shops were often exasperated as she struggled to make herself understood. Yet it wasn't until the judges at the Optimist Club penalized me for not being "home-grown" that my parents truly opened their eyes to the constancy of the discrimination we suffered.

Soon after reuniting with us in 1964, they had been hurt to discover how very American we already were, but four years later their perspectives had dramatically changed. It was simply too costly, too detrimental to claim our Cuban identity any longer, they now believed, and toward that end the first rule they handed down was that henceforth we were *solely* John, Bob, and Bill Vidal. The three of us were fine young American men, and Juan, Roberto, and Guillermo had been Cuban boys who simply didn't exist any more. They forbade us to speak Spanish in front of anyone else—just as vindictive Jim McCoy had done—and increasingly spoke English with us at home, and neither were we allowed to develop friendships with other Hispanics. We were *not* Mexicans, and we would prove it by shunning any contact with anyone of Latino decent; our parents instructed us to be as bigoted as we could be, in other words, to help us deflect the bigotry aimed at us. Every time one of us brought a friend home to the apartment, Mami and Papi were quick to examine his family tree, and if they unearthed roots reaching back to Central or South America—or even to Spain, where our own ancestors were born—they would inform us after the friend had departed that the relationship had to end. If the friend were named Jones but his skin was as olive as ours, he too was black-listed, and even fair-haired kids with Italian names like Bono, Costello, or Rossi—suspiciously Spanish-sounding, Mami and Papi feared—had to be jettisoned as well, since it was obviously better to be safe than sorry, and before long the three of us responded to this idiocy by never bringing friends to our home again.

Much of my parents' growing obsession with race and class had to do with self-protection and the perceived defense of our family, we knew—Mami and Papi even opting not to attend events sponsored by El Círculo Cubano, a Denver organization of Cuban immigrants, out of concern that this affiliation needlessly would label us the aliens we were—yet I know there was something more. They had lived in the midst of, but not quite fully a part of the elite class in Camagüey prior to the revolution, and they stubbornly resisted accepting second- or third-class status in the United States. It was one thing to have been stripped of their prosperity, but they would not blithely acquiesce to being robbed as well of the dignity they believed their social standing provided them. They had looked down on blacks and members of the lower classes in Cuba, and now they instructed us to do so as well—a way for all of us to falsely assure ourselves that we remained on top, never mind the fact that we shopped at the Salvation Army and that Papi worked for half-pay, an assurance that sorely was challenged in the months after my father convinced Monsignor Smith to pay him a little extra for setting up for Bingo on Wednesday nights.

The St. Francis De Sales Bingo operation brought in vital revenue for the school and parish, and it drew hundreds of weekly players from the surrounding community. Our job, just as soon as classes ended on Wednesday afternoons, was to fill the school's cavernous gym with a sea of folding tables and chairs, which in turn had to be dismantled and stored away at the end of the evening. It was janitorial work, plainly and simply, and for seventy dollars a week—five of which Papi gave to each of his sons as our allowance—the extra income it offered was significant. Yet "doing Bingo," as we referred to the tasks, served to remind the four of us during every moment we spent in that gym on those nights that we were different from everyone else. No other teacher ended his taxing school day lugging heavy tables and chairs, and every kid who called us spics closely observed, we had to believe, when Bob, John, and Bill Vidal joined the custodial crew on those afternoons. Dr. Roberto Vidal might be convinced that he belonged among the school's professorial class, but Bingo reminded him of another, more bitter truth. Just because the three of us attended a private school, and just because we had Americanized our names, didn't mean we could dream of moving beyond our station.

There would be no "most likely to" titles for the Vidal brothers at St. Francis De Sales. And as Sister Joan of Arc, the school's guidance counselor, condescendingly helped us understand, we weren't really college material, sad to say. John would have a difficult time becoming a teacher, she told him, but he could probably be a teacher's aide. Becoming a lawyer was more than Bob could aspire to, but perhaps he could work as a legal aide. And no, I wouldn't have a career in science, the good sister explained to me, but she thought I might be a fine car mechanic some day.

As the five of us struggled, each in our own particular way, to come to terms with our second-class lives in a nation that often pretended it had no classes, surely it wasn't surprising that we turned to a boxer for inspiration, nor that this boxer also painfully understood America's inclination to allow some of its citizens to climb toward success on the backs of others for whom the climb was all but impossible. Cassius Clay first fascinated us while we still lived in Camagüey. His gold medal at the 1960 Olympic games in Rome highlighted him as a young boxer of extraordinary promise, and by the time, as a professional, he was scheduled to fight world-champion Sonny Liston in

Miami in February 1964, he had become nothing less than an idol in the hearts and minds of every Cuban kid at Sacred Heart Home.

Since his first victory over the beloved Floyd Patterson in 1962, Liston had emerged as something of a malevolent figure in the minds of many, and since communists clearly were the worst people I ever had heard of, he clearly represented to me the evil advance of Bolshevism across the globe, and it appeared almost impossible that he could ever be stopped. The Clay-Liston match, I feared, would be a repeat of my brother Juan's fight against Robert Duran—the beautiful but weaker boxer against an alley brawler. An angel would be devoured by a demon, and as I anticipated the fight with a deep sense of foreboding, my thoughts had turned to Papi, who, I knew, would be equally worried back home in Camagüey. It was the tactical beauty of the sport my father loved so much, not its inherent violence, and I knew Papi's was as offended as I was that a false prophet like Liston presided over the sport that provided a holy, yet very tenuous bond between my father and me.

When the night of the fight finally arrived, and all of us Cubans at the asylum gathered around the radio to listen to the bout, it seemed astonishing that Clay had survived the first round, then the second. Through the next three rounds, we could hear the rising excitement in the announcer's voice as Clay began to dominate the fight, and then, when the bell rang to open the seventh round, Liston refused to come out of his corner and the fight was over. As Clay was declared the winner, we fell into ecstasy. A miracle of biblical proportion had just occurred; good had triumphed over evil; order had been restored to the world and forevermore Cassius Clay became a god I dependably could believe in, just as I knew Papi was deliriously celebrating his victory far away in embattled Cuba.

It was May 1965 before the two fighters met again; we had become a family and were fledgling Americans by then and Clay was now Muhammad Ali. We listened rapturously as Howard Cosell announced the fight over a Salvation Army radio around which we crowded in our apartment in Denver, and Papi, as I *knew* he would be, was every bit as much in awe of the Kentucky boxer as I was. Ali knocked out Sonny Liston in the first round of the re-match, and on Grant Street all was right with the world. If some people did not, at least *we* understood that your name and your religion were yours to freely choose; we understood that you could love your country and hate its government's policies at the same time, and when Ali announced that he would refuse induction into the army because "no Vietnamese ever called me a nigger," we understood that decision as well.

For the next two years, Ali's fights—and the victories that were foregone conclusions—united our family as nothing else could. When Ali stepped into the ring, he became an artist, a genius, a man without equal in all of our eyes, and nothing else in the world mattered but the pure poetry of his boxing. During the minutes that Muhammad Ali fought, there was no poverty for us to contend with, no difficult jobs, no discrimination, no bitter and tormented marriage. The world was perfect for that focused reach of time, and at the end of each bout, justice prevailed and we loved our lives, even loved the battles each of us was forced to fight. Then, when Ali was stripped of his title, the five of us mourned that terribly misguided decision like the loss of a loved one. Ali was the thread that held the fabric of our beleaguered family together; his was the only virtue we ever could count on, and, once more, this place called America broke our hearts.

With each year that passed, my parents' marriage grew more brittle, more caustic, nearly lethal. Each of them moved like badly wounded animals, and at the slightest provocation, they would bare their fangs and attack. Theirs wasn't a loving relationship terribly tested by the stresses in their lives; instead, they were two people whose hatred for each other was persistently fueled by their many challenges, and we were their triggers, their foils, and their weapons.

An unmade bed or a fork left on a kitchen counter—crimes my brothers and I often were guilty of—could send my mother into violent frenzies, and Papi invariably would respond with cruel laughter, deeply cutting sarcasm, and an uncanny ability to twist her own words into proofs of her insanity. Then the moment he declared her insane, she would hurl dishes at the floor, and break vases, lamps, and virtually anything of some small value in an attempt to strike a wounding blow to the husband who constantly worried about money and who would have to replace what she had in anger destroyed. Papi, in turn, would respond with a slurry of vile words; she would scream at the top of her lungs; he would storm out of the apartment or lock himself in a room, and my brothers and I would be faced with a problematic decision: we could leave as well and escape in search of some peace, but if we did, we would have to deal with what was certain to be far greater devastation when at last we returned. By the time we were in high school, Mami no longer could physically overwhelm us; John, Bob, and I were big enough to block her punches or hold her to prevent the shedding of blood, but when we did, her anger simply intensified and she sought out secondary targets. I would often walk into the bedroom I shared with my brothers to discover that Mami had cut a favorite shirt into small pieces and carefully laid them out on my bed. She would take treasured posters down from the wall and tear them into thin strips, and beloved mementos had a way of simply disappearing from the earth, Mami either blithely insisting that she knew nothing or coldly explaining that it was a punishment richly deserved.

The Old Man would do nothing to prevent these outrages, and instead would rather theatrically offer Bob and John shoulders to cry on, taunting her with a show of empathy toward her two sons, proving his reason, generosity, and superior parenting skills, but because I was "Mami's favorite"—as he had perceived me since I first toddled across the tiled floors of La Villita Candado—that same shoulder seldom was offered to me. In the midst of furious conflict, Papi liked to take John and Bob into another room to privately console them, pointedly excluding me in ways that were every bit as painful as Mami's attacks on me and my possessions ever were. I envied my brothers' relationship with my father; except for the time when he had coached me and stood and cheered my optimistic speech-making, Papi virtually never singled me out as the subject of his attention, and when he would take my brothers with him and leave me alone with my still-raging mother, to whom I felt no allegiance, I believed I was utterly alone in the world.

My mother raged with renewed energy day after day, and never did anything to check or change or even examine her behavior. My father, his fears and shattered dreams so often buried deep inside him, chose to do little more in the context of our calamitous family dynamics than to defend and console my brothers, as proof to my mother that they loved and needed him more than they needed her. Yet it was impossible for me to rush to my mother's side in turn—her unpredictability and the flash of her temper made a real relationship with her almost impossible—and neither did she attempt to draw me in when she repeatedly observed Papi pulling John and Bob into his corner of the brutal boxing ring that was our home. I was alone—hurt and perplexed and filled with a kind of loathing that made me desire nothing more than to flee as far away from that appalling apartment as I could go.

At the end of my sophomore year of high school, my parents decided we could afford to give up the management of the apartment building and rent a two-bedroom bungalow. No longer would we have to clean up after the building's tenants, and no more would *they* be forced to endure the steady cacophony of screaming and shattering dishes that emanated from within our walls. Although the house wasn't much bigger than the apartment had been—my two brothers and I still sharing a single tiny bedroom—the proof for Papi that at last we were making some financial progress was that he now could have a dog. As was his manner, he extensively planned and researched the subject prior to the purchase, and ultimately a wire-haired terrier named Belinda joined the family. Predictably, my parents immediately began to compete for the dog's affections, and when Belinda plainly chose Papi as her alpha companion, my mother sulked and whined and cajoled until finally Papi purchased a second terrier, that Mami named Princesa.

I had adored our mutt Lucky at home in Camagüey and tended to be drawn to animals, just as my father was, but I absolutely hated those fucking dogs, in largest part because they simply refused to be housebroken, as if doing their business outdoors was somehow beneath their pedigreed station. Papi decreed that Colorado's weather was far too severe for the little darlings to live outside, even when we all were away for the day, and so, although my brothers and I no longer had to clean clogged toilets at the apartment building, instead we now constantly cleaned up after these two yapping beasts. The daily dog-shit duties were exclusively my brothers' and mine, even though we knew nothing about housebreaking dogs, and one of us would race home after school each day to rid the house of the offending evidence before either parent returned. It was a repulsive task, but at least we shared it among the three of us, and keeping the house clean was far easier than suffering the consequences of Mami's wrath when it occasionally was not.

Near the end of May 1968, my father received news from Tio Antoñico in Miami that my grandfather, Don Antonio, was dying. Papi had remained in telephone contact with Antoñico since their arrival in the U.S. four years before, and he even had spoken by phone on a couple of occasions with his father, whom he hadn't seen since we had moved to Denver. Father and son never had reconciled; Papi still harbored deep anger because of my grandfather's failure to find us and safeguard us as we reached Miami, yet the news that Don Antonio wouldn't live long was enough to spur Papi to travel to Florida to pay his filial respects and, importantly for him as well, to assert himself as his father's obvious successor—the Vidal family's new *patron* once his father was gone. Papi worried about missing school, and because he couldn't be sure how long he would be away and the trip obviously would be more costly if my mother joined him, he announced that he would travel to Miami as briefly as possible—and alone. Mami was livid.

She, like the rest of us, had traveled nowhere in the four years since we'd moved to Denver. She was eager to visit friends from Camagüey who lived in Miami now, and she worried not only that Papi would conspire with his family against her—as she believed they always had—but also that, once in Florida, he might choose simply never to return. Yet none of her pleas or her histrionics could persuade my father to relent and allow her to join him, and with each day that he was away she became more volatile, her frustration and her swelling fury ever more certain to trigger a cataclysmic explosion. Two weeks into Papi's trip, Mami's mood had grown so simultaneously fragile and intense it seemed certain that virtually anything one of us did could be the event that would tip her over the edge, and we kept our bedroom and the kitchen spotless and the dogs as carefully attended to as we could in hopes that none of us would become directly responsible for sparking the fire we sensed was on its way.

Yet one afternoon just before the school year ended, each of us was suddenly called to the principal's office, where Sister Jarlath informed us that because of a family emergency we were to leave school immediately and get home as soon as possible. As we walked the few blocks to our house on South Clarkson Street, first we presumed as we talked that our grandfather, Don Antonio, had died, but if he had, it soon seemed logical, surely Mami simply would have told us when we arrived home that evening. Was something else wrong? Was Papi okay? Had something happened to Mami at the bank where she now worked as a teller? I was terribly uneasy and filled with real foreboding by the time we reached the house, which made the scene we observed as we opened the front door all the more macabre, all the more impossible to believe.

The house was in utter chaos. Shredded newspaper and paper towels torn into tiny pieces lay everywhere—on the furniture, the counters, the beds—and Mami was in a state of disembodied fury, flailing wildly as she moved from room to room, swinging or kicking at anything in her path, screaming at the top of her lungs about what hideous and irresponsible children we were, incapable even of housebreaking two little and loving dogs. It was then the reason for her rage began to make sense. She had come home from the bank early and had discovered the daily messes Belinda and Princesa made that we otherwise always had cleared out of the way by the time she returned from work. Yet it wasn't until we began to clean the house that we discovered, to our horror, that Mami had smeared the dogs' shit all over the walls in the white-hot throes of her tantrum. But she had spread more shit than those two miserable dogs ever had produced during a school day before, and we began to suspect that the thought that this may have occured was so hideous, Mami had used her own excrement to make the scene as dramatically repugnant as she could, I had to fight to keep from vomiting. Shit and piss were *everywhere*—and my anger at my mother gave way to a sudden fear that made it difficult for me to breathe. The whole of the house stank; the disarray was disgusting and utterly terrifying, and as Mami continued to scream, I was dumbstruck by what I now had not only to consider but accept, by the inescapable truth that my mother's rage no longer had limits. Who knew what acts she was capable of? What horrible scenes would we encounter in the days ahead as we walked in the door of our home? What might she do to Papi in a comparable fury? What could she do to her sons?

John, Bob, and I cleaned the house throughout the long hours of the afternoon and evening, each of us continually sick to his stomach and rushing for the toilet as we washed walls and floors and furniture—as we cleaned shit from the simple but lovely house in which she took so much rightful pride. I wanted to cry, but I couldn't; I wanted to scream but I could not utter a sound, and gradually, inexorably, Mami began to grow calm, her shouted outrage ending at last, the wrath that had consumed her muscles, her bones, and her brain giving way to a kind of unsettled peace. She cooked dinner for us when our hours of cleaning were done and the house was ordered again, the smell masked by Ajax and Pine-Sol and bathroom spray. She smiled affably as she set our plates in front of us at the kitchen table, and after dinner the three of us—still wary and shocked and utterly disbelieving—watched television with her for a time in the living room she had destroyed hours before, Mami cradling her beloved Princesa in her lap.

My grandfather died a few days later and was buried in a Cuban cemetery in Miami's "Little Havana" district. The Old Man flew home and each of us—Mami included, I know—was very happy to see him; he had not abandoned us and our lives could take their commonplace shapes again. My brothers and I said nothing about the bizarre and terrifying afternoon we had endured; we did not confess to him that Mami, unimaginably, had spread the dogs' shit throughout our home. We simply reunited, as we had done four long years before, the five of us delighted for a few hours to be together again despite the hell we could engender in each other's lives, despite the certainty that violence surely would return to South Clarkson Street in only a day or two, buoyed and made hopeful again soon after he had unpacked his bag when Papi asked, as we loved to hear him do, "Who wants to go to McDonald's?"

Going out to a table-service restaurant was something we never had done during our years in Denver; it was a luxury relegated to our Cuban lives, it seemed, or at least it would be until our futures turned in the direction we somehow trusted they would. Yet on rare and blessed occasions—particularly on those Saturdays when Papi's mood was lifted skyward by a particular bargain he had snatched from the shelves at the Salvation Army store—he would feel flush with money and genuinely celebratory and we would shout *yes*, we'd love to go to

McDonald's before his question was entirely out of his mouth.

We would pile into Papi's Studebaker, with him at the wheel, of course, and make the short drive to the McDonald's hamburger stand on Colfax Avenue that lay in the shadow of the Basilica of the Immaculate Heart. And our dinner order was always the same: five hamburgers, three orders of French-fries to split among us, and five milk shakes—four chocolate shakes for the others, and a strawberry shake for me. We ate in the car on every occasion, observing a ritual none of us dared to break. As the rest of us watched with rapt attention, Papi would carefully unwrap his hamburger, take his first bite, then slowly chew, savoring the taste for what seemed to be an eternity before at last he would pronounce the burger delicious and wryly ask what of the rest of us we were waiting for.

Our conversations invariably were the same as we made quick work of our meal. "What *do* they put in these hamburgers?" my mother would ask, astounded that anything could taste so tempting. "These fries are so good. Do you think they're really potatoes?" one of us would query from the backseat. And on the day Papi came home from Miami—as Mami had feared he would not—the ritual of that meal and those inane yet important words mattered more to me than anything I could imagine. Muhammad Ali was still the best boxer the world had ever seen, despite the ongoing efforts of many to wreck his career and destroy his sainted name, and Roberto and Marta Vidal and their boys John, Bob, and Bill still *were* a family sometimes.

There would be a better future, I knew somewhere deep in my bones; I would be free and proud and prosperous one day and would chase dreams of my own—and I would catch them. I was an optimist—just as my embittered and beaten and often-anguished father still was despite it all—and although my mother was at her limits and I feared for the days just round the bend, on that particular evening, Papi had returned from the tropics at least and we were sharing a sacred meal at McDonald's and everything was okay.

Once

The First Cuban on the Moon

Vidals Make Good in America read the headline in the *Denver Post*, the article accompanied by a photograph of the five us sitting in the living room of the house of Clarkson Street that my mother had spread with shit twelve months before. In the photo, Papi is sitting in his easy chair and the mutt Belinda is leaping into his lap; Princesa already sits attentively on Mami's thighs, and John, Bob, and I are seated on the couch behind her, all of us dressed as if we're about to go to mass—something we hadn't done in a very long time.

Feature writer Cindy Parmenter had been interested in chronicling the Robert E. Vidal family in the spring of 1969 because all five of us were enrolled at the moment at the University of Colorado at Denver—my father completing the master's degree that at last would allow him to earn a full salary at St. Francis De Sales, Mami taking art classes as part of her own effort to earn a degree now that she had begun to teach at St. Bernadette Elementary School; John, a freshman majoring in speech and drama; Bob, planning to study political science, and I had been admitted to the university at the close of my high school career, but wouldn't begin taking classes until September. The article briefly outlined our exodus from Cuba, our years at the asylum in Pueblo, and the challenges we had faced since our arrival in Denver, noting that "among Mrs. Vidal's furniture finds is a chair, now sporting an attractive corduroy cover, purchased at a second-hand store for $1.50." Parmenter described Mami as a "gracious, attractive woman," and quoted Papi's proclamation that to succeed in America "you just have to keep trying to win because you have to prove to yourself and to others that you can."

I remember how disingenuous it seemed for us to be making ourselves out to be something of a Cuban-accented version of the "Brady Bunch"—a show that was wildly popular on television that spring—during the reporter's interview and the *Post* photographer's shoot, and there's evidence of how completely our parents ruled our lives in the fact that the three of us acquiesced in helping them act out that bizarre charade. Parmenter did note in her article that in pursuing our educations and supporting ourselves, we five Vidals kept so busy that we seldom saw one another, no one offering her the further explanation that crossing each other's paths as seldom as possible had become the way each of us best coped these days with life in a family whose story would have made a decidedly different sort of TV series. We didn't spill family secrets or express the breadth and intensity of our familial struggles; Papi didn't confess to Cindy Parmenter that life in exile had been far harder than he ever imagined. Instead, we simply talked about how fortunate each of us was and about the critical importance of education—both of which perspectives were absolutely accurate, of course, even if the picture we painted of ourselves was a partial and decidedly gilded one.

That Bob, John, and I would go to college was so much a certainty from the time our parents arrived in America, none of us ever dared to question it. My brothers and I implicitly understood how important university degrees would be to our future lives, and when Papi learned that going to college also would be a way for us to at least temporarily avoid the draft, he would have greeted the suggestion that we take a year or two off between high school and college with the same kind of outrage the news that we had joined the Communist party would have engendered in him.

No one believed more ardently in the domino theory than did my father, and his only argument with the United States's dramatically expanding war in Vietnam was that it should have been preceded by a similar incursion into Cuba. Yet at the same time, Papi was incensed by the notion that one of his sons might be conscripted to go and join the fight. As political refugees, each of us were "resident aliens" in the government's eyes, and citizenship was held back from us. Papi believed he had been prohibited from holding a number of jobs—good, well-paying positions—in the years since his arrival simply because he wasn't a citizen, and it further outraged him that the government had the power to draft resident aliens into the nation's armed forces. "Any country that denies me opportunity because I am not its citizen," he repeatedly proclaimed, "does not deserve the right to ask me to offer up my children to fight for it." He would sanction not a word of debate on the subject, and it wasn't surprising, of course, that on this matter, if few others, we agreed with our father whole-heartedly and welcomed his support at a time when many other American fathers viewed military service in a decidedly different way.

Papi was vocal and often derisive, however, when it came to my brother John's determination to go to college to become a teacher of literature, speech, and drama, and I always shuddered when my father launched into him with one of his high-decibel and condescending lectures. Papi himself was currently a high-school Spanish teacher, of course, and was working toward a master's degree in education, yet he never referenced those ironic details as he berated John for pursuing a career he believed was properly reserved for women and effeminate men. John, in turn, never was swayed by the Old Man's tirades, something I admired as much in him as I had his valiant attempt to out-box Robert Duran at the asylum eight years before. Bob, on the other hand, didn't have to face Papi's ire because his intention was to study political science en route to becoming a lawyer someday, a manly profession of which my father clearly approved, but *my* plans—pursuing a basketball scholarship as a first step toward playing forward for the Boston Celtics—didn't win me similar favor.

"Playing basketball is not a career," announced the man who once had dreamed of his own success as one of Cuba's great professional boxers, and he forbade me to continue my efforts to win a scholarship from one of the small colleges that might have been intrigued by a lanky kid with an impressive jump shot and an abiding passion for the game. It didn't make any sense to me for the Old Man to turn his back on the possibility that my undergraduate education wouldn't cost the family a dime if I was successful in winning a basketball scholarship, but such were his dictatorial powers that I had no choice but to follow my brothers' leads: I would find a way to pay for my own tuition at the University of Colorado at Denver, and I would continue to live at home, the latter prospect far more unsavory than the former. Yet if I couldn't play for the Celtics—as I'd clearly been destined to do—there wasn't any other career to which I truly aspired, at least not until July 20, 1969, when two men first walked on the moon and utterly astounded me and re-directed my life.

Christine Robinson, a popular classmate at St. Francis De Sales, had become my steady girlfriend by the time the two of us graduated from high school, and I spent that singular summer afternoon at her parents' house, my eyes fixed on their living-room television, paying the Apollo astronauts far more attention for hours on end than I did Christine. In the days leading up to the moon walks, I had been fascinated by the technological challenges involved in sending men to the moon, and was awed by the courage and capabilities of astronauts Neil Armstrong, Buzz Aldrin, and Michael Collins. I was transfixed as Armstrong and Aldrin descended toward the desolate surface of the moon, aware as they and billions of people on earth were that their lunar lander had only seconds of fuel remaining when at last the module, dubbed the *Eagle*, settled onto the lunar surface. I watched as CBS news anchor Walter Cronkite removed his glasses and wiped a tear from his eye—a tear both of relief and wonderment—and, like him I knew I had just witnessed one of the most extraordinary events that had ever occurred. When, a few hours later, Armstrong descended the module's ladder and first stood on one of the moon's powdered plains, my career uncertainties had vanished: I was going to be an astronaut.

It was too late for me to apply for admission to the nearby United States Air Force Academy—an obvious avenue toward becoming a fighter pilot, which every astronaut had been up to that time—but my quick research disclosed that an aerospace engineering degree would be essential as well, and—*yes!*—the University of Colorado, where I would start school in a few weeks' time, happened to offer a degree program in that discipline. My "Star Trek" idol Scottie was the *Enterprise*'s engineer, I noted to my further exhilaration, and the rightness of my plan now seemed to be confirmed. If the rest of my family was dumbfounded when I announced my mission—Papi acquiescing to its first stage when I explained that my first degree would be a bachelor's of science, rather than the decidedly suspect bachelor's of arts degree—I, on the other hand, now was entirely at ease with the path my future would take. I would marry Christine and become an aerospace engineer, and then I'd join the air force and learn how to fly jet fighters. We would be wondrously happy together and I would lead a life of thrilling adventure; I'd ascend to the astronaut corps one day, and then be the first Cuban to walk on the distant moon.

Life has an uncanny way of altering even the clearest and firmest of plans, but I did, in fact, marry my high-school sweetheart and I did become an engineer. Yet I didn't join the astronaut corps, and, as had happened before in my life, national and international turmoil ultimately shaped my future in ways completely beyond my control. My life took turns I couldn't possibly have imagined as a young man. I succeeded along the way, and I failed, and over time, my relationships with my mother and father endured far more turmoil than they had even in the years when we were ripped apart by the revolution. I didn't journey to the moon, in the end, but I did return to Cuba one day, discovering there secrets and answers and deep reassurances about the place from which I had come, and about who I was, as well.

Robert F. Kennedy's assassination in June 1968 had stunned and deeply disillusioned me, as it had millions of other Americans—and nearly seven years in Colorado *had* transformed me into an American in myriad ways. I had been elated at the prospect that a Kennedy would return to the White House, and in particular *this* Kennedy, who had been among the very first people to personally welcome me to the United States. I believed he would be elected and that he would turn the nation away from its increasingly disastrous war making in Vietnam. I believed he could restore hope and vision and inspire young people like me to serve their country in vital ways, and his murder—as well as the assassination of Martin Luther King, Jr. a few weeks before—crushed me and left me rudderless and profoundly uncertain about whether I ever would live in a country of which I could be deeply proud.

Yet I continued to want very much to serve as a astronaut, and certainly would have eagerly joined the air force following college in order to sustain that goal, and after a year as an aerospace-engineering student, I now understood the enormity of the challenge I had set before me and was as doggedly committed to it as Papi ever had been in trying to achieve his personal goals. Then two events occurred that rose like great mountains across my path, the first of which was the near collapse of the U.S.'s aerospace industry. Denver-based Martin-Marietta, the nation's largest aerospace contractor, began laying off much of its engineering force as NASA's Apollo program grew to a close; panic spread throughout the aerospace division of the University of Colorado's engineering school, and many of my classmates opted to suddenly change their majors. Because my long-range plans were to become a pilot and an astronaut, however, rather than an engineer, I persevered—that is until a rash of hijackings of commercial airliners commenced and then grew epidemic, more than two dozen of those crimes committed by people who commandeered the planes they captured to Cuba—where the hijackers regularly were offered asylum—in hopes of securing the release of American prisoners from U.S. prisons. Airports scrambled to install metal-detectors and other screening measures, and airlines began to do what they could to profile their pilot candidates, ensuring as best they could that the men and women flying their planes were people who could be counted on to respond appropriately in crises, and to weed out as well any who might have political or criminal agendas themselves.

When Max Peters, the dean of the engineering department and a man who had offered me caring and important advice since the beginning of my freshman year, called me into his cramped office to discuss my plans in light of the aerospace-industry collapse, he pressed me immediately. "Are you really willing to work so hard for the next five years and get this degree knowing that you might not find a job when you graduate?" I explained that the risk didn't concern me because I planned to go to flight school following graduation. He didn't remember that I'd informed him long ago of my astronaut dream, and when I reminded him, the thin and balding professor—who always before had seemed so staunchly supportive—grew visibly exasperated. Becoming a pilot wouldn't by any means guarantee me acceptance into NASA's astronaut program, he wanted me to consider, and what about the fact that I was Cuban?

"What about it?" I asked, and then he was blunt.

"No respectable airline is going to hire a Cuban pilot. They would be the laughingstock of the industry. And you will have spent nine years working toward a goal that won't get you a job. Think about it."

The professor's words almost instantly transformed the fears I already had begun to accumulate into a kind of terror: What if aerospace engineering and becoming a commercial pilot *were* dead-ends for me? What if, alternatively, I enlisted in the air force but was rejected as a pilot candidate, then was shipped to Vietnam to do some perilous job I hated and that offered me no career advancement in the midst of a war to which I was deeply opposed and for which I also could die? And if I couldn't get a job as an aerospace engineer or didn't join the air force, could I *ever* liberate myself from my parents? It was that latter concern—my desperate desire to escape the perpetual cycle of slammed doors, broken dishes, and simmering hatred in my parents' home—that foremost occupied my less-than-entirely seasoned twenty-year old mind, and within weeks I had become a civil-engineering student. I wouldn't build rocket ships or vault into the heavens; instead, I would build buildings, roads, and bridges—perhaps even a highway spanning the sea like the causeway I had seen a decade before and been dazzled by on the short flight from Havana to Miami, on that long-ago day when my life had taken an even more dramatic turn.

Although we continued to live under the same roof, I seldom saw my brothers or my parents for more than a few minutes at a time. It was only on Wednesday evenings that I invariably made a workaday rendezvous with my father and John and Bob, "doing Bingo" at St. Francis De Sales as we had done each week, it seemed, for a lifetime by now. The Old Man needed the help, of course; now that we were no longer students, the crushing embarrassment of the work was far less acute for us, and during the otherwise mindless hours of setting up and taking down hundreds of chairs and tables, we were able to catch up with each other's lives and reconnect in casual but nonetheless important ways. Each of us did his best to assure Papi as we chatted that we were focused and entirely diligent in our academic pursuits, and he joined us in planning the purchase of a second car, which the three of us would drive—this one a Rambler American painted a hideous brown, an American Motors dweeb-mobile that was almost as ugly as Papi's Studebaker, and that I'm sure similarly reminded him of his salad days in Cuba. The car's sole redeeming feature, as far as we were concerned, was the fact that its seats folded flat, an attribute each of the three of us, if perhaps not also our father, understood would be quite accommodating on nights when it was our individual turn to take the car out and devote it to amorous purposes in the waning hours of an important date.

During my sophomore year in college, my parents proudly purchased their first home in America—eight years after their arrival—a green lap-sided, blue-shuttered ranch-style house with a finished basement in an east Denver neighborhood entirely new to us. If our all-too-overtly racist parents didn't recognize the irony in the fact that we had moved to Mexico Street, my brothers and I certainly did, and we laughed as we noted that the universe apparently wanted us to understand that just because we would be college graduates in a year or two, we still would be aliens, exiles forever in the eyes of many of the "home-grown" Americans with whom we studied and worked and struggled to be accepted. Each of us had his own bedroom at the Mexico Street house—a luxury of transcendent importance to young men in college still living with their parents—but I continued to chafe at the proximity to my parents and the confinement, both symbolizing the truth that I wasn't remotely as free and adult as I was desperate to be. I debated dropping out of school for a while—I'd move out and find a cool job in a cool town for a stretch of time—but at the end of the first semester of my junior year I opted instead to travel to Miami over the Christmas holidays. I planned to travel alone and visit my extended family, none of whom I had seen or communicated with since the days of gunfire and mounting fear on the streets of Camagüey half my lifetime before. I wanted to get close to Cuba, at least geographically, and perhaps I would learn at long last why neither my grandfather nor aunt and uncle had taken us in on those days before Father Sierra escorted my brothers and me to Colorado and we began to remake our lives out West.

Papi, predictably, wasn't happy about my plans, seeing in them something of a betrayal of him as well as a failure to understand that the five of us had chosen to live far harder lives in Denver than we might have lived in Miami because we stood on principle—in this case, on the inviolate belief that family defends and rescues family without question or qualification. In the four years since my grandfather, Don Antonio, had died, my father's feud with his sister Elda and her husband Aquiles had expanded beyond their failure to help us in 1961 and now also enveloped Papi's belief that the two claimed more of my grandfather's estate than rightfully was theirs. Although he lived near Elda and Aquiles in Little Havana, Tio Antoñico sided with my father, and the two brothers were locked in fierce battle against their sister and her husband, a resolution of any sort appearing remote. I had heard my father angrily describe Elda and Aquiles's transgressions to John and Bob, yet he wouldn't discuss them with me, and likely for that reason as much as any other, it seemed to me that the siblings and Aquiles were little more than hungry mice fighting over a scrap of cheese—and choosing to go to Miami despite my father's protestations was, in part, my way of demonstrating both to him and to myself that I made my own decisions these days.

I spent my first week in Florida—and the Christmas holiday—with the family of Papi's college roommate, José Ramón Zayasbazan, a physician who somehow had found a way to practice medicine in the United States and who had prospered since his arrival. Dr. Zayasbazan's eldest son, Aonchy, was my age and had been my buddy back in Camagüey, and he and his sister Carmencita and brother Miguelito were wonderfully hospitable to me, despite the fact that, after a decade apart, we were virtual strangers. They were quick to include me in a host of holiday parties where, I discovered to my amazement, I was something of a star attraction—a *compadre camagüeyaño* who nonetheless was an authentic American as well. It was, apparently, a combination that the colorful, stunningly good-looking, and decidedly mature Cuban girls I encountered found particularly intriguing—no doubt in part because of my engineering-student credentials and the promise for my future—and more than a few of their fathers made it clear to me that if I remained in Miami and pursued a relationship with their daughters, they wouldn't stand in my way.

Never before in my life had I been such a center of attention, and it was glorious. I loved the strong hugs and kisses on the cheek that I exchanged with everyone, just as we would have had we been celebrating in Cuba; I loved being offered mojitos despite the fact that I was underage, loved dining at 10:00 p.m. and dancing to salsas and merengues into the exhausted hours of the morning, and I didn't think even once of my girlfriend Christine back in Denver during those heady days and nights of holiday merrymaking.

Before New Year's arrived, my Tia Elda and Tio Aquiles insisted that I come spend some days at their home as well, and when I
arrived they greeted me with those same enveloping hugs and formidable kisses that were so commonplace in my youth, as if I still
were the chubby ten-year-old they had known and loved before they
quietly slipped out of Camagüey and fled Cuba in 1960. It took me
a bit, however, to fully return their affections in kind—they, after
all, were the two who foremost had turned their backs on us, Papi
had proclaimed throughout the succeeding years. It was wonderful
to see my cousins again and they, like the Zayasbazan kids, made
me feel immediately at home, and I was delighted to learn as well
that Elda's older sister, my Tia Mella, and my very old and demented
grandmother at last had immigrated and were living with them. It
would be wonderful to see my Abuelita again, I remember thinking,
but the reality of our brief encounter was very different. Since I was
a small boy, my grandmother had been sickly; whenever we would
visit her at the Hotel Residenciál, she would be sitting in her chair
in the middle of her living room, wearing a housecoat and wrapped
in a thin blanket. By now, in addition to her other maladies, Abuelita's Alzheimer's disease had grown so advanced that she knew no
one; she repeatedly referred to her daughter Mella as "Mama" and
needed to be assured of her constant presence. Tia Mella cautioned
me to be quiet and gentle as I entered her dark and urine-scented
room in the house in Miami, and I was. But as I silently bent to place
a kiss on her cheek for the first time in ten years, Abuelita suddenly reached for my genitals and firmly grabbed hold, exhibiting the
same sexually inappropriate behavior many Alzheimer's patients do,
but nonetheless shocking and perplexing a less-than-worldly twenty-year old who never before had known his fat and infirm grandmother to be so bold.

Tia Mella remained the angel I remembered; she had cared for her
mother for more than a decade without complaint, and steadfastly
had refused to leave the island while her son languished in a Cuban
prison because he had fought for Batista against Fidel and his forces,
but at last she relented, and brought her mother to Miami to join the
rest of the family. She was haunted by the sense that she had abandoned her son Pepito in the process, despite the fact that she seldom

even could visit him in jail while she remained on the island—and that guilt was something I understood from my immediate family's experience—and Mella and I renewed a real bond in that brief time I spent in the Florida sun. Each morning I would walk the short block to the "Sawesera," Southwest Eighth Street, Little Havana's main thoroughfare, where a few shop windows boldly announced "English Spoken Here." I savored hearing nothing but Spanish on street corners and in the bustling *panaderia* where I would drink coffee, remembering the times as a boy when Papi would let me sit on his lap and take sips of his thick black *café cubano*. After a decade without them—even at home with Mami and Papi, where TV dinners were our diet staples—I loved eating *arroz con pollo* and *moros y cristianos*, *plátanos fritos* and *flan* at Elda's table and in neighborhood *cantinas*. What a pleasure it was to watch and listen as old men with cigars in their mouths denounced Fidel as they played cubilete in the shade of coconut palms, the game dear Felix had taught my brothers and me when we were innocent and very young, the tastes and smells and *feel* of my homeland flooding back to me for the first time since I fell asleep to those poignant memories in my first years at the asylum.

It was intriguing for me to discover how very different life in exile had been for my extended family in Florida than it had been for the five of us in Denver. Although everyone except recently arrived Mella spoke at least some English, even my young cousins spoke with thick accents; Spanish remained the language in which they conducted virtually every aspect of their lives, and they remained Cuban in ways I obviously did not. I was indeed a gringo, my cousin Kiki often kidded me—and he was correct—and in faraway Colorado it had been impossible for me to know and appreciate how many challenges *la familia Vidal* had faced in Florida as well as in Denver during the decade past.

With some gentle inquiry, I learned that at the time my brothers and I arrived in Miami in September 1961, neither my grandfather nor uncle nor aunt yet had been able to find a job of any kind. Eleven people lived crowded into every corner of Don Antonio's tiny, two-bedroom house, and only his dwindling savings sustained them. Their financial struggles had been as protracted and defeating as ours, and, like Mami and Papi, they had been forced to accept lives far paler and much less full than those they once thought had been their birthright.

On my arrival in Miami, I had been eager at an appropriate moment during my visit to raise the difficult subject of their collective decision not to come to our aid. I'd wanted to ask directly but without any rancor why, even with a house that overflowed with people, they had chosen not to meet us at the Miami airport. I wanted to understand as best I could why making no contact whatsoever with us had been the best option for them. Once they knew we were in Colorado and couldn't pose hardships for them, why hadn't they ever called or written to us to see how we were and to assure us that we *did* have a family here in America? Yet as I celebrated the arrival of the new year with them for the first time since I was a boy, and as I began to know these people again and understand the turmoil that had wrought *their* lives, my need for answers receded, just as the island of Cuba itself had grown small from the window of the Pan American plane that ferried me to this new world. All of us, whether in Denver or Little Havana, had struggled to contend with circumstances that offered us few simple or easy responses, and, in the end, I hugged each of my aunts and uncles and cousins as warmly as I could when I departed for Colorado, each of us exchanging a *fuerte abrazo* and the certainty that something called family bound us forever together. Then I left without ever asking the questions that had haunted me for a decade, their answers far less important now and perhaps already offered to me as eloquently as anyone ever could.

My years of exile officially ended—or at least they did in a powerfully symbolic way—on the sunny spring morning in 1973 when I graduated from the University of Colorado at Denver. I remained two thousand miles from Cuba, of course, yet at last my credentials as an American seemed firmly and forever established. Like every other college graduate, my future theoretically was bright and full of promise, and if I was willing to work hard I knew I could demonstrate that my adopted home was indeed a land of opportunity.

It's hard, in retrospect, to remember a day in my life when I was happier than I was on that day: I was proud of what I had accomplished, not just during the four previous years, but also in the twelve years since Bob, John, and I had arrived in Colorado; I felt like I had truly become a man—one ready to make his mark—and I welcomed that proof of my maturation. As of that day, I was free from my parents and they were free of me. Liberated at last from the head-slaps and body-blows and soul-killing critiques that were life with Mami and Papi, I knew I never would return to it again, and I was pleased to consider that they no longer had to provide for me in any way or remain in their miserable marriage because of me. My graduation symbolized the completion of their parental responsibilities, and I hoped they now could pursue their own happiness—together or apart—and, God knew, they were entitled to some as their years of exile continued.

Christine and I now were married and lived in a small apartment, but John and Bob, both of whom were at work on their master's degrees, continued to live with Mami and Papi on Mexico Street—a decision the two of them made that was incomprehensible to me. Some years before, surely the three of us could have found a way to go to college without living at home, had we chosen to, and I'm sure that our early separation from our parents played a role in our determination to live with them into our twenties. Perhaps we endured the shattered holidays and the inexorable torture of the family's daily death-dance in the years following high school simply because something inside each of us was very unwilling to let go of our parents a second time.

My Rojugui bond with my brothers long since had been broken, and like many adult brothers, we seldom spent time with each other any longer. There was no conflict between us, and I know I felt enormous respect for John and Bob and the distances we had traveled side by side, yet somehow, leaving my life of exile seemed to necessitate a clear and sharp separation from them as well.

The only job offer I had I received was to go to work for Fluor Contractors and Engineers in Los Angeles, a position I accepted, and at first I was excited by the prospect of moving to California and living near the sea again, but as our moving day approached, I began to feel a sense of foreboding, even dread, about leaving Denver and the family I had been eager to shed only a few weeks before. Perhaps some part of my subconscious had begun to relive once again my wrenching departure from Cuba, but whatever its cause, I did my best to simply ignore my terrible apprehension, even as I often awoke in the middle of the night in a cold sweat, shaking and uncontrollably crying.

In mid June, we drove away from Denver, with me behind the

wheel of a U-Haul van and Christine following in our little Fiat 124. During the long days we spent crossing much of the American West, I often was disconsolate and angry with myself for having brought so much upheaval into our lives. As I drove, I cheered myself up as best I could by vowing to find a way to get us back to Colorado as soon as I could, but the plain reality was that I was entering a new world once more—one far from Denver, and farther still from Camagüey.

Doce

Burial Grounds

ONLY THREE YEARS AFTER MY FATHER COMPLETED his master's degree in education in 1970, the financially troubled St. Francis De Salles closed its doors. He didn't receive a trumpet blast nor a respectful salute—certainly didn't make an exhausted boxer's triumphal parade around the ring—and just like that, the job Papi had worked so hard for was gone.

Determined not to let his years of night school and endless abuse from hormone- and sugar-crazed pupils go for naught, he tried hard to find a job in Denver's public school system. But parochial schools were closing everywhere, and hundreds of teachers were pursuing the same thin hope, and Papi's age decidedly worked against him. No, he heard dozens of times the schools he contacted were not in need of a Spanish teacher. Younger teachers, most of whom had only bachelor's degrees and therefore earned smaller salaries, found the few available jobs, and Papi despaired that he would have to find yet another new line of work until a school district in far southeastern Colorado offered him a one-year appointment implementing its new bilingual-education program. He had to be on the road all week— traveling to a succession of schools in towns with large populations of agricultural workers, the vast majority of whom were Hispanic— and staying in the cheapest motels he could find, but Papi enjoyed the work, and being away so often from my mother, who now worked as a bank teller, also eased the tension between them.

That summer, John married and moved out of the house and my

brother Bob often found himself home alone with the woman who had made him the special target of wrath since he had been a small boy. My mother's depression and internal trauma remained unallayed, her "punishments" still could come at him like a sudden avalanche, and Bob complained to Papi, John, and me that we had cruelly abandoned him, Mami and Bob failing to form even the slimmest kind of truce in the long hours they spent together. When Bob completed his graduate degree in public administration and moved to Ames, Iowa to take a job in the early summer of 1974, Papi too found a way—this time a truly startling one—to move far away, opting to make an enormous career and financial gamble, just like he often had rolled the dice before.

The state of Florida, my father learned to his fascination, finally had agreed to allow Cuban exiles who had been professionals in their home-land a one-time opportunity to take state licensing exams, and, if they passed them, to resume their careers as doctors, lawyers, engineers—and pharmacists. Concluding that it was now or never for him, and freed from any responsibility for providing for his sons, Papi abruptly determined to do whatever it took to get his pharmacist's license. He packed only a single small bag and marched off to Miami, leaving my mother and the miserable dogs alone in the house on Mexico Street.

It was no surprise for me to learn that Papi had rented for himself the cheapest, most run-down dung-hole in all of south Florida. I knew full well how minimally he could live if he set his mind to it, and his choice in a domicile, as he framed it, was an appropriate measure taken in challenging times, particularly given the fact that he felt obligated to pay the mortgage on the house in Denver. Determining that he would need to spend virtually every waking moment study-ing during the coming year, he lived solely on his savings, working very occasionally as a substitute teacher but otherwise remaining locked in his grim little cell. It had been a quarter-century since my father last worked as a pharmacist, a profession he had pursued for only five years. He had seen nothing of medicine, chemistry, or phar-macology after that time, and everything he needed to relearn and learn for the first time he had to accomplish in English, a language he now spoke comfortably but certainly had not mastered. Yet the stubborn, self-driven son of a bitch did it. It took him half a year longer than he had hoped, but finally he took the Florida licensing exam and aced it. He was a pharmacist once more, but, as was his perennial style, he notified none of us, and, in turn, I'm sorry to say that none of his sons offered him the congratulations he richly deserved when at last we learned of his achievement.

He shared his good news with my mother only after he had secured a job working the night shift at a twenty-four-hour Eckerd Drugs, and, to my huge surprise, soon she announced in turn that she was moving to Miami to join him. Even more astonishingly, Papi agreed to let her join him, and John, Bob, and I spent long telephone conversations asking ourselves what good could possibly come of this? During their time apart, our parents had the opportunity to separately recreate their lives, but neither had opted to do so. Yet they separately acknowledged to us that they hadn't missed each other at all during their eighteen-month separation, and neither had acquired an even fractionally better opinion of the other. What possessed them to return to the hell they had known for so long with each other?, my brothers and I repeatedly asked ourselves, yet there didn't seem to be a compelling answer, except for the fact that, unlike the three of us, both of them remained psychologically in exile. They were Cubans still, and Cubans of their generation simply didn't divorce. My father resolutely believed he was financially responsible for my mother until the day one of them died, and he could meet that responsibility more easily if they shared a single home; Mami, for her part, was secure in the truth that she had pledged her life to a single man— no matter how much she happened to despise him—and her *marido* was the pharmacist-businessman-wage-earner-Spanish-teacher-pharmacist Roberto Emiliano Vidal.

Not long after my mother moved to Miami—just three hundred miles from Camagüey but still far from her truest home in Cuba—Christine and I returned to Colorado when I accepted a job with Stearns-Roger, a Denver-based engineering company. I had been plagued by dark moods during the eight months we spent in Los Angeles, and I hoped our return to Colorado would set me emotionally straight again, yet my malaise—and my fears—never abated.

Within a few months of beginning my new job, the bottom fell out of the petrochemical industry and people in the engineering department in which I worked began to be laid off. Every Friday I attended a going-away luncheon for someone the company had abandoned, and it didn't take long for me to understand that it was only a matter of time until my own special Friday came round. We had just purchased a small house, and I began to worry obsessively that we would lose it, and, like Papi had been years before, I was terrified that we would be forced onto the streets. Once again, the feelings of uncertainty and enveloping panic I had known when I left Cuba came roaring back to me as I slept—or tried to sleep—and my chronic exhaustion began to affect my concentration at work and my health started to falter. I couldn't keep food down; I lost weight dramatically, and temporarily I even lost sight in my right eye. Doctors diagnosed my ailments as severe colitis, but I recognize now that their diagnoses might have been different had I confessed to them the emotional turmoil I suffered, something I chose to share with no one, in fact.

My number at last came up in the spring of 1976 when I received a two-week notice of the end of my employment, and with this news my greatest fears appeared to have been realized, and I bitterly blamed myself for bringing turmoil to our lives once more. Part of me understood that my feelings were grossly exaggerated—after all, I had an engineering degree and work experience by now, and Christine was working as a second-grade teacher. Nevertheless, I couldn't stop obsessing about the terrible things the future was certain to bring, and I finally concluded that not only would I never leave Colorado again, I'd also scour the state to find a job in which I was utterly secure.

When at last I was offered an entry-level engineering position at the Colorado Department of Transportation—one I was sure would be far more stable than anything I could encounter in the private sector—God seemed to have heard my unspoken prayer, and at last I began to thrive again. CDOT's institutional bureaucracy offered a kind of stability that allowed me to flourish in ways I had fifteen years before in the rigid environment of Sacred Heart Home, and I soon started climbing the organizational chart—secure and at ease and at home again, at least for the time being.

By this point in our lives, Christine and I had three small children, Sarah and Molly, half-Hispanic babies whom we had adopted when each was just a few days old—and whom I was thrilled to have saved from lives in an asylum—and Joshua, our own biological son. I know I failed to see the sad irony in the fact that I had dismissed my parents and brothers from my life as I began to raise a family of my own, and although the kids were acquainted with their grandparents and uncles, at least, they had virtually no interaction with them. I made no attempt to teach them Spanish, nor did we socialize with other Hispanics. Unconsciously, I suspect, I had reprised the same fear my parents had suffered when I was young, worrying that their children would be discriminated against if their true heritage were revealed. In a way I sadly couldn't see at the time, my diligent work to limit my family's influence on my children—the only Hispanic people who might have been a truly significant part of their lives—taught Sarah, Molly and Josh to disdain precisely the same culture and values I had chosen to shun, a culture they were biologically linked to as well. And now a related problem had emerged in my marriage and my young family.

My adamant refusal to incorporate my parents' perspectives and traditions into our family enabled Christine to assume a powerfully superior role in raising the children. Whenever we would disagree on something regarding one of the kids, she would caution me, "Remember Bill, you grew up in a really bad situation, and you can't know how to raise children properly." Early on, I believed she surely was right and always acquiesced to what I assumed was her better judgment. I concentrated instead on simply giving the kids my love and attention; I attended all their school and sporting events and spent lots of time playing with them, reading to them, helping them with homework, coaching their teams, and taking them on myriad trips. Yet increasingly, I grew uneasy with Christine's parenting style—one highlighted by her refusal to clearly define boundaries for the kids or discipline them when they acted out. Each of the kids seemed to grow progressively more defiant and aggressive over time, and as they did, I began to disagree with Christine's approach to dealing with them, did my best to establish stricter discipline and enforce consequences for their bad behavior, something Christine—who continued her laid-back approach—strongly opposed. She became the children's defender against what she saw as my harsh and unforgiving brand of fatherhood, and I began to see, unimaginably, the repetition of a pattern I'd known far too well as a child—with me in my mother's role as the unreasonable and unpredictable parent and Christine assuming the role Papi always had played, consoling my brothers and me and assuring us that our mother didn't deserve to be honored or obeyed. I know fully understood how we had imprisoned my mother with loneliness during all the years my brothers and I shunned her. Because of her erratic behavior, we chose to believe that all her actions were inherently mean or perhaps evil, just as my kids were now doing with me.

My brother John had become a high-school teacher, as he long had planned, and Bob had returned to Colorado as well to work in the city government of a Denver suburb. Yet the three of us still seldom saw each other and we never saw our parents. On the rare occasions when we would gather, we would compare notes about the challenges of raising children of our own and the incessant demands of mortgages, about the checkered fortunes of the Denver Broncos and John's newfound passion for fishing, and would remind ourselves how lucky we were that Mami and Papi were too far away to confound our lives any longer.

Yet without our parents to provide a nucleus around which we could shape some semblance of a family, the three of us inexorably grew even farther apart. We literally had depended on each other for our survival a couple of decades before; John had fought for us and battled for our beloved Cuba in Jim McCoy's makeshift boxing ring; hundreds of times we had shielded each other from Mami's physical blows and the knife-slash of Papi's words, yet now we were nothing more than brothers, and the bond between us that Papi called the planet of Rojugui simply was no more, our three lives spinning in widely diverging orbits. Separately, we focused our attentions on our spouses, our children, and our spouse's families, discovering and becoming part of their family traditions, their pleasures and particular sorrows, the three of us avoiding each other in part, I know, to protect ourselves from memories of our own family life that remained tender and raw.

I spoke with my parents by telephone on major holidays and their birthdays, but they never asked for information about the shape and substance of my life, never were curious to ascertain what kind of father I had become, or to consider that we now shared the enormity of that experience. Our infrequent conversations focused almost exclusively on them, and I was pleased to learn that Papi had reconnected with *his* family—people he always had loved dearly, even during the long years during which he sustained the most complete rupture from them he could, and there were subtleties in what he said that assured me he now understood that during the earliest days of exile everyone in our family was focused on nothing more substantial than survival, and that it no longer made sense for him to hold his family members accountable for what they once did or failed to do.

It was clear as well that my mother—always suspicious of her in-laws and jealous during the years when my father was close to them—hadn't joined him in his reconnection with his family. In fact, she and Papi lived the most separate lives they could fashion for themselves while still sleeping under the same roof, and Mami spent her days renewing relationships with dear friends from her country-club years in Camagüey as well as a few Ramos-family cousins, all of whom had immigrated to Miami early in the 1960s. It appeared to me from afar that she was as happy as I ever had known her; she was anything but ebullient during our conversations, yet it seemed that as she inevitably grew old and as friends and family members began to die, her huge anger at life eased a bit and she increasingly spent her days more readily accepting the circumstances of her life than she ever had before.

I instantly knew something was wrong when my mother called me out of the blue in the fall of 1982. Papi had fainted several times during his all-night shift at the drugstore, she explained, and a subsequent examination had determined that he would require immediate triple-bypass surgery, his coronary arteries massively occluded by his fifty-year, three-pack-a-day smoking addiction. His condition was precarious, she said; he could have no visitors other than her, nor could we speak with him by phone. We were deeply suspicious, of course, when we learned that she also refused to allow anyone in his family to visit him in the hospital following the successful open-heart surgery, and in Denver the three of us debated what she was up to: was this just an all-too-predictable effort on her part to make herself the center of attention at a moment of crisis? Was it an attempt to punish us for the distance we had allowed to grow between us? Or was it a profoundly cruel effort on her part to isolate him from his immediate kin at a moment when his life lay in the balance? We never did ascertain what she hoped to accomplish by making herself the sole conduit of information about his condition; the two of them certainly didn't communicate successfully with each other, after all, and it was a bit late to pretend for the sake of appearances that she was his helpmate in difficult moments, but despite my dawning recognition that my estranged father might die, Papi instead recovered remarkably well, and once more he surprised me with his stubborn will to accomplish a gargantuan task.

This sixty-two-year-old man whose only exercise in the years since he no longer could swim in the sea at Santa Lucia had been those hours each week of setting-up and taking-down tables for Bingo suddenly resolved to begin walking and swimming every day of the week. Since I had been a small boy there had been a tea-colored stain on the ceiling of each house he had lived in, precisely above the spot where he reclined in his easy chair, and by now he was as physically dependent on his Chesterfield Longs as any junkie hooked on heroin, yet the day of his surgery he quit smoking cold turkey. He loudly complained that his greatest pleasure in life now was gone, to be sure, but he never lit another cigarette, and I was surprised to discover how much he evidently believed he still had to live for.

Yet just as Papi resolved to make the most of the time that remained to him, those dearest to him began to die. The move to Florida and my father's subsequent success in becoming a pharmacist once more had allowed him to begin building for his and my mother's retirement—something he'd never been able to focus on during his years in the United States—and it also had allowed him to resume his role as the de facto head of his larger family and to draw near his brother and sisters before their lives came to a close. But my father's achievements had always been met with a measure of heartbreak throughout his life, and that pattern somehow continued. The death of my grandmother—her brain destroyed by Alzheimer's disease—was something of a blessing, everyone agreed, yet her passing was deeply sad nonetheless. Then all the family rejoiced in 1980 when my Tia Mella's son Pepito was released from prison and allowed to come to the United States as a *Marielito*, one of the 125,000 former prisoners—many of them violent criminals and drug addicts—and their families Fidel cynically set free and dumped on the United States, more *gusanos*, worms, he was quite willing to be rid of. Mella was ecstatic that Pepito was free at last and that she could be with her son, his wife and children again, but for Pepito, the challenges of living in society again—one that was entirely foreign to him—learning a new language, and struggling to support his family were overwhelming. He shot himself in the head within a few months of his arrival in Miami, and my aunt fell into a despair from which she could not recover. With her mother, father, and only son now no longer alive and in need of the constancy of her loving care, Mella simply withered until she too passed away, Papi reporting tearfully to us that an angel had rejoined her maker.

Tia Elda's son Jorge died of AIDS soon thereafter, then Elda's own life came to a close, and Papi and my Tio Antoñico were the only Vidal siblings who remained alive. Antoñico never had recovered the psychological equilibrium he lost as a young man in Camagüey, and his life in Miami had been a one of constant turmoil. He divorced his wife Nenita soon after his arrival because she had fallen in love with another man, then later re-married a woman named Neida who was fifteen years his junior, and her daughter had joined them in a life that promised to be more stable than the three had known theretofore. Antoñico and Neida fought bitterly, however, and their battles intensified with each passing year. Papi didn't devote much concern to their discord—it was a kind of conflict with which he was profoundly familiar, after all, and he counseled his brother simply to accept the relationship's shortcomings and to focus his attentions elsewhere. Married couples lived their lives at war, Papi understood from his own experience; that simply was the way it was, but he was overwhelmed with disbelief on the night of October 26, 1989 when he received a call from the Miami police informing him that Antoñico and Neida's bodies had been discovered inside their home by her daughter Neidita—now grown, married, and six-months pregnant—who had arrived at the house planning to go shopping for a crib with her mother.

Papi's shock was mammoth. How could his beloved brother—once handsome, all-talented, and the envy of every young man in

Camagüey—be suddenly dead? Yes, Antoñico had been met with challenges even Papi had not been forced to face, he understood, and he recognized as well his brother's flaws and destructive tendencies that he had been blind to in their youth. Accepting that Antoñico, *Antoñico*, was dead was impossible for Papi, yet the truth of his death became even more unconscionable as the police described to him what they believed had occurred.

Neida's skull had been shattered as she suffered three severe blows to the back of her head with a sharpened ax, then she was stabbed three times in the chest with a long knife. Antoñico had been her killer, the police insisted, before—unimaginably—he had turned the knife on himself, stabbing himself in the neck and chest until he slumped to the floor beside his wife's bloody body and died. The macabre murder-suicide was immediately the focus of lurid stories on the city's television news and in English- and Spanish-language newspapers around the region, but Papi was utterly convinced the police were wrong. Antoñico could not possibly have committed acts so barbarous, so vicious, and inhuman. Surely the crime was the work of a psychotic intruder who remained on the loose, and Papi was furious when the Miami police soon closed the case and refused to investigate it further. *No,* their deaths couldn't have come at Antoñico's hands, my father desperately pleaded, and as the days passed, he found it increasingly hard to accept the reality and the depth of the tragedy.

Papi was deeply grieved by the thought that Neida, an elementary-school teacher and only fifty-five years old, had been cut down so horribly. He was filled with sorrow for Neidita, who had had to discover the bloody scene and who had lost her mother and the grandmother of her unborn child. And as Papi slowly began to accept that his beloved brother *had* been the murderer, he was wracked with guilt over his own failure to help combat the demons inside Antoñico that were loosed on that terrible night. He might have prevented the crime, the gruesome and senseless deaths he berated himself, if only he had been more sensitive to his brother's plight and the dramatically escalating tensions in Antoñico's home.

The children at Neida's school were deeply traumatized by her loss and the manner of her murder, and the efforts of counselors and psychologists to comfort and support them kept the sensational case foremost in the news for many days. The media coverage seemed to grow ever more intensive, and each story horrifically repeated the events of that night and the name of the perpetrator, Antonio Alvaro Vidal, a Cuban exile who was survived only by his brother Roberto Vidal, a Miami pharmacist. Not only was dear Antoñico gone; not only had he committed a crime beyond believing, but now no one remained in Miami whom Papi deeply loved, and the profound shame the murder and suicide brought to his family and to his name was much more than he could bear. He could no longer face his few friends, his neighbors, or the colleagues with whom he worked at the drugstore; his relationship with my mother didn't sustain him in any way, and Miami's Little Havana—the closest approximation of Cuba outside the island itself and the vital center of the collective belief that one day Fidel would be overthrown and hundreds of thousands Cubans would resume their Batista-era lives—had become a place in which my father no longer could live.

One day less than a month after Antoñico and Neida's deaths, Papi announced to my mother that he was leaving. He had paid off the small mortgage on the condominium they shared, and he had worked his last shift at the drugstore. The two did not even briefly discuss his plans, nor did my mother object or inquire where he planned to go. My sixty-nine year-old father simply loaded his clothes in his car and drove away, and Roberto and Marta Vidal never saw each other again.

Close to midnight on a late-autumn evening that year, I answered the doorbell and before me stood a grizzled old man in a tattered Hawaiian shirt, baggy shorts, and sneakers. His dark, deep-set eyes and punch-flattened nose were somehow familiar, but it wasn't until he offered me a thin smile that I recognized my father; it had been thirteen years since we last had seen each other.

Two days before, Papi had called me in Pueblo, of all places, where I had recently moved to become a regional director for the Department of Transportation—ironically at home again in that city, yet very careful to drive past the red-stone asylum, now a low-income apartment complex, as infrequently as I could. My father was calling from a roadside stop in Georgia, he said. He was moving back to

Denver and wanted to stop to visit me en route. But before I could give him directions, he had hung up.

Soon after I had received the promotion that sent me to Pueblo—where I lived alone until our house in Denver sold and Christine and the kids could join me—I had been blindsided in my sleep one night by the darkest and most menacing terror I had felt in my life. A voice inside my head screamed, "What have you done? How could you have fucked up your life so badly? Why did you let your ambition put your family's financial welfare at risk? How could you be such a terrible father and live apart from your kids?" From that night forward, these incessant questions would capture my conscious thinking for days at a time. My moods became dark and forlorn, and once again I believed I must be guilty of doing something unforgivable to my family. Surely God was punishing me for becoming like Papi, I thought to myself on that blustery spring night, for allowing myself to be blinded to what really mattered, by my single-minded ambition to succeed.

Despite the late hour, when at last he reached Pueblo, my father had made repeated stops at gas stations, convenience stores, and even a couple of homes before, amazingly, the crazy old fool encountered someone who knew me and offered him directions to my house. I shook his hand in the porch-light, and then invited him in. As the two of us sat in the living room and began to talk, we quickly discovered how little we knew each other. Papi's full head of hair now was completely white; there were new scars on his face and neck from his ongoing battles with skin cancer; he was far paler than I remembered, and much more bent and shrunken. I was aware almost immediately that something else was unusual, and then it struck me: he didn't have a cigarette in his hand; he wasn't stubbing one out as he lit its successor in the way that always before had defined him. He was proud that he hadn't touched a cigarette in the weeks since his surgery, but confessed that not a minute passed when he didn't desperately crave one, and I understood that only a man with my father's mulish and unmovable resolve could have stopped smoking so suddenly and successfully after an addiction of fifty years.

When I asked about Mami, it was strangely out of character for him when he chose not to complain or express his exasperation with her, not to fume about what a madwoman she was, as he always had done before. That night he spoke only in measured and very matter-of-fact tones: he had left her; he had endured enough of their hellish marriage, and under no circumstances would he allow her to rejoin him in Denver. As he perceived it, he had provided her with a comfortable and secure situation in which she could care for herself: her condo was paid for; she had a good job, health insurance via Medicare, and income for her retirement. "She won't be a load for you boys to carry after I'm gone," he assured me.

As for himself, he said he planned to return to the house on Mexico Street; its renters had agreed to vacate quickly, and he would be able to move in as soon as he arrived in Denver. When I drove up to check on him a few weeks later, I had to smile as I entered the house. The three-bedroom house with a finished basement was utterly empty except for an easy chair, a bed, a small table on which he had placed an old TV, and small boom box on which he could play his Big Band favorites. He explained proudly that he had purchased everything, including a few pots and pans, sheets and towels, at garage sales— which evidently now captivated him as completely as the thrift-stores once had done—yet he made it clear that he planned to make few additional purchases, and I sensed that he was more than a little fearful of the future and whether he had money with which to retire. Quite poignantly, it seemed to me, as he entered his seventh decade Papi was starting from scratch once again, just as he had done in Mexico City, in Denver in the Sixties, and in Miami. And I believed—or wanted to believe—that something in each of those fresh starts invigorated him in spite of his myriad struggles and assured him that no matter its trials, life also always offered true possibility. "You just have to keep trying to win because you have to prove to yourself and to others that you can," he had told the *Denver Post* twenty years before, and it seemed certain to me that nothing—including a terrible tragedy—had yet dissuaded him from those bywords.

When Christine and the kids were able to join me in Pueblo, my black moods finally began to ebb, but—because I was convinced that my depression had been triggered by my return to Pueblo and the memories it brought back to me of the asylum—I fashioned a solution I believed would end my internal misery once and for all: I'd find a way, somehow, to move us back to Denver.

My plan took two years to achieve, and, in the end, I enjoyed my return to Pueblo—a cordial city where I was warmly welcomed as a returning orphan who had made his mark in the world—and in 1990 I accepted a position as director of the Department of Transportation's Denver region. I remember being ecstatic on the day the announcement was made, and that night Christine and the kids and I celebrated in ways we hadn't in a long time. But the ecstasy was short-lived, blown to pieces by the insidious return of my depression. It had crippled me before, but this time I felt—quite literally— as though I was falling into a bottomless, pitch-black pit. Yet how could this be happening to me again? Everything was working out as I hoped it would; life was better than fine, but nonetheless—and just as had happened four times before—a strange and stark terror of losing *everything* invaded my mind and I could consider nothing else. What made my depression far worse this time was the fact that I seemed utterly incapable of crafting answers to resolve my predicament—our predicament—unable to imagine solutions I believed might possibly save us. Alone in Denver now while Christine and the kids once more waited for a house to sell before joining me, I went night after night without sleep, the impossibility of my setting my life straight as unimaginable to me in those despairing hours as, long ago, was the idea of ever seeing my parents again on the cold and endless nights at the asylum when I cried alone in my bed.

Christine's response to my crisis was simply to announce that she and the children would remain in Pueblo until I settled this strange distress, and absent any support from her, I even went to Papi, now settled again in Denver, to enlist his advice. In a moment of rare openness, I confessed to him the totality of what I was experiencing. He listened, hesitated for a moment, then angrily shook a finger at me and exhorted, "Be a man, damn it. I have never allowed myself the luxury to feel sorry for myself, as you are now. I have always surged forward and conquered my problems." Next, he recounted everything he had suffered in his life and assured me my troubles didn't remotely compare to his. My God, I was hurt. My circumstance was a luxury as far as the Old Man was concerned? I vowed in that instant that I never would share my problems with him again. I felt abandoned by my father, abandoned by my wife, even by God. I was trapped all over again at Sacred Heart Home, abandoned by my Abuelito, my uncles and aunts, and no one—not even Mr. Eddy—was able to save me.

My depression deepened as the months progressed. Although I functioned well at work, I was constantly overwhelmed by dark storms that invaded my moods. Invariably, the worst suffering came in the night, when I was most alone. As I struggled to find some release, for the first time in my life I saw therapists; I read every self-help book I could find, and I even attended twelve-step meetings despite the fact I wasn't addicted to anything. I was desperate.

After a year caught in the closing vice of depression, I began to worry about my sanity. It seemed my personality had splintered in two, the competing parts of me battling to dominate my thinking. I was terribly sleep deprived and utterly exhausted, and I often doubted whether I could hold things together much longer. I considered Mami's many breakdowns and feared that my mind—and my life—were beginning to mirror hers. Yet another possibility was even more terrifying: was my depression less like hers than it was Tio Antoñico's? Like him, was I moving—inevitably—toward an unimaginable suicidal rampage? There were days when I concluded that was precisely where I was headed.

Despite my ongoing anger with him, I was pleased when Papi began to reveal to Bob, John, and I—and our families—an engaging, even warm and sentimental side we never had seen before, and it was clear that he now wanted to be the grandfather he had not been during his years in Miami. He carefully noted each of his grandkids' birthdays and always purchased a present, a true gesture of love for someone who hated to spend money as much as he did. He seemed eager to spend time visiting each of us, and during the summer following his return, he began to spend every other weekend at John's home in the mountains west of Denver, getting to know John's children so well they eagerly anticipated his company, and learning the art of trout fishing from John with the same tenacity, dedication—and skill—John long ago had applied when Papi taught him to box.

Then slowly—and sadly—Papi began to draw away from us, and in time he seemed quite comfortable seeing his family only on holidays and talking only infrequently by phone. My brothers and I asked ourselves why we had dared to presume that a man his age really could so dramatically change. *"Aunque un mono se vista de seda, mono se queda"*, we remembered. You can dress a monkey in silk, but it's still a monkey. And Papi proved he was still Papi—growing offended if the kids didn't greet him as respectfully as his Cuban perspective made him believe he should be, and quickly irritated if they were too loud on the few occasions he saw them, carping miserably that my brothers and I didn't go to him for advice about the important personal and career issues in our lives. He wanted to be the family's honored patron, it seemed, yet only very occasionally.

When one of us would stop by his house to check on him, increasingly he wasn't at home, no matter the time of day and even late at night; regularly, there wasn't an answer when we called, and sometimes many days would pass before he responded to messages we left for him. He assured everyone he felt well and was doing fine, and it didn't seem right to ask him to outline his comings and goings for us. Then finally one day, as John was en route to his house to see if by chance he could catch him at home, he observed from half a block away, Papi at his door, collecting his mail. Yet he didn't take it inside; instead he walked to his car—where a woman waited for him. Papi had a girl-friend!

The three of us were relieved and delighted for him, and we joked about how desperate for companionship the woman must be to endure our father's moods, opinions, and idiosyncrasies. For years the three of us had joked about our parents, that "it was a good thing they married each other and thereby did not wreck two couples." Now Papi's relationship was going to prove this before long, we chortled as we spoke about it. Yet she remained a mystery. For months he continued to hide his relationship with her from us—perhaps because, in his own mind, he remained married to Mami despite the all-but-legal dissolution of their marriage, perhaps because once more he had taken some kind of pleasure in starting anew, and didn't want to introduce the reality of his past life—and his children—to her. Like amateur sleuths, my brothers and I tried to learn what little we could about this new turn our father's life had taken, and we were fascinated when we discovered a young family moving into the house. Surely Papi had rented it and now was spending all his time with this woman—and the crazy Old Man somehow presumed that he could continue to keep his new life secret from us. We were brave enough to ask a few leading questions of him on the rare occasions he called, and yet he resolutely never came clean. Yes, everything was fine. No, he wasn't lonely. No, there wasn't anything he needed at the house. And no, he couldn't attend our barbeque on the Fourth of July—none of us, to our regret, ever simply saying to him, "Papi, we know about the lady, and we're very happy for you, and we hope you'll be comfortable introducing her to us sometime."

Her name was Virginia. She had been widowed following a fifty-two-year marriage. She was seven years older than Papi, and bright, cheerful, and full of spirit and energy. They had met not long after he had joined a seniors' club—surely because he did seek friends and companionship and hadn't wanted to sit alone in his empty house in the way we had feared—and when Virginia had introduced my father to *her* children, they had welcomed him into their family with open arms, delighted that their mother had found a good man with whom to spend the last chapter of her life. Papi relished his life with Virginia, relished the loving and convivial time he spent with her larger family—becoming truly a part of it, celebrating most holidays with them and adopting their traditions. And none of this we knew about her or their lives together for more than two years after the day John first saw him collecting his mail.

On the rare occasions when he would agree to join us for his birthday or another special occasion, Papi always seemed curiously non-specific about the shape of his days. We suspected he continued to be with the woman John had seen, but we knew nothing more. Papi seemed increasingly uncomfortable during the short time he spent with any of us, often nervous, inattentive, and always eager to be on his way. Yet Papi was odd, we reminded ourselves and we presumed he was happy, and we were at ease with his un-secret secret just as we similarly had to accept the other ways in which he made decisions far different than ours, and in which he remained in exile.

When my father returned from Miami, I had been surprised to discover what a dramatic turn his political views seemed to have taken. In south Florida's sultry and rabidly anti-Castro air, he had hooked far to the right, so much so that the former Nixonian conservative and a man who held Ronald Reagan in high esteem as one of America's greatest presidents, now seemed to see communists under every bed and to believe that Democrats and liberals were Satan's spawn at the very least, and, more likely, the products of Fidel's despicable loins. Papi haughtily dismissed any mention of Cuba's great three-time Olympic heavyweight champion Teofilo Stevenson, insisting that anyone who boxed for Cuba was communist and a chump. He listened religiously to Rush Limbaugh—calling him "the only man in America who tells the truth"—and like the bilious radio talk-show host, my father increasingly appeared happiest when he was viciously attacking anyone who had the freedom-hating gall to disagree with him. But the truth was that I didn't entirely realize that Papi's current political perspective—seared in the profound personal losses and deep indignities he had suffered in Cuba and sustained by his continuing belief, well after the dissolution of the Soviet Union, that communism could be blamed for every one of the world's myriad ills—had become truly perverse. It was a truth that I didn't begin to comprehend until a day that otherwise might have been one of the proudest days of my life—and, at least I hoped, of his.

During an eighteen-year career at the Department of Transportation, I had advanced from an entry-level engineering job to a top management position in charge of the agency's Denver metropolitan engineering district. Yet I was surprised—overwhelmed is surely a better word—when Colorado's three-term Democratic governor, Roy Romer, asked me to become executive director of the department in the late winter of 1993. Because this was a political appointment, I knew I'd lose my much-treasured job security if I accepted, and, once more, I was forced to battle a round or two with the darkness as I considered the offer, my depression triggered this time, as it always had been, by a sense that I simply couldn't survive if my safety net were pulled from beneath me. And for the first time in my career, I turned the promotion down.

Soon after I informed the governor of my decision, my dark moods predictably vanished. I spent time in the following days imagining what it might have been like to become a key member of the governor's cabinet, but I trusted that other opportunities would come my way that wouldn't leave me so vulnerable. Then, just a month later, Romer approached me again with the same offer, but this time he guaranteed me a return to my old job when he left office, and this time I said yes. Despite the fact that I was about to undertake the biggest career challenge of my life, my depression never returned and at last I felt at peace, certain in a way I'd never been before that I had discarded the demons that had haunted me since my childhood. I would become the first Hispanic ever to direct the Department of Transportation, and it pleased me to think that I'd also be able demonstrate to my father what his many sacrifices for his sons had made possible.

In the days leading up to my swearing-in, my thoughts returned constantly to the path my life had taken from La Villita Candado to the Colorado capitol building—the trauma of leaving Cuba, the loneliness and hopelessness of the long years at Sacred Heart Home, the impoverished fear for our survival as a family in the decade after we were reunited, the protracted war my parents endured in order to keep us together. I couldn't tear my mind away from the clear and simple truth that I never would have been given this wonderful opportunity if it weren't for the decisions and sacrifices made by both my mother and my father, and, despite all our pains and sorrows, I wanted to find a way to express my gratitude to them.

When Romer's spokesperson Cindy Parmenter—by amazing coincidence the former *Denver Post* reporter who had written about the five Vidals twenty-four years before—informed me that the governor would hold a press conference to announce my appointment and wanted me to say a few words as well, I invited Papi to go the capitol with me, specifically because I wanted him to hear from my lips at last how indebted to him I was and to publicly receive my thanks. But my father was strangely reluctant to join me when I invited him, and under other circumstances, I would have let it go at that, but this time I insisted, pushed past his objections, and finally he relented and agreed to go.

I was more than a little awe-struck as Papi and I entered the governor's expansive office, which was filled with dozens of people, and quickly something about the occasion seemed surreal: I hadn't found myself in front of a bank of television cameras in the thirty-two years since Robert F. Kennedy had welcomed me, my brothers, and seven other Cuban kids to his country. By now, it had become my country too, and the governor of Colorado had asked me to join his high-level administrative team; I had traveled a complex distance from Camagüey, and I was both proud and humbled.

Governor Romer and I were both seated as he began his remarks, briefly describing my professional background and the reasons why he had selected me to head the state's transportation department. When he invited me to speak, I began by saying, "Before I make any other comments or answer questions, I want to acknowledge my father, Roberto Vidal." I motioned to Papi to stand, which he awkwardly did. "Had it not been for the sacrifices he made," I continued, "I would never be getting this opportunity. Thank you, Dad." I then stood, and began to clap, and was joined by everyone in the room.

Papi's face flushed red and he clearly was ill at ease in a way that unsettled me and made me nervous. Private man that he was, I presumed he was embarrassed by my very public expression of gratitude, but I trusted that he did appreciate my words nonetheless. After I had answered the reporters questions and the press conference had given way to a few minutes of casual conversation among those who were present, I noticed out of the corner of my eye Papi standing alone in a corner of the office, speaking to no one. Again, I presumed he was simply awkward among people he didn't know, but he was strangely quiet as well when I drove him home to Virginia's house.

We didn't speak again until he came to my house weeks later for a Father's Day celebration, and even as he arrived, he obviously was agitated about something, behaving in a manner I'd never precisely observed before. He repeatedly snapped at the kids, seemed irked by every topic of conversation, then began hurling insults at me in response to even the most innocuous things I said. His verbal battering finally got under my skin, and angered me, and at last I bluntly asked him, "What the fuck is your problem?" I'd never spoken that sharply or coarsely to my father in my life, and he exploded.

"I'll tell you what my problem is. I can't believe my own flesh and blood has gone to work for the communists. I can't believe you are working for a Democrat. How many asses did you kiss or bribe to get this job? Everybody knows this is what Democrats do, and this is how they have destroyed this country. I now have to live with the knowledge that my son has become like the people who destroyed my Cuba. And on top of everything else, I had to *witness* it. That press conference was the most shameful day of my life."

I was stunned. The son of a bitch's words were like a knife plunged into my heart, and in that moment he and his brother Antoñico seemed utterly capable of the same crimes. For forty-two years, I had longed for and tried so hard to win my father's acceptance, and now my real and meaningful achievement had *shamed* him. Yet instead of dissolving into tears the way I had done countless times before, at last a lifetime of suppressed anger shot out of me. "Get your sorry ass out of my home, motherfucker," I roared. "You are no longer welcome here." I grabbed him by his thin arm and pulled him across the room to the front door. I let go of him only after both of us were outside, and as he regained his balance, he punched me in the chest.

I flashed white hot—as if I were confronting one of the Roldan brothers at the asylum once more—pressed my face only an inch from his, and I screamed, "I am not the helpless little boy any more who you got used to mistreating. You do that again, Old Man, and you'll find yourself flat on your back!"

My words wounded him this time, I could see his body enfold and could sense his sorrow. "Fine, I'll go," he quietly said as he straightened his shirt.

"You're damn right you'll go," I persisted, "and you will not be welcome here until you are willing to show me some respect."

"Well, you're always welcome in my home," he said, but I would not, *could* not lessen my rage, as he hoped I would.

"That's the problem between us," I said, my eyes burning into his. "I may be welcome in your house, but you've *never* welcomed me into your heart."

I didn't say anything else to my father for the next four years. Finally, I had successfully rid him from my life; he was a toxic person with whom I needed to have no contact in order to protect my sanity, I convinced myself. Occasionally I would hear about him from my brothers, and their reports reaffirmed for me the wisdom of banishing him from my world. Months later, after I shared with my brothers the fact that I had begun to contemplate divorce, they reported to me that my father's response to the news had been understanding and supportive—as theirs certainly also had been—yet I was astonished to learn that he had gone on to expound about how quickly people in my generation gave up on marriage, saying, "Look at your mother and I. We have been married for forty-three years, and in spite of all our problems, we are still married." The fact that he spoke those ridiculous words from a telephone in Virginia's home evidenced for me the predictable fact that the kind of willful ignorance and upside-down thinking he had brought to the subject of my going to work for Colorado's Democratic governor he continued to widely apply. And I renewed my resolve to shun him forevermore. Neither did my father attempt to contact me—certainly never to express that, yes, he had come to understand that we rightly had earned each other's respect. In time, he seldom crossed my mind, and I was relieved, even happy, to have utterly disconnected my father from my life once and for all.

Three years had passed before my family rejoined me in Denver. During those years, I drove to Pueblo each weekend to be with Christine and the kids and reconnect myself to their lives, attempting as best I could to reassure all of us that we remained a family. In the midst of those weekly commutes, I discovered how even internal chaos could become the norm over time, and, little by little, I learned to accept the mistakes I'd made in my life. I now understood that my childhood trauma had rendered me abnormally risk-adverse, particularly when it came to my personal and financial security. But in my drive to succeed, I had accepted the Pueblo and Denver promotions without adequately considering how I could remain with my family, provide them a home and assure our financial stability. My responses to our early move to Los Angeles and the loss of my job at Stearns-Roger had illuminated the fear I'd carried with me since my childhood, but I had failed to recognize it. And in being blind to that fear, I'd gambled my safety net and thereby triggered the depressions.

But if I had resolved my turmoil as I accepted the position the governor's cabinet, I'd also been forced in those days to recognize that seeing each other only on weekends inevitably had damaged my relationship with Christine. It remained difficult for me to reconcile the fact that during the years we had been apart—a time in which I had suffered more than at any other point in my life—Christine, for her part, never had been happier or more fulfilled. Together again in Denver, neither of us could ignore the truth that we had grown at ease with being apart, nor could I fail to see how much my relationship with my kids also had deteriorated—or how troubled they now seemed to be.

Sarah, the eldest, entered middle school as she returned to Denver. Soon, her grades plummeted, she began to rage, and was inexplicably violent, intentionally breaking things in ways that reminded me all-too-much of her grandmother, Sarah's language often vile and filled with hate. As far as Christine was concerned, this was just a "phase" she was going through, but by now I had begun to realize that my parents had been right about more than a few things along the way, particularly the need for children to respect their parents and other adults. Yet the more I became a parental enforcer—the uncaring asshole with lots of rules, expectations, and consequences, from the kids' perspective—the more they could count on Christine being understanding, supportive, and immediately forgiving, as when Sarah flunked out of school simply because she refused to attend. Tensions grew ever greater, the conflicts becoming more intense and protracted with every passing month, and ultimately, my home became the same madhouse I had grown up in. Except for the violence I still shuddered to remember, the war that once had raged between my parents now was part of my marriage as well.

Finally, I concluded that I had to move out of the house an into an apartment, both to reclaim some personal peace and also with the hope that in a different and more stable environment, perhaps I could become more effective in establishing boundaries and discipline and setting the kids' lives on a clearer course. I knew this would be very hard for me to accomplish, and I was heartbroken when I failed.

In choosing allegiances between a house in which any kind of behavior was entirely acceptable and one in which I made demands of them and held them accountable for their actions, it surely wasn't all that surprising that my children inevitably dismissed me from their lives as completely as they could, joining their mother in blaming me for their failures, and accusing me of abandoning them. They viewed Christine, on the other hand, as their rescuer, depending on her to console them when their mean father would go so far as to ground them, their mother even allowing them to stay with her if they happened to be angry with me on days they were scheduled to join me at my house.

Having dropped out of school, Sarah's problems worsened; she was briefly jailed, then utterly disappeared for almost three years, a time during which not even her mother knew where she was. In turn, Molly and Josh didn't make great choices with their lives either as far as I was concerned, and like their sister, ultimately decided to remove all traces of me from their lives. Their decisions twice more broke my heart, and I suffered further from the understanding that I'd personally demonstrated to them long before how to blame their parents for their problems and how to lock them out of their lives.

Four-and-a-half years after Papi punched me, Papi's secret girlfriend, Virginia, telephoned John to say that my father had been diagnosed with lung cancer. The three of us conferred by phone, and I agreed to join them in visiting him at Virginia's home. It was the first time I had met her in the seven years they had lived together; she was warm and remarkably kind, and although Papi, in turn, didn't appear thrilled to see us, he did agree to sit and talk with us for a bit and explain his diagnosis to us. As I looked at that pale and shrunken relic and listened to his thin and raspy voice, it seemed clear to me that he didn't have long to live, yet as was usual with him, the Old Man was far from ready to concede the fight. X-rays had determined, he said, that the cancer was very advanced and even had begun to deteriorate the bones of his rib cage. He would have to begin intense radiation therapy immediately to slow the cancer's advance, something he had agreed to and would begin the following day.

But he had more to say. His name was no longer Roberto; it was Robert, and he was an American, not a Cuban any longer. He refused to speak Spanish ever again, a tongue foully polluted by the fact that it was the language with which Fidel Castro barked his hideous orders. He wanted us to know too that he would not participate in a Father's Day celebration in a few days because to do so would be a mockery of the truth he now accepted: he had been cruelly abandoned by his three sons.

Each time during the short conversation that Papi erupted in anger, Virginia would intercede by assuring us, "This is not the real Robert." The real Robert, she wanted us to know, "has always been the perfect gentleman to me for all these years." Virginia believed the terrible pain Papi suffered brought on hostility and anger; anyone who had to endure what he did would be irritable, she was sure. Then she confessed that she would need help getting my father to his radiation treatments. He could no longer drive because he tended to forget where he was going and to get lost on his way home. He was beginning to present early symptoms of Alzheimer's disease, the terrible malady his mother had suffered, although Papi angrily snarled at her that she was wrong and that his mind was fine. Virginia had a hard time driving as well these days, she said, and yes, the three of us immediately responded, of course, we would see to it that Papi got to his appointments and safely home again each day. That was all the help they needed, he snapped, and they wouldn't accept any more than that—not from ungrateful sons who were his sons no longer.

Within a week of beginning his radiation therapy, Papi's condition worsened dramatically. He lost what little energy still remained to him, and, even with the help of a walker, he could barely negotiate the distance from the house to the car. It was essential for one of us to be with him and Virginia much of the time, and although both my father and the circumstances often were difficult, in the end it became an experience for which I was deeply grateful.

I still had to endure his long and disconnected ranting about the tribulations and people who, he believed, had so unfairly limited his life—stolen his property, blocked his work opportunities, and destroyed his country and much of the world. But I discovered that if I simply ignored him in the midst of his tirades, they would stop in time, and, almost certainly, a good conversation would follow. It was as if—together—we were lancing his emotional boils in ways that gave him real relief at last, and when I learned how to tune out his wild venting, I was able to learn remarkable things about my father and his life I had not known.

He and Virginia had traveled widely during their seven years together, vacationing in several parts of the world and taking cruises. The two of them loved each other completely, something I readily observed, and which they also expressed. I'd never seen my father convey such physical and emotional affection before, certainly not to my mother, and Virginia's efforts to ensure that he was fed, and bathed, and comfortable—despite the fact that her health too had begun to fail—moved me too. During long stretches when Papi slept, Virginia told me how much she had loved to dance with my father, and I was floored. Imagine, Papi a *dancer*; it was an image I found both wonderful and impossible to believe because I'd never seen him go near a dance floor. Unlike my statuesque and beautiful mother, Virginia was petite and very plain, yet she swore that together they dazzled the crowds when they danced to swing-era songs aboard the ships on which they sailed. She told me my father often spoke of how being separated from his three sons when we were young was harder than anything else he'd endured in his life, that he often spoke not only of his love but also his admiration for us, and she whispered as well that in recent days he had told her how much it meant to him that we had immediately come to his aid when we learned of his cancer. We *hadn't* abandoned him; he now was reassured.

One day in mid-July, Papi had grown very weary after talking with me for hours. He asked if he could close his eyes for a while and whether I still would be there when he awoke. I assured him I would, and as he napped, I simply sat and watched him. Then suddenly, he awakened, grabbed my arm, and said, "Son, I have to tell you something." He paused, "You know, all I ever asked of the three of you was that you should be good people and always do the absolute best you could. But I guess I just lost sight of that along the way. The three of you far exceeded anything I could ask for." As he spoke, his eyes watered and a tear rolled down his right cheek.

"It's okay, Dad," I whispered. "I know what you mean."

That was all he said, but it was enough. His was an apology as full and redemptive as any I'd ever heard, and I'd *never* heard one from him before. Even as he neared death, I understood that his enormous pride wouldn't allow him to literally tell me he was sorry, but the few words he did speak forever washed away the rancor and anger I'd borne inside me since the time more than four years before when he had hit me and had told me that one of my proudest days was his moment of greatest shame.

I felt as though angels had descended and offered me a profound and important gift because from that moment forward, I was bonded to Papi—and him to me—in a way we never had been before. And as he continued to weaken, Papi asked me to promise that if he deteriorated to a point where his mind no longer functioned, if he couldn't converse and express his thoughts, I would refuse on his behalf any medication or mechanical assistance that might keep him alive, and this he asked of both John and Bob as well.

One bright day near the end of July, he presented me with a typed piece of paper on which he had outlined the properties he and his family had owned in Cuba, and that had been confiscated by Castro's government. The list was far longer than I might have imagined, and included the Hotel Residenciál and the Casa Vidal building that housed the furniture store, two warehouses, eleven rental homes and apartment buildings in Camagüey and Havana, the lot in the Monte Carlo development where Papi once hoped to build a wonderful home, and, of course, La Villita Candado and our beloved beach cottage at Santa Lucia. At the end of the list, he had written in English: "All documents of ownership of these properties were given to relatives for safekeeping. The relatives are all dead and the houses confiscated, so we don't know where these papers are. The government office where these documents were registered are all gone or the documents destroyed."

Yet nonetheless, Papi wanted me to promise, to *swear* to him that one day I would return to Cuba and reclaim these properties. They were his legacy, and the legacy of his father and mother and brother and sisters, and they rightfully belonged to the family's next generations. They belonged to *us*, not to Fidel, he insisted as forcefully as a dying man could, and despite the impossibility of doing so, I found myself assuring my father that yes, yes I would go to Cuba and find the documents and reclaim the hotel and buildings and houses. Yes, of course I would do that for him.

Late in July, Papi had to be hospitalized to remove massive amounts of fluid from his lungs, and he didn't return to Virginia's home again. At his doctors' suggestion—and on the information from them that they could do nothing more for him—we moved Papi to a hospice, and he was able to subtly express that he was ready to die, a decision he'd clearly made with both body and soul. He no longer spoke except to whisper his love for Virginia and for us; and to assure us that the four people who had mattered most in his life were with him, and that he was *happy*. He refused any food or drink—clearly a conscious decision to help his body shut down, and after two days, he barely spoke at all any more, and it had become difficult for him even to hold Virginia's hand.

At the hospital and now at the hospice, we had asked his caregivers to address him as Dr. Vidal, believing he would appreciate and be honored by that simple—and final—show of respect, and they were wonderful about doing so. Papi hadn't spoken a word for a couple of days when, one afternoon, an orderly came into his room to adjust his position to help him avoid bedsores. "Dr. Vidal, Dr. Vidal," the young man gently called out, hoping to rouse Papi from his sleep and alert him to what he was about to do. "We need to move you." As the man bent and attended to him, I heard Papi faintly say, "That's okay. You don't need to call me doctor. It really doesn't matter anymore." That was the last time I heard his voice. And I'm sure what he meant was that now he was finished with striving; he had lived a life of challenge and struggle and now he was ready to rest.

My brothers and I—and Virginia as well, of course—took the opportunity over the next days to spend time with him privately, Papi motionless and silent except for the gentle rasp of his breaths. I spoke to him often during those hours we were alone, and it seemed to me that he could hear me and that he welcomed my words. I told him how much I loved him. I thanked him for everything he had done for me and for helping me become a man. I apologized for not always having understood him and for the time we had wasted quarreling. I expressed my *respeto profundo*, my abiding *admiración*, and I assured him that he would live in me for the rest of my days. Then I urged him to let himself go, and in the early morning hours of August 4, 1998, surrounded by his beloved Virginia and the three sons who had been his planet of Rojugui, my father took his final breath, and then was on his way.

At the moment of my father's death, I was overwhelmed by deep sadness, but I was also filled with joy; Papi no longer suffered and now was at peace, and the experience of his dying and his death had transformed me in ways for which I was deeply grateful. I spent all my years up till now believing my father's life had been tragic, yet at the end he had encountered true love with Virginia, expressed his deep pride in three sons, and had died surrounded not by rancor and resentment and grief, but by love. His ultimately had been a story of triumph, I understood, and for the first time in my life, I was genuinely proud of who my father had been, proud to be Roberto Emiliano Vidal's youngest son.

We had discussed Papi's funeral wishes with him, which were straightforward and simple to set in motion, but then immediately after his death the three of us made a decision I'll always regret, yet it too was grounded in the love and profound sense of familial reconnection my father's dying had rekindled in each of us. John, Bob, and I *did* want to remain a family, for all of us to become a real family for the first time, if we possibly could, and if we had reconciled with Papi as wonderfully as we had over the past months, surely, it seemed, we should attempt to do so with Mami as well. Following ten years absent any kind of contact with our father or with us, we called our mother in Miami to say that he had died and to invite her to his funeral.

To be fair to her, Mami had no reason to suspect that my brothers and I had grown close as we helped our father die, nor that we briefly had forged the kinds of father-son bonds with him we always had longed for. She knew nothing of Virginia or his deep happiness, and she flew into Denver presuming that the five of us simply would go through the family motions once more during the funeral. Driving into the city from the airport, Mami inquired whether Bob, who had gone alone to meet her, knew what my father had left her in his will—that was her only question, evidently her sole concern. When she learned that Papi had named John the executor of his will, next she pressed him. What did Roberto leave her?

My brothers and I had been so moved by our father's death, so grateful to have lived his last days with him, and her singular focus offended and angered us, but what did we expect? Our first blissful and celebratory night together with our parents after at last we left the asylum thirty-four years before had been followed the next morning by Mami's absurd and brutal attack on Bob. And the pattern had repeated itself once more: in the first days after Papi's death, we joyously had imagined reconciling with our mother, drawing close to her, getting to know her again and reintroducing her to the grandchildren who, we knew, would delight her. Papi's death would initiate the renewal of our family in myriad ways we prayed, but then Mami's arrival, her indifference to any emotion we might be experiencing, her selfishness, and interest only in money and property dashed our hopes and refueled our decades of hurt and anger.

Virginia, kind and gentle as always, informed us that, because my mother would be present, she would not, *could not* attend Papi's funeral. It was an entirely reasonable response, of course, and one we immediately understood: why would she want to meet my father's tormentor or to see her conduct herself as his grieving wife? Yet we couldn't find a way to keep Mami away, particularly since we had invited her, and our best intentions, in the end, led to our utter failure to meet one of Papi's most basic requests, simply that the four of us—my brothers and I and Virginia—represent at the funeral the family that mattered to him most.

In the end, at the funeral and at the cemetery where we interred his ashes, what occurred was far more akin to the careful façade we long ago crafted for the readers of the *Denver Post* than it was the extraordinary familial experience we had shared with my father and Virginia in the days that led to his death. Despite the summer heat, the day of the funeral was cold and bitterly sobering; it brought back into my mind the grim and ruptured and wasted reality of our lives as a family. It wasn't the way I wanted to say farewell to the man I now knew deep inside me had been *my father*, and I ached and I cried as we icily laid him to rest.

Trece

Volver a Cuba

My life, like many lives, often has moved in circular motion; events that occurred long ago have come round to visit me again, and I've repeatedly been blessed to see with new eyes people and places that were important parts of my life in years now distant. Time seems less a straight line than an imprecise freehand circle to me, and I seldom call it a coincidence when people I encounter link me directly to my earlier life—my several lives—and take me back to them.

Not long after I'd received the promotion to head the Pueblo district of the Colorado's Department of Transportation in 1983, for example, the department's executive director, Joe Dolan, called me into his office to get acquainted with me. During our conversation, I casually told him I'd been born in Cuba, that my parents had elected to send their three sons to the United States as part of Operation Peter Pan, that I'd ended up in Colorado because my brothers and I had been sent to an orphanage in Pueblo. When Dolan, in turn, told me he had worked for Robert F. Kennedy while he was attorney general, I told him about the afternoon at Chicago's O'Hare airport 22 years before, when Kennedy had shaken my hand and welcomed me and a rag-tag group of Cuban kids to the United States.

Dolan's eyes filled with tears before he asked, incredulously, "You were one of those kids?" I nodded affirmatively but said nothing more in the awkward moments before he was able to add, "I set up that meeting." Both of us were amazed to discover that we had met before, in effect, that our paths had crossed in the autumn of 1961 when the attorney general heard that exiled Cuban kids were passing through the airport, just as he was, and he asked his assistant—this same Joe Dolan—to arrange a press event on a moment's notice at which he would greet us and assure us that all would be well.

It was Dolan, too, who suggested later that year that, as an immigrant from a Latin American country myself, I might want to introduce myself and make welcome a young woman from Chile who recently had joined the department. I did so; our brief meeting went badly—she was disgusted by me, to be blunt—but as we worked in close proximity over the years, eventually we became friends. The man she married, an Argentinean, became a good friend as well, and when the two of us were single again in 1998, we began to date—at precisely the moment my father was dying and I was endeavoring for the first time in decades to tentatively reconnect myself once more to my family and to my roots. Gabriela Cornejo and I fell deeply in love, and later were married, and she, more than anyone else, helped me see that I was living parts of my life in a precarious limbo. I readily acknowledged my Cuban background—and liked doing so—yet little in my life truly reflected it or paid it honor. My early years in Cuba lent me a single aspect of my identity—I was a father, an engineer, a basketball fanatic, a Cuban—yet something was missing, something that linked my roots to my soul. Gabriela—whose profound sense of her Chilean selfhood still defines her after nearly three decades in the United States—understood my predicament, and was troubled by it, and I know that without her insight, her steadfast encouragement, and her passion for the true meaning of family and home, I might never have gotten to know—and to like—the man who I fully am, a man shaped by two cultures as well as two parents, by experiences both wondrous and horrific, and by each of the eras in which I've lived. Without Gabi, I might never have returned to Cuba.

As she likes to tell the story, I walked into Gabi's office on the long-ago day we met, and announced, "Hi, I'm Bill Vidal," pronouncing "Vidal" as if I'd been raised in Arkansas—or Colorado—and she needed to hear nothing more before she knew I was trouble. I claimed I was

Cuban, she still reminisces in mock repugnance, yet I spoke to her in English. I called myself Bill—*Bill!*—then suggested that we might have lunch sometime before I said anything else. No self-respecting Cuban man, no proud and self-possessed *latino*, would abandon his real name, or ignore an opportunity to speak his language, or be so forward as to immediately suggest a shared meal. If I was a Cuban, she believed, then I was surely a Cuban *gusano*, one of the worms who had abandoned his nation rather than work for the betterment of all its people in the first years after the revolution.

Gabi came of age in the optimistic years surrounding Salvador Allende's election as president of Chile; on her bedroom walls hung posters of Fidel and Che Guevara rather than rock stars, and she was heartsick and frightened when—following the CIA-sponsored coup in which Allende died, General Augusto Pinochet came to power, and thousands of pro-Allende Chileans began to "disappear"—her family was forced to flee to the United States. She studied engineering at the University of Colorado, became an American citizen, and raised two brilliant bi-lingual daughters, and always, her pride in her family, her native country, her language, and what it meant to be a *latina* remained focal for her. As dark and beautiful, bright and strong-willed Gabriela and I began to grow close in the months surrounding my father's death and to explore the essences of each other's lives, Gabi couldn't comprehend why my parents had wanted so desperately for all of us to hide the fact that we were Cuban; to her, that attempt was akin to trying to hide your nose, or pretending somehow that your heart didn't pump in your chest.

I quickly grew to love Gabi calling me "Guille," the name that always had seemed most essentially my own, even during the decades when I'd virtually never heard it spoken or used it myself; I loved speaking Spanish with her and hearing her read Pablo Neruda's poetry in a voice suffused with rich Chilean emotion, and along the way I discovered that, like her, I longed to travel to Cuba. Gabi, still hopeful, as she had been for decades, about the promise of the revolution for Cuba's poor, would go for the first time and I—it began to be a word I could speak again in the context of that place—would go *home* for the first time in forty years.

Yet the truth was that I was *afraid* to go home, and I procrastinated for months about making specific plans. What if Fidel's government still had an issue with something Papi had said or done and held me responsible when I arrived? Would I be followed everywhere I went by shadowy G-2 agents? Would I be arrested and jailed? And, even if spared that horror, how would ordinary Cubans treat me? I was a *gusano*, after all, and people might take great pleasure in taunting me, even robbing or assaulting me in the good name of the revolution. What if I wasn't allowed to leave?

My nascent desire to return to my homeland also had reawakened the profound fears I had known as a child in the two years before my brothers and I boarded a plane to America; they were irrational fears, I understood, yet they were dramatic and potent as well, and I drug my feet and insisted my workload was too heavy for me to travel just now and fretted about the cost of the trip before finally Gabi offered me an ultimatum: *she* was going to Cuba, whether with me or without me, and I knew my strong-willed mate was quite serious and I did not want to be left behind.

As I finally began to carefully plan the trip, my fears abated a bit. Yet as we flew from Denver to Cancún on Mexico's Yucatán peninsula on the first leg of our journey in April 2001, they roared back, hijacking my thoughts, and seemingly paralyzing me in my seat, trepidation aggravated by the fact that—because we wouldn't be able to use credit cards issued by U.S. banks while in Cuba—earlier in the day I had placed a large and seemingly dangerous amount of cash in a money belt I wore strapped to my belly beneath my clothes.

Because Mexicana Airlines flew from the Cancún airport to Havana only on Saturday nights at ten p.m., we spent much of the day relaxing on a nearby beach, yet by the time we returned to the airport for our flight, I was chilled and clammy and nearing panic. When a gate agent announced that instead of assigned seating, passengers on the flight could claim their seats on a first come, first served basis, I suddenly imagined a way in which I could avoid boarding the plane. Gabi and I would simply wait until everyone else had boarded—and surely every seat eventually would be occupied—and because of our generosity, we would be left behind. It seemed like a perfect plan until Gabi grabbed me by the arm and wrestled me to the front of the line. A final time she announced, "I'm going with or without you, Guille. You can either join me or wait for me here until I get back." I *wanted* to wait—God, I wanted to wait—yet I longed to see Cuba again as well, and we boarded the plane and soon were underway. Only a ninety-mile reach of the Yucatán Channel separates Cancún from the island of Cuba; no sooner had the plane reached its cruising altitude, it seemed, than it began to descend, and I broke into a cold sweat and now visibly trembled in fear. What had I done? Why had I taken such a wild and foolhardy risk? A powerful sense of foreboding now insisted that something terrible was about to happen, and Gabi—seeing the apoplectic shape I was in—took my hand in hers and caressed it, assuring me that all would be well until we had landed safely and were approaching customs in an airport that had been the scene of my life's greatest trauma forty years before.

I wasn't surprised when Gabi passed through immigration quickly and without incident, the immigration agent flirting with her lightheartedly, but then she disappeared behind a wall and I stood terribly alone in front of a now-taciturn Cuban who studied my passport a moment before announcing sternly in Spanish, "This isn't you," insisting that I didn't look at all like my passport photo. Obviously, I concluded—my terror seeming to explode out of my chest—the man also had noted that my birthplace was "Camagüey, Cuba," and I'm sure I turned white as a ghost. This was exactly what I'd been afraid of: the instant this *chico* or anyone else in Cuba learned I was a *gusano*, I would suffer his venomous wrath, yet, in fact, all the agent subsequently asked of me was to see my driver's license, and its photograph reassured him that I was indeed Guillermo Vicente Vidal. *Bienvendio a su casa*, he offered, "Welcome home," and I was free to go.

I could hear a loud commotion behind the wall as I moved toward it, yet, as I turned the corner, I was stunned to see a great mob of people packed into the Havana night, each of these *cubanos*, it seemed, agitated and talking loudly and very urgently. *My god, they're all here because of me*, I thought in a rush of panic. *They want to tear me to shreds.* And then, quite suddenly, someone grabbed my arm and yanked me into the chaotic heart of the crowd, and I was petrified in the seconds before I realized it was Gabi, who simply was leading me toward the van that would take us to our hotel. No one was trying to hurt me, I realized as I began to take breaths again, and the only people paying me any kind of attention to me were the two women who struggled to determine who would carry my luggage as I clutched it ever tighter, afraid that their aim was to steal it. As we drove away from the airport a few minutes later, our guide explained that hordes of people recently had begun to wait for every international flight, hoping to carry arriving tourists' baggage for a few meters in return for a tip in American dollars—U.S. currency, ironically, having become a kind of Cuban gold. It was well past midnight by now, and I felt both relief and a sense of excitement inside the van; I was alive and well and in *mi Cuba* again; I squeezed Gabi's hand as if to say yes, yes I'm here and I'm okay, and I studied the dark streets as we drove in hopes that something familiar remained in my country after so long an absence.

From our room high in the Hotel Nacionál, we had a grand view of *La Habana* the following morning, and I was eager to reacquaint myself with the city that had seemed the most magical place in the world when I was a boy. I recalled a beautiful, enchanting city with towering buildings and streets teeming with traffic, and when we ventured out in the morning sun, I was struck immediately by both the similarities modern Havana bore to the metropolis I remembered and the dramatic differences. American cars from the late 1950s— most of them meticulously maintained and repainted—still plied the streets; there were boxy old Russian Ladas too, and joining the cars on the cobblestone streets were thousands of bicycles, mopeds and scooters, ear-shattering motorcycles, three-wheeled "coco-taxis" that looked like enormous yellow eggs, and more than a few horses pulling buggies. *Habaneros* got around, it was clear, by whatever means they could, and as I admired the gleaming Chrysler Saratogas, Buick Roadmasters, and even a Studebaker Silver Hawk or two—with their dramatically pointed rear fins that forever captured Papi's eye—it seemed to me that contemporary Cubans surely must be the world's best mechanics, cannibalizing even the smallest parts from cars now junked but still very valuable, and crafting new parts entirely from scratch as they needed them.

As we made our way through the streets near the hotel, I couldn't help but see the city as a beautiful and sophisticated woman, now past her prime and a bit past caring as well, but still very lovely. Virtually all of Havana's exquisite colonial buildings still stood, but many of them—like the Hotel Riviera, where I had stayed with my family in September 1961 in the days before my brothers and I boarded a plane to Miami—were terribly careworn and neglected, and some even seemed near collapse. Yet every building—whether newly constructed, renovated and freshly painted, or derelict—was occupied, and clothes hanging from lines that stretched between windows and draped over balcony rails attested to the fact that the city was filled to its rooftops with people. Pedestrians jammed the narrow sidewalks, and everywhere we walked, the blend of the architecturally beleaguered and the carefully restored seemed haphazard and absent a plan. Some people we spoke with told us they had no idea why particular buildings were chosen for renovation; others insisted that the homes of government officials always were the first to be targeted for renewal, but everyone agreed that it was critically important to retain the city's unique colonial character. We take great *orgullo*, pride, in our history, people always were quick to tell us, and nowhere did we see American-style in-fill development, where old buildings were bulldozed to make room for crass new structures out of sync with period styles.

What was quickly surprising as we spent that first day wandering in contemporary Havana was how vitally important to the nation's precarious economy foreign currencies were and how people from every walk of life were forced to focus on dollars, euros, and a curious Cuban über-currency above all else. In recent years, the combination of the forty-year-old U.S. economic embargo against Cuba, a variety of internal government economic initiatives that proved unsuccessful and ill-advised, and the 1989 collapse of the Soviet Union and the end of its three-billion dollar a year subsidy had collectively spiraled the Cuban economy into a severe depression known as the *período especial*, the special period, during which Fidel responded by opening the nation's doors to massive foreign investment in tourism, initiating a huge influx of tourists from Europe and Latin American and their respective currencies. But the decision ultimately had created two separate and very unequal economies.

In 1993, as the depression grew ever worse, Fidel had legalized the circulation of the U.S. dollar, then a year later established a *second* Cuban currency, the *peso convertible*, whose value was pegged to the dollar. To further capture foreign currencies, the government subsequently opened stores throughout the country that only accepted dollars, euros or *chavitos*, the slang term for the new "convertible" peso-shops that sold goods otherwise unavailable to ordinary Cubans. If people wanted to purchase those goods—high-quality foods, certain household items, and expensive pharmaceuticals among them—they had to acquire dollars or chavitos with which to do so, and inevitably, soon the most lucrative jobs in the nation were those closest to the tourists—because they were where the money was.

In a country that still rhetorically spurned everything capitalist and American, it was a strange and unsettling sight—the dollar and its equivalents having become the source of all marketplace passion and the best means with which individual Cubans could improve their economic lot in life. Old pesos, the *moneda nacionál*, remained the official currency of the revolution—trading at roughly twenty-five to a dollar—while dollars, euros, and chavitos had become the de facto currency of a free-market-style government that Castro both encouraged and decried. Everywhere, people clamored to find ways to earn what they perceived as *real* money; scientists and academicians fought for jobs in tourist hotels, and Cuba's black market—always thriving and always dollar-based—boomed as never before.

I've successfully avoided my father's cigarette addiction, but the occasional good cigar is a true pleasure, I'll confess, and the opportunity to purchase—with dollars, of course—fine Cuban *puros* at bargain prices was irresistible. We set out one afternoon to find the renowned Romeo y Julieta factory, and, as often happened during our Cuban sojourn, two outgoing and engaging young men of whom we asked directions kindly offered to escort us to the factory themselves, which, they assured us, was nearby.

We chatted about life in Cuba and life in the U.S. as we walked—and walked—and after a while I thought I recognized streets we already had trod. They assured us we'd nearly arrived, and, after what must have been five miles of walking, we did indeed reach the factory gate, only to discover that it had just shut down operations for the day, and our informal guides were very apologetic. We would have to return the next day if we wanted to tour the factory, but if it was an excellent price on cigars we foremost were seeking then perhaps they still could be of help. The two *chicos* explained that workers in Havana's major cigar factories were given two of their fine, hand-rolled creations at the end of each shift, provided they met their daily quotas, and that many simply saved them, cached them in branded boxes, and sold them to tourists for a fraction of their price in the hotel shops. They happened to know someone who sold Romeo y Julietas and other brands on the *mercado negro*, the black market, and because they felt bad about us reaching the factory too late, they could take us to that person, but only if we wanted.

We agreed to forge on—we had devoted hours to the pursuit of *puros* already, hadn't we?—but the kinds of fears I'd experienced as we flew into the city began to return to me when I noticed other young men in doorways and alleys making subtle signals to our escorts as we journeyed on through a twisting thicket of streets. I was carrying several thousand dollars in my money belt, and increasingly was sure that our escorts' plan was to rob us. Finally, my worries overcame me, and I refused to continue. When I did, Gabi immediately scolded me for my lack of trust. "This isn't America where you get mugged everywhere. In our culture, this doesn't happen, so stop worrying and come on." Gabi's blanket assurance that no one in Latin America ever initiated a mugging was far from comforting to me, but when she willingly continued, I had little choice but to follow.

Finally we turned down a deserted street and stopped in front of a bolted steel door. As it opened, the brave—or naïve —Gabriela, stepped immediately inside. I followed her with the others. I suddenly imagined news reports of our deaths with the loud metallic thud of the door closing behind me. But we remained alive and well as we climbed three flights of stairs to a small apartment where we were met by a young couple. Their flat was clean, if not spacious, and I noticed new appliances and state-of-the-art electronics, and the cordial and accommodating couple soon presented several boxes of carefully packed cigars for our inspection. We opted for a box of twenty-five Cohibas—reportedly Fidel's favorite cigar—at a cost of ninety dollars, a fraction of the $425 the cigar's sold for in a shop at the Hotel Nacionál; our new acquaintances hailed us a "gypsy" cab in the street—one of the thousands of illegal taxis that flourish in the city—then we offered them our thank yous and bade them farewell, Gabi letting go of the opportunity as we drove back to the hotel to remind me that my sense of foreboding continued to be quite faulty.

After dinner that night, I lit my life's first Cohiba, and Gabi took a snapshot of the Colorado *gusano* about to enjoy one of Fidel's signature cigars, but I couldn't get my *puro* to light. I got dizzy, I sucked so hard, and the people with whom we were dining had the same problem with the cigars I had offered them. They were duds, all twenty-five of them, and at last it dawned on us that we'd been the victims of an elaborately orchestrated scam. Who knew how often our escorts and their *compañeros* executed their impressive con—including the timing required to reach the factory in the minutes after it closed—but we'd had an afternoon of adventure, at least, we reminded ourselves, and I had to acknowledge too that even though we had been brilliantly played for fools, no one had done us the physical harm the memories of my childhood continued to cause me to fear.

Having spent several days in Havana by now, I realized that, while I'd certainly been royally conned, I hadn't been the victim of, nor had I witnessed any other crime or civil disorder—a far cry from what I remembered from the early 1960s, when thousands of people carried weapons in public and fired them indiscriminately. I was struck not only by how safe the streets of contemporary Havana appeared to be, but how genial the Cuban people—the vast majority of whom had little by way of economic opportunity—nonetheless were as they went about their daily lives. We encountered no street confrontations, no begging or open drug use, no machine-gun wielding soldiers, and surprisingly few policemen. Prostitution appeared alive and well at the tourist hotels, but not in the city at large, and compared with other third-world countries I'd visited, the Castro government clearly had succeeded in eliminating the bleakest levels of poverty: if virtually no one was wealthy in Cuba any more, at least no one died of starvation or lacked medical care any longer, and the Cubans with whom we had surprisingly candid conversations were openly proud of that truth.

It was difficult to be critical of the fact that illiteracy was nearly non-existent on the island now, and that everyone received at least a high-school education, tuition-free. And perhaps most impressive to me was the reality that in the forty years I'd been away, racial integration among Cuba's whites, blacks, and browns had become complete.

It was true that a bit of the bigotry and focused class-consciousness that I remembered from my childhood still survived among the eldest Cubans—those who had come of age well before the revolution—but for subsequent generations, that societal scourge now was entirely gone, and it was remarkable to spend time among people who so successfully had learned to look beyond color. And we were amazed as well to observe first-hand one evening how *habaneros* readily accept the shortcomings of their collective lives in return for the basic societal safety net Castro's government has afforded them.

We had traveled for dinner to a highly recommended *paladar*, one of the thousands of in-home restaurants in the city and throughout the country—some licensed and carefully controlled, many others thriving despite having to hide from the gaze of the authorities—and I was eager that night, as I was throughout the trip, to dine once again on the food that always recalls for me the abundance and security of my earliest days. Legal *paladares*, we learned, can include no more than three tables, each seating no more than eight people, and are allowed to serve only chicken and pork—never beef or seafood—in order not to compete with the often-woeful state-owned restaurants. But by common consensus, the black-market paladares tend to serve far better food, and without any menu restrictions, and we discovered that any gypsy-cab driver—the cardboard sign reading TAXI each one kept on his dashboard easy to hide when necessary—was happy to recommend a good restaurant or two in return for a decidedly capitalistic kickback from the paladar's owners.

Gabi and I found we were irresistibly drawn to the illegal cabs and restaurants during our time in Havana, which perhaps was a bit surprising in my case, since I had brought such fear with me to the island. We were impressed by the chances these entrepreneurial people took—getting caught could result in harsh penalties, and, of course, the loss of the businesses they vitally depended on—and too, people who operated in the underground always were willing to speak their minds openly, we observed, whether they were praising the Cuban government or bitterly chastising it or both. On that particular night, we just had sat down at one of the few tables in the leafy courtyard of a careworn Havana house when the power failed. We sat in utter darkness for a few moments before our hosts approached us with candles and bad news: this loss of electricity was an *apagón*, a "big blackout," one of the rolling blackouts that are a regular, if inconvenient, part of life in every Cuban city, a means of helping make do with oil imports slashed in half since the fall of the Soviet Union and the drastic curtailment of that nation's economic support.

The paladar's owners, a young couple who clearly were committed to this free-market means of making a living, were apologetic and expressed their hope that we would join them again on another evening. They explained too that, since taxis—licensed or otherwise— were almost impossible to find in the midst of the *apagón*, we likely would be forced to walk. Once out in the street, in every direction the city appeared as dark as a cave, and for the first time on this trip, Gabriela was as uneasy as I was about the circumstances in which we found ourselves; neither of us could entirely escape our American sensibilities, after all, and we associated power blackouts with muggings, lootings, and many kinds of mischief of which we wanted no part. Very tentatively, and blind as bats, we set off in the direction we presumed would eventually lead us to our hotel, but then something remarkable began to occur: people came out of their doorways with candles in their hands, then their neighbors joined them, most bringing chairs as well. The light from their candles allowed us to make our way through the narrow and winding streets, and as more people emerged from their homes, so did an unmistakable air of festivity. People chatted warmly; they drank and laughed and embraced, as though it had been far too long since an *apagón* had brought them together. On some streets, guitar players sang songs I remembered from my childhood, and on others, battery-operated boom boxes played salsas while children scampered about and occasional couples danced. Sometimes, people called out greetings to us as we passed, and always they were eager to help when we asked for directions; no one appeared angered by the inconvenience of losing power, at least not out in the streets, and everyone we encountered seemed to accept the shared proposition that some nights you simply made the most of the darkness and let your *compañeros* in other neighborhoods use ranges and refrigerators, ceiling fans and lights so you, in turn, could enjoy electricity on another night. This was a collectivist society after all, and with it came both opportunity and sacrifice—as these impromptu gatherings languorously unfolded in the dark and thick-aired city.

The lights of the Hotel Nacionál were blazing as we approached it after we'd walked a couple of hours, and *no, señor*, a doorman offered with an air of pride, the *apagón* hadn't affected the hotel; it and the other tourist hotels always were spared the blackouts. We were hungry and ready to relax after our curious trek, and we drank mojitos and began our meal in the elegant surroundings of the hotel, aware as we perhaps wouldn't have realized before that foreign tourists, in point of fact, now comprise Cuba's elite class, and that the citizens eager to serve them have become the equivalents of people like my parents in years long past—members of an entrepreneurial class willing to work very diligently in order to approximate the living standards of those at the very top. Ordinary Cuban citizens weren't allowed to stay in the tourist hotels, we discovered—even if they somehow had the means to do so, but although they couldn't spend the night at the Nacionál, anyone could pay fifteen dollars a day to enjoy its beautiful swimming pools, a fee more than half of the nation's average monthly wage. Clearly, some people were more equal than others in contemporary Cuba, and the tourism industry—critically important once Soviet support of the economy disappeared—had emerged as the nation's leading source of foreign exchange, bringing two billion dollars a year to the country, more now than the sugar-cane industry, and creating super-classes of foreign visitors and those who attended to them, Fidel focusing his efforts to entice Spanish, Portuguese, Italian, and other developers to invest in massive resort hotels scattered throughout the island.

A few days before, we'd enjoyed an open and interesting conversation with a middle-aged Havana couple, both of who were scientists proud of their contribution to their nation and its revolutionary goals. Yet together, they earned an equivalent of only about fifty dollars a month. In comparison, the enterprising young men who sold us cigars—hard at work in Cuba's underground economy—earned nearly twice that amount in only a couple of hours, and even in the legitimate tourist trade, people lucky enough to find jobs that paid them *pesos convertibles* were assured far better incomes than they otherwise could hope to earn. The dream of every Cuban physician, people cynically told us several times, was to become a bellboy one day at a tourist hotel.

We had hoped prior to arriving in Havana that the people we met would speak frankly with us about their nation and their lives, and in these few days, everyone to whom we put questions seemed to respond candidly and to be eager to share their perspectives, in fact. Universally, people expressed pride and gratitude in the absence of crime and the availability to all of health care and education. But if the foremost measure of the revolution's success was the state of the economy, on the other hand, then it had to be labeled a dismal failure, many insisted. Yet people saw the economy's precarious condition as much more the result of the longstanding U.S. embargo against Cuba than poorly planned and executed internal economic strategies, and it was fascinating to note how enormously popular *el jefe* remained, even when his government did not.

Fidel and his army had accomplished something miraculous in ousting the despotic and corrupt Batista, then, in ways people plainly saw as analogous, he had boldly stood up to the always uneasy and often-threatening power of the United States for two generations by now. It was the insufferable Cuban bureaucracy that was responsible for the terrible over-regulation people endured and the too-constant presence of the government in their lives. Fidel, on the other hand, people insisted, could visit their neighborhoods and examine a problem, then *fix* it; even in his advancing age he remained accessible to the people, they said, and their love and respect for him was very real.

I've always seen intriguing similarities in the early lives of Fidel Castro and my father; yet their fortunes began to veer in dramatically different directions in their thirties. By any measure, Fidel had lived an enormously influential and successful life, and despite the fact that I remained personally aggrieved by how his early edicts and policies shattered the lives of so many middle-class families like my own, I had to acknowledge that, in doing so, he had secured better lives for the poorest in Cuba and who theretofore had suffered the most.

Yet did it have to be one or the other? I hoped the answer was no, as we sat in the sultry and fragrant night, surrounded by opulence and looking forward to traveling tomorrow to a decidedly different Cuba and to the place where my life had commenced. I was convinced that Fidel tragically had missed an opportunity in the immediate aftermath of the revolution to shape an utterly new and democratic society, one in which the terrible inequities of the past were addressed and in which the wealthy were required to share their good fortune and to become responsible—and indeed patri- otic—citizens in ways never before required of them. I believed his long and stubborn adherence to a political and economic ideology now widely discredited and virtually abandoned around the world had cost his nation dearly, and his failure to foster political and per- sonal freedom had been inexcusable. But I felt equally strongly that the U.S. embargo against Cuba had been disastrous—for both coun- tries—and that, ironically, it had empowered Fidel by allowing him to constantly and cunningly remind his people over the years how directly the giant nation to the north interfered with and impeded Cuba's self-government. Even the most insightful people with whom we spoke feared a U.S. invasion, and they were frightened as well that America would work devilishly following Castro's death to foment a civil war, a prospect utterly no one favored.

I understood, and I shared, the huge anger of a legion of Cuban Americans who lost everything they'd worked for at the hands of Fidel—homes, businesses, careers, families, and cultures destroyed in the name of an ideology nobody believed in anymore. But the embargo served only Fidel; it kept Cuba's people locked in isolated poverty—even paper and pencils for schoolchildren were in chroni- cally short supply—and the only succor it offered in the United States was the toxic soup of revenge. I hadn't returned to Cuba to reclaim Papi's properties, as I'd told him I would; that was an impossibili- ty, I'd known all along. Yet I wanted to believe on the night before we set out to discover what remnants, if any, we could find of my father's life on the island, that I honored him nonetheless by trust- ing deep in my heart that Cuba *could* have a robust economy one day and that its people could revel in meaningful personal freedoms. Papi believed in a Cuba in which people made their own way in the best ways they could, and I was getting to know Cuba again, and increas- ingly, I could imagine his dream.

La Villita Candado, with our beloved mango tree still towering in back forty years later

Catorce

The House and the Mango Tree

W E ARRIVED IN SANTA LUCIA AT DUSK, and—I might have predicted it—a swarm of mosquitoes was waiting to greet us. I'd told Gabi shocking mosquito tales from my boyhood, of course, but she'd only imagined Chilean coastal mosquitoes, or Colorado's timid alpine types; she hadn't been prepared for *Santa Lucia* mosquitoes, and she instantly knew she'd never encountered such pests in her life.

I was amazed that the once-very remote beach now boasted a tourist resort, and our hotel's registration desk was located outdoors, as poor luck would have it. In the minutes we waited to check in, we tried futilely to keep the mosquitoes at bay; and my assurance that, at least as my memory served, this was a rather mild invasion did nothing to make us more comfortable or to help us keep the fiends at bay. Then a pesticide truck rolled past and loosed a fine mist into the nearby street that wafted its way toward us. The chemical? I asked. "Es DDT, Señor Vidal," was the answer from the desk clerk, and I turned to Gabriela and managed a humble smile.

We had flown from Havana on Cubana, the country's national airline, and I had the uneasy sense during the journey in an old Russian four-engine prop that a proudly patriotic ground crew kept it in flying trim with little more than baling wire and duct tape. When, a few minutes into the flight, our co-captain began to serve us coffee and I found myself longing to ask him to attend to more pressing matters like keeping us alive, I was reminded how very American I'd become in many ways. But we landed without incident at Camagüey's airport, and I was surprised to discover that the once-primitive road to Santa Lucia had been paved, the three-hour drive I remembered lasting just an hour now.

Relaxing in our room that evening—delighted to be in one of my favorite places in the world and who cared about a few small mosquitoes and a smidgen of DDT?—we attended to our bites, and napped, then went to dinner. When our waiter at the beachside hotel asked us what had brought us to Santa Lucia, I briefly explained that my family had a cottage here in the 1950s before my brothers and I traveled to the United States via *Operación Pedro Pan*. I was a bit taken aback when his eyes quickly filled with tears, and more surprised still when he hugged me. *"Bienvenido a su casa,"* he warmly said. Welcome home. As Gabriela and I enjoyed our dinner, other waiters came to our table to introduce themselves and welcome me back to Santa Lucia, and when even the chef and his kitchen crew came out to similarly make me feel at home, I was both overwhelmed and perplexed.

None of these people knew me, yet the briefest sharing of my story had clearly moved them. Then, at last, we learned that a recent and enormously successful book by Cuban authors Ramón Torreira Crespo and José Buajasan Marrawi had exposed an alleged and incredibly complex CIA plot from early in the 1960s to send unaccompanied Peter Pan kids to the U.S. as a lure to entice their parents to leave the island, the book comparing the fourteen thousand youngsters like me with Elian Gonzalez, the Cuban boy who, a year before our trip, had fled to Florida by raft with his mother before becoming the subject of an international tug-of-war and a media frenzy in both nations. Throughout Cuba, six-year old Elian by now had achieved a stature little short of Che Guevara's, we'd learned in the week since our arrival, and for everyone at the hotel, I became in the subsequent days the next best thing to meeting the boy himself. I'd already angered friends and family members in the U.S. with my opinion that because his mother had died, Elian's father alone now had the right to determine where Elian would live, the same right the parents of every Peter Pan child once had. Since I therefore belonged in the Elian-in-Cuba camp—a position few Cuban Americans took, to my chagrin—it was easy for me to serve as his stand-in in Santa Lucia, and the hotel's staff unofficially adopted me throughout our stay.

The following morning, I set out early along the beach to see if I could find the houses my parents and aunts and uncles once had owned. After walking for about a kilometer, I found the houses that belonged to Tio Antoñico and Tio Aquiles and their families, exactly where I expected them to be; one had been converted into a small shop, the other into a folksy sea-creature museum, filled with stiff sea-horses and clear jars containing pickled octupi. Our house, to my surprise, was even closer at hand—it was part of the hotel complex where we were staying, and was used now to house the deep-sea divers who escorted tourists like us on excursions to the enormous coral reef that lay offshore. The house was far smaller than it had been in the 1950s—or at least I remembered a much larger and grander place—but the carport Papi had transformed into our boxing ring still stood and appeared capable of yet hosting another fight. Papi loved to dive—he'd always been enchanted by fish and the surreal and silent world that lay beneath the surface of the sea—and it seemed fitting somehow that divers now occupied his house, that they lived in the place where he had been happiest, above the water and below it.

Santa Lucia had been substantially developed in the four decades since my last visit, yet these three houses quite wonderfully remained, and my mind was flooded with memories of the most carefree days of my life. The small *muellecito* that reached out in the shallow bay had all but collapsed, but parts of it still stood, derelict and forlorn, yet how I remembered the pleasures of fishing from that pier on long, sun-drenched days and soft and humid nights, my brothers and I the young men of the sea in that place, sometimes even landing barracudas and small sharks that swam too close to the shore. I loved the warm and crystalline water, the sand crabs we battled after dark on the wet and sloping beach, and I loved being a part of my big extended family, none of us acknowledging a care in the world during the days we spent beside the sea, and a *real* family we were in the memories that overwhelmed me that morning while Gabi still slept and the sun remained low in the sky. For the first time in forty years, I was truly at home. I stood with my toes dug into the sand in a place that was *mine* in a way Pueblo and Denver simply never had been. I'd never live here again, I knew—and knew, too, I didn't want to—but to *have* a home, one I could name and return to was a gift I didn't know I needed until it was given to me.

Before we'd left Denver that April, I had written to my mother's first cousin, Josefina De Para, to tell her of our journey and our hope that we could visit her at her home in Camagüey. She and my mother had corresponded enough over the years that I knew Josefina's husband, Gonzalo Acosta, and their son, Gonzalito, spent much of their time in Santa Lucia, finding whatever work they could among the tourists. When I explained my relation to the two men to my new and dear friends at the hotel, they were eager to help me reconnect with them. Gabi and I would need to take a taxi to a nearby hamlet called Playa del Coco, they told us as someone summoned a cab-driver—I never would have dreamed of cabs in Santa Lucia—who said, yes, of course, he would be honored to ferry us to Gonzalo's door.

But I was shocked when, after a short drive, he pulled to a stop in front of shack built out of salvaged boards, with no windows or doors and a tin roof that left parts of tiny building exposed to the open sky. The driver waited while I got out and went to the doorway, knocked on its teetering frame and calling out, "Hello, is this the home of Gonzalo Acosta?" And from far within the dark shack I heard a reply: "Guille, Guille, could that possibly be you?"

Gonzalo had grown very old; I shouldn't have been surprised. He wore only a pair of khaki shorts and sandals, and was so arthritic that he was literally bent in half at the waist as he moved toward me. He walked with a cane as he made his way to the shaft of light at the doorway, and, as I rushed to him, he ignored his pain, stood upright, and gave me a powerful embrace, our eyes filling with tears. Gabi joined us and the two of them met each other with a warm hug as well, and when Gonzalo shouted the news of our arrival, Gonzalito limped toward us from around the corner. He was only a year older than I was, but he too had grown old; one leg appeared much shorter than the other and it was hard to imagine that he was the athletic cousin I once ran with for hours. The two of us embraced again for the first time in forty years, and then Gonzalo insisted that the occasion called for a *vasito* of rum.

Inside, the shack was utterly empty except for two small beds with mosquito nets hanging above them, a small wooden table and two chairs. Gonzalito found two boxes that could serve as chairs as well, and his father filled the only two glasses they possessed with rum and we shared them all around. Gonzalo's eyes remained clear and astonishingly blue and Gabi quickly could see what a handsome man he had been in his prime, yet now his eyes also evidenced deep sadness and resignation. As we chatted, he described how his charterboat business had slowly collapsed after the revolution, how he was solely devoted now to selling rum and cigars to tourists for a few dollars a week, most of which money he sent to Josefina in Camagüey. Months often passed, father and son explained, without seeing their families; hitchhiking was their only means of travel between the beach and the city, and there was little assurance that other travelers would offer them rides.

Gonzalito's life might have taken a different turn, he explained. He had been such a promising baseball player that he had been selected for entry into the national Olympic-training program, but a severely broken leg in 1969 had abruptly ended his athletic career. He had struggled for years to find good work and now was a cabana boy who attended to the needs of the tourists at Playa del Coco, and he too sent all the dollars to Camagüey that he could. I told both men how proud I was of the ways in which they had endured their hardships, assuring them, too blithely, that even with their struggles there was always something to live for.

But Gonzalito turned, then calmly and without meaning to challenge me said something that haunted me. "What *is* there to live for?" He paused to take a sip of rum, "I have no dreams. I have no aspirations. I get up every morning and do the same thing. I hope I will make a dollar or two—or I will not—and there is nothing else I can do. Every day will be this way until the day I die."

I was stunned by his words—for an instant I imagined myself as a young man full of hope who'd had to settle for a destitute life as a cabana boy—so I offered no other platitudes. No one spoke again, until Gonzalo told us we should be on our way. Dusk was approaching and the mosquitoes soon would arrive; he and his son would need to crawl under their nets for the night and we would need to be in the taxi to avoid the swarm. But we made plans before we quickly departed to return for them the following evening and to take them to dinner, and yes, said Gonzalo, they would love to dine with us.

Inside the cab and out of my cousins' sight, I wept. I couldn't be sure why I was so moved, except that I understood now that my family's suffering over the years had been nothing compared to theirs. Whatever had befallen us, we always could cling to hope, and always—inevitably—our lives changed for the better. But hope had abandoned Gonzalito and his father decades before, and I cried, thinking what my life might have been like had I remained in Cuba; my tears flowed so powerfully, I suppose, because for the first time in my life perhaps I could confirm that leaving this island had been the best thing to do, the *only* choice Papi and Mami could make.

Gonzalo and Gonzalito were washed, shaved, carefully combed and perfumed and dressed in their very best clothes when we arrived the following evening, and we were delighted to see them again. Gone from their faces was the resignation they wore so heavily the day before, and in its place was eager anticipation: neither man had dined in a restaurant in more than forty years.

Before we reached our hotel, Gonzalo insisted we make a brief detour to the see our old beach house. As it happened, his grandson Macao was one of the young scuba-divers who lived in the house, and Gonzalo therefore wasn't reticent to make an unannounced visit. But I was taken aback when, just seconds after we were invited in, he proclaimed to the several deeply sun-darkened men who were at home, "The real owner of the house is here." It seems he wanted these men who were still young and full of life that once the world had been a different place, and that it was a world to which he still bore allegiance. I didn't know what to say, and it was an awkward moment for everyone; we stood uncomfortably and simply talked about the reef and the diving and all the changes I'd noted in Santa Lucia, then Gonzalo put his arm around me and added, "Don't forget, this is all still yours."

My father always had liked Gonzalo—he was willing to forgive the fact that Gonzalo had married into my mother's family—and I know Gonzalo cared for him in turn, and as he spoke those words I was chilled by a sudden sense that Papi was speaking to me through his old friend, reminding me of the promise I'd made to him to reclaim what once was his. Old and wizened and bent Gonzalo had become Papi's accomplice in this quest, and my father's spirit suddenly seemed to fill the small house, now divided into two apartments and home to six of the young divers. I lingered alone for a few moments in the carport as we left, remembering how purposeful, and how happy, Papi had been as he taught us to box, and I silently thanked him for what he'd taught me there long ago. Unlike my brother Juan, I'd never amounted to much as a fighter, but I understood, thanks to Papi, that in some ways I'd always been boxing for Cuba—believing in the paradise I was certain it could be, cheering for the good fortune of all its people—and struggling too for the best life I could make for myself in all the years since my father first had tied gloves to my fists and asked me to show him what I could do. Boxing was art, Papi believed, as well as a sweet science; boxing was survival against great odds, boxing was proving to yourself that you were strong and secure and that your single life mattered—under the roof of a carport, in an island nation, and abroad in the wide and exigent world.

Once more, the staff at the hotel restaurant eagerly awaited our arrival that evening, but they were taken aback and suddenly uneasy when they saw that we planned for Gonzalo and Gonzalito to join us; in a country purportedly absent class divisions and where everyone is equal, these two Cuban men—and simply *because* they were Cuban—technically were not allowed to dine in the hotel. Yet as soon as I made it clear that they were my guests and that they *would* be joining us and that I wanted them not only to be served all the food and drink they desired, but to be treated with great respect as well, the waiters' attitudes immediately softened and they welcomed us into the dining room as if the four of us were Fidel's closest of kin, bustling quickly about to ensure that Gonzalo was comfortably seated and that both men had rum drinks in their hands before they could ask for them. And the hours we spent at the table were wonderful. Eighty-five year-old Gonzalo joined the restaurant's roaming musicians to sing dozens of songs from the old days, and Gonzalito ate and drank with obvious pleasure and appreciation, this day, at least, very different from every other. All of us laughed, told stories, offered toasts to each other's heath—Gonzalo telling me he would live five more years if I would promise to return in that time—and toasts as well to our beloved Cuba, to the United States, to friendship and peace and the promise of lives well lived.

The following morning, we rented a car at the resort to take us to Camagüey, but as soon as I'd completed the rental transaction at the front desk, I was astonished to be informed that, should we hit and kill a cow en route, that transgression could be punished by a twenty-year imprisonment without possibility of parole. What? I asked, presuming he was joking, but then quickly seeing in his expression that he decidedly was not. "How could this be so?"

He explained that this law against bovi-slaughter was a peculiarity of the "special period," and had been made necessary when, in the depths of the depression, accidents involving cars and cows sharply increased, and the Castro government determined that the increase in road kill was a clever means for individuals to augment their food supply. To stop it, government officials chose to implement an unimaginably stiff penalty, one that dramatically slashed the cow-killing incidents, yet the law remained on the books, and I, it goes without saying, slowed the rented car to a crawl every time we so much as saw a shadow cross the road during our drive to Camagüey.

Gonzalo and Gonzalito had told us how difficult it could be to hitchhike between the beach and the city, despite the fact—and again by law—that Cubans were required to ferry hitchhikers when they had room for them, private automobiles in Cuba meant to serve everyone's need, at least in theory. Yet that regulation, the desk-agent assured us, didn't apply to us—tourists were more equal in this regard than were Cuban citizens. But in solidarity with my cousins, and because we remained eager to speak with everyone we could throughout the trip, we offered rides to a young mother and her daughter, three older women, a very old man and a middle-aged couple in the sixty kilometers between Santa Lucia and Camagüey, as well as a furiously angry mulatto woman in her mid-sixties whose experience in traveling that day echoed those that commonly befell Gonzalo and Gonzalito. She had an important medical appointment in the city, she shouted, but no one would stop for her. "What the hell is the matter with these, Cubans?" she asked, her voice still loud and acidic. "Who do they think they are? Do they think these cars are theirs only? They are mine, too." In the spirit of the revolution, we couldn't disagree and we drove her to the door of the hospital where she was overdue before she bade us a perfunctory, and still embittered, goodbye.

Gabriela was impressed that I could readily find my way to the Plaza de las Mercedes after having been away from my hometown for four decades, but as we negotiated the warren of winding and narrow streets, I was shocked by how rural, how poor, and how forlorn Camagüey appeared. It was Cuba's third-largest city, after all, and in my youth I had been certain that it was a very sophisticated and surpassingly important place, but modern Camagüey felt captured in time somehow, a time even before my own. The city was crowded with people, to be sure, but there were few cars; and these *camagüeyanos* simply walked, rode bicycles, or whatever farm animals they owned that were stout enough to carry them.

When we reached it, the plaza was far smaller than I was sure it once had been, and that same tendency to shrink over time had transformed the capacious storehouse of furniture that once was Casa Vidal into something more akin to a small corner store. The first floor of the building still was turquoise, I was surprised to see, but was so faded and chipped that it seemed possible that it hadn't been received a new coat of paint since the days when my brothers and I would burst into the store in search of Papi. The space was now occupied by an artisan center, and was filled with local arts and crafts, and the four apartments on the upper two floors that my father had begun to build had been completed sometime after he fled the city in 1964. It seemed strange to me, but the large sign that hung on one side of the building reading "Casa Vidal" never had been taken down, but each of the letters were gone, leaving only their outlines in darker, less sun-bleached and weathered paint. Yet discovering a different sign, this one above the door that led up to the apartments, brought tears to my eyes in ways that caught me by surprise. It was painted turquoise still, just as I remembered it, and was roughly a meter square. Edificio Vidal, Padre Valencia N° 2, it read in black letters, and seeing it filled me with a curious but deeply satisfying kind of joy. I'd never forgotten the building's address, of course, and remembered seeing that same small sign every time I visited the plaza, the building, my father, and my Tio Antoñico, but I never dreamed the name of the street would remain the same, let alone the possibility that the structure would remain the "Vidal Building."

"They still remember him! They still remember him," I shouted gleefully, and I hoped in that moment that, akin to the literal way in which my father remained alive in me, he knew now that this evidence still existed of what he had built and what once had given him great pride. No one I spoke with—people inside the artisan's center, shopkeepers in adjacent stores, a woman who lived in a second-story apartment—knew the name Roberto Emiliano Vidal, but, to a person, they seemed genuinely interested to hear a bit of the building's history and to meet the proud son of this Señor Vidal who had ensured that his building would last for a very long time. Papi was with me again, I began to be sure, and although, just as in Santa Lucia, I couldn't claim this building in my father's name as he had hoped, I could at least further his memory, and the recollection not just of him but of the work he had done and the measure of the man he was, and a sense of accomplishment and of peace swelled inside me. I thought for a moment of Ernesto LaRua, who I hadn't considered in a long time—Papi's employee who had so doggedly persecuted him and hoped to see him rot in prison or die. LaRua hadn't succeeded, and Papi's life, though challenged repeatedly, had not been utterly destroyed. That was certain, and it seemed sure now as well that, in a country where stories from the past kept the present animated and meaningful, these few camagüeyanos now would tell stories about my father for as long, at least, as I remained alive.

We had promised Gonzalo and Gonzalito that we would visit their families during our time in Camagüey, and although I wanted to in any case, I think I understood during the hours we spent with Gonzalo's wife Josefina and her family why it had been important to father and son for us to have a sense of the fruits of their labors and what their hard work in Santa Lucia had accomplished. In contrast to the windowless shack at the beach where the two men lived in such stark conditions, Josefina and two of her grown children, and Gonzalito's wife Mirna and their two children lived in adjacent well-kept homes on a leafy Camagüey street. The two houses were modern and attractive, and the two families' lives were good, they reported. Everyone had jobs that suited them and that helped them contribute to their collective prosperity; they were proud of what they had accomplished and deeply appreciative of the sacrifices their husbands in Santa Lucia made on their behalf. But we encountered something quite different when we visited Josefina's first-cousin, my mother's brother Nene.

In his seventies now, Nene still was whispered about throughout the city as *el jorobado*, the hunchback, Josefina confided in us. He never had worked for anyone other than my grandfather and had utterly depended on his family during his long life for his survival. Yet despite his terrible disability, he had two grown children—Juancito, named after my grandfather, Dr. Ramos, and Martica, named in honor of my mother. In the years following the revolution Nene had been able to remain in the large and once-opulent home that had housed my grandfather's clinic, several of his assistants, and his family. It was on the street in front of that grand house that Fidel had taken my hand in the first days of January 1959, at a time when Papi and Mami assured us that Cuba had been blessed by him and his great courage and resolve, and that the future was very bright. The street seemed little changed when Gabriela and I arrived, and from the exterior, the house continued to have a look of substance, even grace about it.

Nene's daughter, my cousin Martica, who hadn't yet been born when my brothers and I left the island, answered the door. She was dark-haired and pretty and the shape of her face made her look like someone to whom I was closely related. Martica had been expecting us, and greeted us warmly, and as we went inside, the house appeared familiar and quite different at the same time, but I couldn't immediately ascertain why. The ornate and beautiful furniture, mirrors, and paintings were long gone, all of them, either bartered or sold over the years for the few pesos they brought. The same was true, Martica said, of the wing that had housed the clinic; all its medical equipment had been pressed into use elsewhere many years before. Yet there was something else that wasn't as I remembered it, and at last I recognized that a courtyard had been created where the dining room once had been. But as we moved in that direction I was stunned to recognize that the room was open to the air simply because its roof had collapsed. The fallen tiles and stringers and trusses had been carted away, and Martica's brother Juancito now kept a goat and a handful of chickens there, the milk and eggs they provided evidently an acceptable tradeoff to their dung and the wind and the rain.

Sitting alone on a wooden stool in a room adjacent to this unanticipated modification of the house sat a tiny man I knew must be Nene. The shafts of bright light angling in from above the dining room silhouetted him where he sat—his head sunk into his shoulders and his spine sharply crowned and bent—and he seemed from a short distance away to be a kind of gnome. I had warned Gabi that Tio Nene, even forty years before, had been deeply disfigured, doing what little I could to help her prepare to meet him, yet it was I who had to struggle to retain my composure when Martica escorted us over to her father.

Nene wasn't wearing a shirt—a piece of clothing I'd certainly never seen him go without when I was a boy—and I was horrified by what his semi-nakedness exposed. Great dark, fatty tumors bulged out from his skin everywhere on his body; his arms and legs were pocked like the tentacles of an octopus. The bones of his trunk were twisted into impossible shapes, and his back was far more than hunched, I could see: an enormous growth made a mountain out of his spine, and a hole the size of a tennis ball burrowed deep into the front of his chest beneath his ribs. His head, though small, was normally shaped, but his face also was spotted with dark, fleshy tumors. I had to consciously suppress an automatic gag reflex, and I was struck as I struggled to do so how very diligently, if lovingly, my grandparents and my mother had worked over the years to keep the totality of Nene's disfigurement a protected family secret. I knew from long ago that Mami's brother had been dealt an extremely difficult hand, but I hadn't understood until that moment precisely why people always had whispered that the two of them were the beauty and the beast. Nene *was* bestial, and he had grown totally deaf, Martica explained. When we moved in front of him so he could see that we had arrived, he responded only subtly, nodding more than smiling, and as Martica formally introduced Gabriela to her father, my remarkable wife smiled broadly and went to Nene and gave him a warm embrace. Following her lead, I gave my uncle a hug as well and caught his eyes and told him, honestly, how happy I was to see him after all these years. I told him I was Guille, as Martica already had done, and told him my mother had asked me to give him her deep love.

Nene offered no words in return, and ending a brief but awkward silence, Martica said her father now was very old and had grown tired of living. Losing his hearing had robbed him of the connection to his family that always had sustained him, she said, and he had only two remaining wishes—to die in this house in which he'd lived since he was born and in which his parents had died, and to see his beloved sister Marta again.

I didn't try to explain to my uncle how my mother *could* return to Cuba to see him—just as I had returned—but how she also was deeply convinced she could not. Even a brief trip to Camagüey would be impossibly painful for her to endure, she repeatedly had said; she couldn't bear being reminded again of everything that was gone, couldn't face the absence of all she had loved in Cuba except her brother himself.

Martica insisted that we stay for lunch, and although she, her brother, and her father lived with a gaping hole in the roof of their house, Gabi and I noted to our relief that their refrigerator was full of food. Neither Martica nor Juancito had jobs and the three lived solely on the minimal disability income Nene received from the national government. They owned the house, of course, and apparently weren't forced by housing authorities to have others live there with them, but, of course, money always was scarce. The only few words Nene spoke directly to me during our visit, in fact, were to say he knew Marta had sent money with me and that he wanted it—money we offered him after we'd augmented hers with some of our own.

As the five of us ate, Gabi and I began to get to know these two cousins I'd never met before; Nene couldn't hear our conversation, and he seemed caught inside a dismal and very isolated world of his own, and as I spent time with him and the lovely young woman he'd named after his absent sister, I began to see in ways I never had before what my mother had been challenged by since she was a very small girl.

Mami always had called Nene's disorder polio—that was the term her physician father always insisted on—but, of course, my uncle suffered a condition far more uncommon, complex, and profound.

As I sat across the table from him, I couldn't help thinking of Joseph Merrick, the nineteenth-century "elephant man" in England who suffered from an extremely rare disease called Proteus syndrome; I knew, too, that a disease called neurofibromatosis caused malformations of bones and the growth of benign but terrible tumors along nerve pathways. Perhaps one of those two, or yet some other disorder that began to beset him very early in his life, was the thing that had destroyed his parents happiness, and his own, and had severely compromised my mother in ways she never overcame.

I began to see, as I sat in my grandparents' collapsing house in Camagüey, what devastating mistakes they had made in responding to Nene's illness. They smothered Nene with their love and care, but never allowed him to make a life for himself, never assured him that he had anything to offer. They smothered their son with pity, and he had lived his life believing that his parents' and his children's mercy were all that allowed him to survive. The mother of his children had worked as a maid for Nene's parents, and her attentions too, he surely believed, were born out of pity as well.

Toward my mother, my grandparents had shown only indifference once Nene's disability became acute. They abandoned her to be raised by maids, I now truly understood, and she was able only to wonder whether her parents loved her in the way they so obviously loved their son, wondering too whether they blamed *her* for her brother's illness, whether they wished it had befallen her instead. She deeply loved her parents and her brother, but she received solely her brother's love in return, and, as she matured, the only love she knew was directly linked to terrible infirmity and isolation from the rest of the world.

My mother had *wanted* to love her three sons with all her heart, I began to understand, but she had never been taught how. And if my brothers and I had been briefly orphaned and suffered for it, I now could see that Mami had been orphaned far longer and in ways much more brutalizing to her. When she became an adult, she likely believed she could do nothing more than expose that lifelong and festering wound in hopes of winning sympathy from those around her, presuming, like Nene, that pity was the world's sole route to love.

Nothing else in my return to Cuba had taught me as much as this visit and this meal had allowed me to begin to see. I'd discovered at Gonzalo's shack that my parents *did* do the right thing when they chose to send their sons away; I'd discovered in the Plaza de las Mercedes that Papi had built something in his home country that endured, and that something of *him* remained here as well. But as I watched my aged and nearly lifeless uncle pick at his food, unable to hear the words we spoke around him, I'd begun to see something immensely important about who my mother was and what she had undergone. Deeply loving her brother had brought her only inextinguishable pain, and throughout the remainder of her life, she had been as twisted internally as her brother was for all of Camagüey to see. Mami, could no more completely love us, I began to understand that day, than Tio Nene could stand up tall and proud. I could now see that she had been asked to overcome many more obstacles than Papi, my brothers and I could ever dream of.

I had been able to steer us without a misstep through Camagüey's maze of streets to Casa Vidal and my uncle and cousins' houses, so I wasn't surprised when I similarly found La Villita Candado at Carretera Central 160 Oeste, precisely where it had stood for sixty years. But we had lived in a palace, my memory assured me, one surrounded by a wilderness rich with adventure and delight. This house—this place that both was and wasn't the house where I was born, I could see from the street—was small and modest, even by Cuban measures. Its stucco walls still were cream-colored and its flat roof still extended over a porch supported by twin arches. But how could I once have hidden behind the wall that surrounded the house? It was far too short for that. Gabi and I stood near our rented car and studied the place that had meant so much to me in so many ways— the house where I'd first known belonging and protection, where I began to explore and to discover, the house in which I first cowered in fear of my mother and witnessed my parents' awful wars, the house I longed for on cold and endless nights at the asylum when I had traveled far away.

The two of us no doubt were an unusual sight, and it wasn't long before a young man walked up to us and asked, "What are you doing here? Why do you keep staring at this house?" My latent and still potent fears rushed back to me. Was he G-2? Would my former neighbors assault me if they discovered the *gusano* had returned? But Gabi spoke up immediately. "This is the house he was born in," she explained, and the *chico*'s eyes brightened, and as they did I began to relax.

"Why didn't you say so? See that man over there?" he asked, pointing to a lean and angular man in the cluster of people who had begun to gather nearby. As the young man pointed, we caught the other fellow's eye and he began to run toward us, and once more I had to fight a desperate urge to flee. But he held out his hand as he approached, asking, somewhat breathlessly, "Are you one of the Vidal children?" When I told him I was, he smiled broadly and gestured as if to usher us toward the porch. "You must come in. I insist."

The man didn't tell us his name, and I was too overwhelmed to ask, but he was one of the house's eight residents, he explained, and, of course, he understood that surely I very much wanted to see my childhood home again after such a long absence. As we neared the front door, it suddenly seemed as if I were watching the scene unfold from a short distance away, watching myself at fifty years of age entering a house I'd last walked out of forty years before. It all seemed other-worldly, surreal, and yet unmistakably, there I was to observe it with my own eyes.

Inside, we met the other residents who were at home, some of whom were related to each other, and others who were not. A very elderly woman had lived in the house since my parents' departure; she had been the *arrimada*, common-law wife, of the military officer to whom my father had given the house in return for his assistance securing my parents' visas. She was frail and weak and said little, except to offer that she remembered my parents and that she had been happy here during the half of her life she had spent in the house.

Virtually nothing inside had been changed in the years since Papi lovingly attended to his fish in the aquarium near the dining room table and my brothers and I bounded like supermen from bed to bed in our room. In many rooms, the plaster was falling away from the walls, and it seemed very possible that the house's interior hadn't been painted in all those years. The tub, toilet, and sink in the bathroom were the same ones I remembered, but they were chipped and rusted, and many tiles had fallen from the walls. The kitchen too was just as we'd left it, and simply in stepping inside, I could smell again the wonderful aromas Gladis divined from her pots and pans. I remembered how Kiko and Toto and I had loved to play with our toys in the room Emilita shared with Romelia—to their chagrin, no doubt—remembered too how Mami's perfume was a subtle constancy, remembered Papi's big-band records filling the house with music.

Outside, the once-lush garden had been stripped virtually bare. The palm trees had been cut down, and all the fruit trees were gone except for the towering mango in which I had climbed so high in my youth. I was happy to see the old *tinajon*, the clay pot in which tadpoles swam in the collected rainwater and fascinated my brothers and me, and I laughed as I showed Gabi the neighbor's window through which my brothers and I and our buddies Kiko and Oriol had thrown dog shit onto the freshly made love-bed. Every house surrounding La Villita Candado appeared to remain virtually unchanged, and all that appeared new anywhere in my field of vision was the master suite on the back of the house Papi had just begun to build at the time we went away. Once completed, it had become the habitat of the man who had invited us into the house. Then I noticed too that the old garden shed had been converted into a kitchen; the residents planned to operate a paladar, seating guests beneath the great mango tree, the man explained, but in the seven months since they had been licensed they had had no diners, and because Camagüey was far from most tourist routes, it seemed unlikely that their restaurant ever would thrive.

While we stood near the dusty, rain-splattered tables, a boy came up to announce that his grandfather had known my parents and hoped to speak with me, and a friend accompanying him was bursting with the separate news that our neighbors, the Marin family, still lived next door, and that Kiko and Oriol lived only a block from here. He would run to get them, he said, before he bounded away. We excused ourselves to go out to the sidewalk to greet these people, and as we did I was stunned to see that *hundreds* of people now stood in front of the house. Neighborhood children had rushed to spread the news that one of Pedro Pan's lost boys had found his way home, and fully three hundred of them blocked the Carretera Central, traffic stopped, the crowd animated and festive and apparently fascinated to catch a glimpse of the Vidal *niño* who very few of them remembered, to witness this very rare homecoming and be a tangential part of it, at least.

Following close behind the boy whose grandfather was eager to meet me, we walked to an adjacent house where a man missing a leg at the hip sat on his front step. He had lost his limb in the war of liberation in Angola, he explained, while a soldier in the Cuban army, but in the days long before, he wanted me to know, his father had tended my father's car, tuning it, changing its oil, washing and waxing it regularly on my father's behalf. As he continued to speak, remembering how beautiful my mother was, and how her brother had been badly crippled, I realized suddenly and with a start that this *had* to be Pillin Castellano, the same man who incessantly harassed my parents in the years following the revolution, who had been so eager to turn them in as traitors and seize control of their house. But he didn't mention that damaging role he'd played in our lives, thinking perhaps that I had been too young to know of it, or perhaps he'd even forgotten it himself: that was decades ago, and animosities and ill will do, over time, crumble and collapse like plaster and tiled roofs. Speaking with Pillin certainly raised no resentment in me, but it was odd to hear him remembering my mother and father so warmly and with such respect, and I couldn't help wonder whether instead of viewing them as traitors to the revolution, he now imagined my parents as people who had made a sound, if profoundly difficult choice. And part of me, I'll admit, was pleased to note that in a kind of atonement for those aged misdeeds, Pillin Castellano now was on record among the huge crowd that Roberto and Marta Vidal had been fine people, neighbors he was proud to know.

Our playmate Kiko Marin had lived on the edge as a kid, always getting himself into self-inflicted trouble, and it seemed he had lived the balance of his life in much the same manner. In the moments after he arrived on this crowded and curious scene, offering me a warm and enveloping embrace as he did, still-handsome Kiko laughed at himself as he explained that he been *arrimado* to ten different women over the years, a number he seemed both proud of and bemused by, yet he assured me that he had set his life on a new track and that now he lived alone. He'd been a schoolteacher since completing school himself, he said, and there was one more thing: he had a brain tumor, and the doctor had told him he didn't have long to live.

Kiko's brother, Oriol, had been married only a single time, had three children, and recently had retired from the factory where he'd worked making farm equipment for thirty-three years. It was hard to imagine that he had done precisely the same labor during every one of those nine thousand days on the job, and, no older than I was, Oriol now was stooped and aged and all his teeth were gone. Both brothers wanted me to know that they never had gone hungry and that they and their families always had met their basic needs, but life had possessed little luster or color or possibility, they agreed, and they didn't envision how it ever would. I was saddened when Kiko, whose life would end soon, used the word *monótono*, monotonous, to describe the shape of most all his days, yet this clearly had become a very special day and the two brothers were delighted to see me, as I was to see them, and for a few moments we remembered much of our mischief, remembered our assaults on the summit of the mighty mango tree, remembered our trips to Santa Lucia and our bouts in the boxing ring.

As the three of us posed for photographs, my arms around these stalwart allies of my youth, they swore that they forgave me for failing to say goodbye as we rushed away in September 1961, and they said they could see that I'd married well and clearly had made a good life. The crowd—this astonishingly large group of people who evidently wanted only to glimpse what a *camagüeyano* who had made his way to America was like—never pressed us too close. People seemed to respect my desire to chat privately for a time with old and dear friends; no one ever approached me with a flurry of questions, nor did people collectively offer applause, but I was a true fascination for them, and the crowd didn't dissipate in all the time we were there. They were utter strangers, yet they had gathered because we bore roots in common, and just as I couldn't help but imagine what my life might have been like had I remained among them, surely much of their interest that day was in similarly sensing the lives they might have had if *they* had fled like me. "They're proud of you," Kiko whispered to me as he saw me momentarily attempting to take in the totality of the impromptu *reunión* underway in the Carretera Central. "We're proud of you."

I wanted to be alone for a moment, to sort it all out, if I could— to silently see that house without the intrusion of conversation and to determine if it truly still meant something to me, to gather too a sense of whether I deserved or could be comfortable with this extraordinary outpouring of interest and good will. I whispered a few words to Gabi, and then made my way to the back of the house once more, where I could be alone. I considered climbing high in the mango tree, but opted instead only to give its stalwart trunk a strong hug. I'm not entirely sure why I did, yet I knew that singular tree mattered immensely to me, more perhaps than anything else I'd been lucky to encounter again at La Villita Candado, this house that someone had found inside a bar of soap sometime before I was born. Like those long-ago people who had won the house, I too had been blessed with good fortune. Returning to Cuba had made that huge truth far more apparent than ever before, and as I stood in the shade of the mango, words I hadn't remembered in decades entered my mind again—an old Cuban saying I heard spoken in Papi's ciga-rette-graveled voice: *No hay mal que por bien no venga*. Out of the worst of it all, good things come.

And it was true, wasn't it? For all of us. Had Papi opted to stay in Cuba, how could he have endured a life like Gonzalo had been forced to accept? He was far too proud, and his pride and his stubbornness might well have been met with bullets in the end. Watching every-thing in her world collapse—including her childhood home—would, without question, have driven my mother over the edge on which she precariously had been able to maintain her life in the United States. For our parts, my brothers and I would have lived lives like Gonzal-ito, Kiko, and Oriol had we remained in Cuba, and nothing about that would have been impossible for me to accept save the monoto-ny. I had been seized by that word when Kiko spoke it, and I realized that a drift into boredom and ennui was the one turn I could nev-er allow my life to take. I hadn't spent a monotonous moment until now, and everything with which I'd had to struggle and endure had enriched me. I'd long since made my peace with Jim McCoy—who, after all, had grown up in the asylum himself and knew nothing else, nothing better. I'd come to freeing and forgiving terms, too, with the Catholic Church and the Optimist Club, with the blue-eyed bullies with whom I'd always had to battle and the America that kept me an outsider forever. I'd been fortunate to bond with my father—not at the beginning of my life but at the end of his—and I held hard to the hope, to the certainty, that one day my children and I similarly would strike the peace that would allow us to recognize and appreciate the depth of what links us together. I had the love of an amazing woman who helped make me whole, two remarkable stepdaughters, Nicol and Veronica, who had warmly welcomed me into their lives and allowed me a second opportunity for fatherhood, and two brothers to whom I'd be indebted forever. And I realized, too, that I was eager to see Mami again, and tell her with a flurry of words in English and Spanish everything I could about the Cuba that still held her heart and the Cuba where she no longer belonged.

Out of the worst of it all, good things come, my dead father had seemed to whisper into my head as I stood beside the house in which I first had struggled to make him proud. Out of everything that had befallen me since I fled La Villita Candado, *I* had emerged—humble and grateful and sometimes bowed, yet proud of myself in ways that Papi indeed had become proud of me in the end. Like the mango tree against which I leaned and quietly cried, I understood that I was deeply and stoutly rooted in the rich black soil of the island of Cuba. Yet like that tree, too, I knew what it was like to live beyond the ground, battered by weather and torrents but blessed too by bright sun and the breezes of independence and possibility. I wanted to believe I was a man made of many branches, and that I would grow and reach out and upward until my days were done.

No hay mal que por bien no venga.

CASA VIDAL: Remnants of Papi's Cuban dreams.

Guillermo Vincente Vidal at Casa Vidal

A Final Word

or five years, I labored to write this book. Somehow afraid that the story would never be told and die off with me, I spent many long hours on late and sleepless nights reliving events from my early life and remembering the stories chronicled by my parents that were part of my family's folklore. I had often thought about writing this story in my younger days, but I never found the motivation to do so until, following my father's death, I returned to Cuba in 2001 for the first time in forty years. The memories of my family's life before and after the revolution, and then in exile in the United States, became so vivid that I seemed unable to escape them, and it was only in writing about my family's history that I was able to free myself from the burdens those memories imposed on my contemporary life.

For decades, I had struggled to reconcile myself to my parents' decisions and actions. I could see their myriad faults all-too-clearly, but it was exceedingly hard for me to recognize the value and purpose in what they had done. Aided by the perspective and wisdom that time offers, I came to understand the profound difficulty and true significance of the sacrifices they made. This understanding offered the spiritual fuel I needed to write, and this book is my attempt to make amends to my parents for my lack of comprehension of what they had been forced to endure and to do.

It would be a shame if the memories of my family's struggles to leave Cuba and survive in this country became a casualty of the forgetfulness that plagues so many sons and daughters of immigrants, who rush to assimilate and join the great homogeneous American society. Many children of immigrants like me know so little of the pain and sacrifices their parents made that they no longer feel any connection to their early family or to the lands their ancestors came from. It is my hope that my story not only serves as a reminder for my own children of the route our family has taken into the twenty-first century, but that it also causes others to reflect on their unique histories and to reclaim for themselves the courage, strength, and pride of their ancestors who immigrated to the United States. Perhaps all of us can develop greater compassion for those who now forge similar paths as immigrants.

Boxing For Cuba is formally dedicated to my parents and my two brothers, the four people who foremost helped me survive, yet the readers I imagined as I wrote were my children, Sarah, Molly, and Joshua. When they read the book, I hope they will reach an understanding of their father that is similar to the one I reached about my own. I look forward to the day they claim with pride the roots of their Cuban family, and I pray they will also be assured of my love for them and my hope that they find fulfillment in their lives.

I also found great comfort in knowing that my two stepdaughters, Nicol and Veronica, would also read this book. Although I realize I can never replace their real father, I hope the book helps them gain an insight into their stepfather that will enhance the loving relationship that already flourishes between us. Their beauty as people, their thoughtfulness, and their undying commitment to social justice fills me with great hope that a better future for our world is within their reach.

I could never have written this book had it not been for the loving support and influence of my soul mate and wife, Gabriela. Although she is nine years younger than I am, she is, in many ways, far wiser. She understood much better and far sooner than I did that my assimilation to American culture did not need to include the cutting off of my own Cuban roots. It was her persistence that allowed me to reconnect with my past and reclaim a key part of my soul. When it came to writing this book, she was my muse and my sage.

At times, I struggled with my conscience as I wrote, because my parents warned us never to show our dirty laundry in public, and this book does hang much of that laundry on a line for all to see. Although I am mindful that some of its revelations may cause embarrassment for my mother, my brothers, and my family members in Miami and Cuba, but that was never my intent. I deeply admire all of them and the ways in which they have overcome their many hardships. This book chronicles the profound difficulties of immigration—challenges that can shatter bodies and souls and even the closest relationships, sometimes triggering behavior that is difficult to reconcile. Although it can take an entire lifetime, as it did for my father, we can all find forgiveness, and redemption, and the true meaning of our lives.

In the end, I realized that to tell this story without describing the very hardest times would have rendered the story incomplete, creating a façade of our lives that would hide the most important lessons to be learned from them, and taken from me my own blessed opportunity for redemption.

—Guillermo V. Vidal, Denver, Colorado

8574987R0

Made in the USA
Lexington, KY
14 February 2011